ROBERT GROSSETESTE

GREAT MEDIEVAL THINKERS

Series Editor
Brian Davies
Blackfriars College, University of Oxford,
and Fordham University

DUNS SCOTUS
Richard Cross

BERNARD OF CLAIRVAUX
G. R. Evans

JOHN SCOTUS ERIUGENA
Deirdre Carabine

ROBERT GROSSETESTE

James McEvoy

OXFORD
UNIVERSITY PRESS

2000

OXFORD
UNIVERSITY PRESS

Oxford   New York

Athens   Auckland   Bangkok   Bogotá   Buenos Aires   Calcutta
Cape Town   Chennai   Dar es Salaam   Delhi   Florence   Hong Kong   Istanbul
Karachi   Kuala Lumpur   Madrid   Melbourne   Mexico City   Mumbai
Nairobi   Paris   São Paulo   Singapore   Taipei   Tokyo   Toronto   Warsaw

and associated companies in
Berlin   Ibadan

Copyright © 2000 by James McEvoy

Published by Oxford University Press, Inc.
198 Madison Avenue, New York, New York 10016

Oxford is a registered trademark of Oxford University Press

Library of Congress Cataloging-in-Publication Data
McEvoy, J. J.
Robert Grosseteste / James McEvoy.
p.   cm. — (Great medival thinkers)
Includes bibliographical references.
ISBN 0-19-511449-3; ISBN 0-19-511450-7 (pbk.)
1. Grosseteste, Robert, 1175?–1253.   2. Philosophy, Medieval.
I. Title.   II. Series.
B765.G74M34   2000
189'.4—dc21   99-36238

1 3 5 7 9 8 6 4 2

Printed in the United States of America
on acid-free paper

To Werner Beierwaltes
Professor Emeritus of the University of Munich
this book is dedicated

Maynooth, Feast of St. Patrick,
17 March 2000

SERIES FOREWORD

Many people would be surprised to be told that there *were* any great medieval thinkers. If a *great* thinker is one from whom we can learn today, and if "medieval" serves as an adjective for describing anything which existed from (roughly) the years A.D. 600 to 1500, then—so it is often supposed—medieval thinkers cannot be called "great."

But why not? One answer often given appeals to ways in which medieval authors with a taste for argument and speculation tend to invoke "authorities," especially religious ones. Such invocation of authority is not the stuff of which great thought is made—so it is often said today. It is also frequently said that greatness is not to be found in the thinking of those who lived before the rise of modern science, not to mention that of modern philosophy and theology. Students of science are nowadays hardly ever referred to literature earlier than the seventeenth century. Students of philosophy in the twentieth century have often been taught nothing about the history of ideas between Aristotle (384–322 B.C.) and Descartes (A.D. 1596–1650). Modern students of theology have been frequently encouraged to believe that significant theological thinking is a product of the nineteenth century.

Yet the origins of modern science lie in the conviction that the world is open to rational investigation and is orderly rather than chaotic—a conviction which came fully to birth, and was systematically explored and developed, during the Middle Ages. And it is in medieval thinking that we find some of the most sophisticated and rigorous discussions in the areas of philosophy and theology ever offered for human consumption. This is, perhaps, not surprising if we note that medieval philosophers and theologians, like their counterparts today, were mostly university teachers, participating in an ongoing debate with contributors from different countries, and who—unlike many seventeenth-, eighteenth-, and even nineteenth-century philosophers and theologians—did not work in relative isolation from the community of teachers and students with whom they were regularly involved. As for the question of appeal to authority: It is certainly true that many medieval thinkers believed in authority (especially religious authority) as a serious court of appeal; and it is true that most people today would say that they cannot do this. Yet authority is as much an ingredient in our thinking as it was for medieval thinkers. For most of what we take ourselves to know derives from the trust we have reposed in our various teachers, colleagues, friends, and general contacts. When it comes to reliance on authority, the main difference between us and medieval thinkers lies in the fact that their reliance on authority (insofar as they had it) was more often focused and explicitly acknowledged than is ours. The difference does not lie in the fact that their appeal to authority was uncritical and naive in a way that ours is not.

In recent years, such truths have come to be increasingly recognized at what we might call the "academic" level. No longer disposed to think of the Middle Ages as "dark" (meaning "lacking in intellectual richness"), many university departments (and many publishers of books and journals) now devote a lot of their energy to the study of medieval thinking. And they do so not simply on the assumption that it is historically significant. They do so in the light of the increasingly developed insight that medieval thinking is full of things with which to dialogue and from which to learn. Following a long period in which medieval thinking was thought to be of only antiquarian interest, we are now witnessing its revival as a contemporary voice—one to converse with, one from which we might learn.

The *Great Medieval Thinkers* series reflects and is part of this exciting revival. Written by a distinguished team of experts, it aims to provide substantial introductions to a range of medieval authors. And it does so on the assumption that they are as worth reading today as they were when they wrote. Students of medieval "literature" (e.g., the writings of Chaucer) are currently well supplied (if not oversupplied) with secondary works to aid them when reading the objects of their concern. But those with an interest in medieval philosophy and theology are by no means so fortunate when it comes to reliable and accessible volumes to help them. The *Great Medieval Thinkers* series, therefore, aspires to remedy that deficiency by concentrating on medieval philosophers and theologians, coupled with modern reflections on what they had to say. Taken individually, the volumes in the series will provide valuable treatments of single thinkers many of whom are not currently covered by any comparable works. Taken together, the volumes of the series will constitute a rich and distinguished history and discussion of medieval philosophy and theology considered as a whole. With an eye on college and university students, and with an eye on the general reader, the authors of the series write in a clear and accessible manner, so that the medieval thinkers they take as their subjects can be learned about by those readers who have no previous knowledge in the field. Each contributor to the series will also strive to inform, engage, and generally entertain even those readers with specialist knowledge in the area of medieval thinking. As well as surveying and introducing, volumes in the series will advance the state of medieval studies at both the historical and the speculative levels.

In this respect, the present volume is typical. Robert Grosseteste (d.1253) was one of the most influential Englishmen of his day. A distinguished mathematician, philosopher, scientist, and theologian, he was also bishop of Lincoln, a Father of the First Council of Lyons, and chancellor of Oxford University. But his writings have not been much translated into English. And most published studies on him are technical and chiefly aimed at professional medievalists. In what follows, however, readers will find a straightforward survey and appraisal of every aspect of Grosseteste's achievement together with a guide to the scholarship on him. They will also find a selection of notable passages from his writings not accessible to general readers and of sayings attributed to him by medieval chroniclers—materials that illustrate his original personality, his wisdom, and his humor. James McEvoy is one of the world's leading experts on Grosseteste. So he brings to this book a lifetime of research and scholarship. But he also writes for beginners who want clear and painless access to one of the great personalities of the Middle Ages.

BRIAN DAVIES

PREFACE

Robert Grosseteste was born to a poor Anglo-Norman family in England (perhaps in Suffolk) in 1168 or shortly before then. Before 1198 he was attached to the *familia* of the bishop of Hereford, which was known for its cathedral school, where renowned masters such as Roger of Hereford and Alfred of Sareshel had taught the "new" Greek and Arabic science. Little is known of Grosseteste's career as a teacher of the liberal arts. It is likely that he studied theology at Paris. He returned to Oxford at the foundation of the university (1214) or shortly after, and he was chancellor in its earliest years. He lectured in theology there for about twenty years, and in 1229–1230 he undertook the theological education of the Franciscans at the invitation of their provincial minister for the five years before he was elected bishop of Lincoln (1235). He was present at the Council of Lyons in 1245 and returned there in 1250 as a critic of the current centralized policy of Church appointments. He died on 8/9 October 1253 with a reputation for sanctity.

Grosseteste made an outstanding contribution to the thought and the culture of his time. The generation that witnessed the chartering of the universities of Paris and Oxford (in 1200 and 1214, respectively) was full of a sense of vigorous academic renewal and intellectual innovation. Grosseteste made a distinctive contribution to the University of Oxford, the earliest years of which (up to 1235) he may fairly be said to have dominated, intellectually speaking. His life was full of initiatives of the most varied kind, which, when we take them all together, can be seen to have resulted in an exceptionally diversified output of writing: philosophical and scientific treatises; commentaries on Aristotle; biblical exegesis and theological reflection; sermons; letters; and, not the least in importance, translations from the Greek. During his eighteen years as bishop of Lincoln, from 1235 to his death in 1253, he continued to pursue his translating activities, while adding considerably to his output of sermons and pastoral writings, and framing an influential set of constitutions for the diocese.

His abundant and diversified writings have not all been edited. In philosophy, he showed his mastery of Aristotelian logic in a commentary on the *Posterior Analytics*. His genuine appreciation of the natural philosophy of Aristotle was qualified by his own conviction that mathematics, especially geometry, holds an important key to the understanding of natural phenomena, such as light rays, the colors and the rainbow, the climates, sight and vision, form and movement. His philosophical and theological interests combined in the metaphysics of light. God is light, whence the creation and all it contains is some kind of light; the energy exhibited in the universe derives from a primordial, radiating point of light created by God. As he learned Greek, somewhat late in life, he came to admire the *Ethics* of Aristotle, which he translated together with its Greek commentators. Further translations (of works by Damascene and the Pseudo-Dionysius, the *Testaments of the Twelve Patriarchs*, the letters of St. Ignatius, articles from the *Suda Lexicon*, etc.) deepened his own theological vision, as his *Hexaëmeron* (or study of the first two chapters of the book of Genesis) reveals. Although he was a strict traditionalist in theology, Grosseteste held some original, or at least distinctive, views; for instance, he argued that the divine Word would have become incarnate even if Adam had not fallen. He wrote in the Anglo-Norman dialect a long allegorical poem on the Redemption. He was by far the most prominent of the first generation of masters at Oxford, where he left his intellectual stamp on several generations of thinkers.

This book takes its nature, and its limits, from the series in which it appears. It must aim at a general coverage of Grosseteste's intellectual pursuits, while remaining within a relatively brief compass. At present, it must be admitted, the state of Grosseteste studies scarcely admits of the realization of both these requirements together. New impulses to research, competing hypotheses about the shape of his early life, editions of hitherto unpublished Latin writings attributed to him, and studies of his intellectual and religious significance have all given immense stimulation to specialist readers. The

historian cannot hope in a short work like this to resolve far-reaching disagreements among experts, or to look in any detail at even the most important of his subject's works.

   In a previous book (1982) I developed those aspects of Grosseteste's
thought that might be considered philosophical either in a narrower or in a
broader sense.[1] The focus of this work differs from that: here the emphasis
will be placed on his actual writings in the many genres he cultivated; on
the whole it is scriptural exegesis and theology that lie at the center of attention. Philosophy is not entirely neglected, but in the chapter devoted to it
much has had to be summarized, or even set aside, in what is essentially a
review of the philosophical writings he produced. Full account has been
taken of all the most recent editions of works by Grosseteste himself, as well
as of the scholarly literature that has appeared since 1982. However, the
chronicling of current scholarly discussions and controversies has been
avoided in favor of the statement of the bundle of conclusions, convictions,
hypotheses, and even incertitudes that are my own.

   I have had to make choices, and consequently sacrifices. The primary aim
of the book is to afford the reader who is not acquainted with the specialized literature on Grosseteste an overall view of his life and of his achievement, especially regarding philosophical and theological ideas. Since
Grosseteste is not well known even to the educated public (few versions of
his writings exist in any modern language), it has seemed appropriate to
include translations of some of his best and most original or characteristic
pages (in addition to referring the reader to existing versions), so that he
might sometimes speak to the reader in his own voice and make an impact
in independence of glossation. It also seemed advisable to depict this tower-
ing figure against the background of Oxford University in the earliest years
of its existence, and to give some idea of the schools that preceded its emergence (chap. 1).

   In the second chapter some sense is conveyed of the difficulty with which
historians arrive at what are of necessity tentative and very piecemeal conclusions concerning the shape of his life up to the point where he became
well known; documentary evidence of his movements and occupations is
extremely scarce before circa 1230. Hurried readers, or those more interested
in the history of theology and philosophy, may prefer to skim over this chapter in order to get directly to the ideas Grosseteste developed. Should they
choose to do so, however, they should be aware that they are offending against
a healthy and enlightened practice of Grosseteste himself, who, being by

inclination something of a humanist, tended to be curious about the historical origins of ideas and the kind of men who had originally thought them up, or who in the course of time passed them on. Grosseteste's participation as bishop of Lincoln in the general council of the Church held at Lyons in 1245 is awarded a chapter to itself, since it may be regarded as the high point of his episcopal career. The aftermath of that council, his return to the papal curia in 1250, and his final letter to the representatives of the pope in 1253 are given some discussion, as is the myth that grew up in medieval England around his name, and which kept being added to in modern times.

A primary aim has been to expound Grosseteste's thought on the basis of his authentic writings, and insofar as possible to understand his own ideas and initiatives in the light of developments taking place around him, in England, in France, in Western Europe, and even in the Middle East.

Grosseteste's contribution to intellectual life is best understood against the scholastic background of Oxford, from the origin of the schools there down to about 1250. By the latter date the character of theological teaching and research had begun to enter a phase of rapid evolution.

Long before there was a University of Oxford there were schools conducted by individual masters, some of whom are known to us through the few writings that survive from this early period, others of whom have left only their name; of many (no doubt the great majority) we have not even that. The university was founded in 1214 by a legate sent to England by the pope. From the 1220s onward the activities of its faculty of theology begin to be discernible. Early Oxford merits a place in the history of theology even though it was, and knew that it was, only a candle compared to the great light of Paris.

By the middle of the century theology was in a fairly flourishing state, and it continued so until there came upon it a period of real distinction, which was marked by the renowned names of John Duns Scotus and William of Ockham. In its first decades it had the good fortune to number among its several honest masters a single intellectual giant, Robert Grosseteste, who became its chancellor at an early but unascertainable date. He was the one really outstanding personality the university produced during the first generations of its existence. Grosseteste chose to devote what proved to be his last years in academic life to preparing the newly arrived Franciscans for their ministry of preaching. Oxford was to know the benefit of this autumnal period of his teaching, for the Franciscans consistently supplied the best minds of the faculty of theology for a century and more.

The story of Grosseteste's impact on Oxford life can suitably be brought to a close at the point when new theological impulses were taking over. By the year 1250 it would have been clear to any well-placed observer that a change had been made in the curriculum, one that brought the teaching of theology at Oxford into line with fairly recent developments at Paris. Oxford was not, after all, to continue in the paths (either the well beaten or the novel ones) that its first genius had walked. Theology would thenceforth become more specialized; it would accord a prominent place to lecturing from the *Book of Sentences* of Peter Lombard; it would be more speculative than exegetical in its ambition, more scientifically organized and more philosophically based, than the endeavors of the founding generation had been. The present account of the development of theology and philosophy at Oxford, which has Grosseteste as its centerpiece, can legitimately regard the importation of the *Sentences* into its curriculum (1240–1250) as a convenient and justifiable point for closing the chapter of history that began with the origins of the university itself as a corporate body, and hence of its faculty of theology.

St. Anselm of Canterbury had a biographer, and a very perceptive one, in Eadmer. Although Grosseteste did not have a like posthumous good fortune (he did not belong to a religious order), his imposing personality and his celebrity in the last phase of his life were such that memories of his deeds and sayings abounded, and many of these have been preserved. I would venture to say that between Alcuin and Nicholas of Cusa no thinker emerges more vividly in his human dimension than does Robert Grosseteste. This truth strikes us with particular clarity if we compare his case with those of his most prominent contemporaries, such as St. Edmund of Abingdon, William of Auxerre, William of Auvergne, and Philip the Chancellor. The personalities of the subsequent generations, whose intellectual achievements were often better recorded and were decidedly more influential (such as Albert the Great, Bonaventure, Thomas Aquinas, Henry of Ghent, and Duns Scotus), elude the historian, by comparison with his. The natural result of this contrast is that, knowing so much (comparatively, at any rate) of Grosseteste the man, we wish to know more and are driven to feel we know all too little. It is a wholesome thing to rejoice in the abundance of the evidence we do possess, and which enables us to come close to his uniqueness.

Tantalized, however, by gaps in the evidence and by silences among witnesses to his activities, historians feel restless. My hope is that they will always do so. My conviction is that further discoveries will be made, in the course of time, that will change the picture we have of Robert Grosseteste. My fear is that the decline in the knowledge of Latin together with the general secularization of society will render inquiry of this kind not, certainly, less fascinating, but less accessible, and even perhaps less desired. Every man may not have his price (Grosseteste himself clearly did not), but historical research is costly, and contemporary society is less prepared to pay the bill. The personal cost of scholarship, on the other hand, will never deflect some minds from the desire to know, and to learn what we do not as yet know; these ambitions are at the very bottom of what we are.

ACKNOWLEDGMENTS

Over a long period of time I have run up scholarly debts that can never be repaid, so many are those who have helped me, by their publications, through hospitality extended to me at research centers, in correspondence, and not least by personal encouragement. Rather than risk offending the living through selective thanksgiving, I have preferred here to praise the dead: first of all, Grosseteste himself. I could never have suspected, when I first took up the study of his writings, the extent to which his influence would insinuate itself, discreetly but progressively, into my own life as teacher, researcher, traveler, and priest. In a word, I have been infiltrated by him in the dimension of the spirit. Much of what I have read over a good number of years has led me back again and again to his extensive (and mostly lost) library—or else I have begun, again and again, by taking up books that are known to have been present therein. The better parts of what I have been able to read and write have brought me closer than I would ever have thought possible to the reader of ancient philosophy, the biblical exegete, the priest, and the bishop that he was.

My greatest intellectual debt is owed to my predecessor as Professor of Scholastic Philosophy at the Queen's University, Belfast, the late (d. 1990) Professor Theodore Crowley, O.F.M., who introduced me to the study of Grosseteste. At the Université catholique de Louvain the late (d. 1992) Professor Fernand Van Steenberghen encouraged me throughout my research,

with great learning and unforgettable kindness. The late Professor Simone
Van Riet (d. 1993) gave me an initiation into palaeography of a kind that I
have never been able to live up to, in point either of finesse or of productiv-
ity. The late Fr. Leonard Boyle, O.P., stimulated my interest in Grosseteste's
writings on pastoral care. *Requiescant in pace*.

I am grateful to Professor Brian Davies, O.P., for proposing to include
a work on Robert Grosseteste in this series, of which he is the general
editor. He has at every stage been patient and encouraging. Professor
Joseph Goering kindly agreed to read my typescript completely; it has bene-
fited greatly from the criticisms and suggestions with which he generously
supplied me. I would like to acknowledge the help I have received from him,
in this and in other regards. Dr. Philipp Rosemann has been good enough
to read portions of the typescript and to make numerous suggestions toward
its improvement. Dr. Michael Dunn gave valued practical assistance.

Finally, my thanks are due to the Alexander von Humboldt-Stiftung
(Bonn) for four months of financial support, during which time this work
was begun (1994). A generous publication grant was made by the National
University of Ireland, Maynooth.

These acknowledgments would not be complete without gratitude being
expressed for the efficiency and unfailing courtesy of the representatives of
the Press, and in particular Mr. Robert Milks.

Faculty of Philosophy, National University of Ireland,   J. M.
Maynooth, and Pontifical University, Maynooth
January 2000

CONTENTS

ROBERT GROSSETESTE

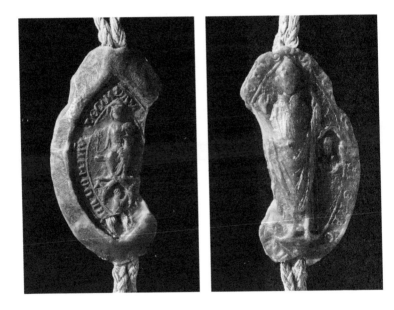

Top: Detail from the first folio of the *Transsumpta* of Lyons. Robert Grosseteste's name (Robt Lincolniensis) appears near the center of the third full line from the bottom. Bottom: Both sides of Bishop Grosseteste's seal. Left: the verso side. Right: the recto side. Photos courtesy the Vatican Archive. Reprinted with permission.

FROM SCHOOLS TO UNIVERSITY

The University of Oxford was not in any way predestined, either in the form it eventually came to take or in its very existence; on the other hand, its emergence was not wholly fortuitous, for it had a prehistory in the various schools that were conducted there in the course of the twelfth century. If the story of the university, properly speaking, begins in 1214, with the ordinance of the papal legate that gave the masters and their students the outline of a corporate identity, the remote beginnings of theological teaching in the town can be traced back as far as circa 1130, in ways that illuminate both the foundation of the university, when it eventually came about, and the character of its earliest faculty of theology, in the years after 1220.

Schools and Scholars at Oxford in the Twelfth Century

By around 1100 Oxford was growing, after a lengthy period of depopulation.[1] Within a few years three new religious houses were established, a new parish church (St. Giles) came into existence, and the king built a residence, so that the town became a center of royal administration (even though only one among many) from this time onward. This growth still did not make it a town of any great significance; it remained small by comparison with the

leading centers of population. Not being a cathedral town it did not have an
established school. Besides, similar growth was being witnessed at many
other centers, and nearby Northampton, in particular, appeared to be out-
pacing Oxford. Even if the times were favorable to the growth of schools, in
England as elsewhere in northern Europe, Oxford did not seem to stand a
very good chance of attracting a significant number of masters and students,
when compared with more favored centers of population, administration,
and trade.

The cathedral and monastic schools of England during the twelfth century could not hope to compete with the schools of France and Italy in attracting students of higher learning. No English student during the period
1066–1190 chose to stay in his country for higher studies if he could go
abroad; and all the schoolmasters who can be named during this period had
studied in some foreign school. The French and North Italian schools had
established their superiority in every branch of learning more than a century before centers in England began their tentative development. However,
the establishment of higher schools presupposed an increase in the number
of grammar schools, and in this regard the precondition was rapidly being
met in England. Documentary evidence bearing on the existence of individual schools is scarce, but enough exists to show that every sizable town,
and even many smaller ones, possessed a grammar school; the forty or so such
schools that have left some trace should probably be doubled in number to
give a rough idea of the total in existence. Education of an elementary kind
was in profitable demand, due to the increasing number of clergy, the need
for basic literacy and numeracy, and the requirement for increasing numbers of administrators to serve the monasteries, the dioceses, and the mon-
archy, as well as the needs of merchants and the urban communities. The
higher places in government, in the Church and in the royal administration,
demanded a broader range of knowledge than the grammar school, with its
basic instruction in Latin, arithmetic, poetry, and chant, could possibly provide. Students whose ambition urged them in such directions left England
for destinations like Paris and Bologna, Laon, Montpellier, and Salerno, to
acquire there knowledge and skills in arts, law, medicine, and theology, such
as were not to be found in their home country. Yet by the close of the twelfth
century a number of centers had come into existence in England and were
enjoying a modest flowering.

To return now to Oxford, which was entering a period of growth in the
decades following 1100: what evidence have we of higher learning being

offered there in the twelfth century? The first teacher known by name, Theobald of Etampes, moved from Caen to Britain and was established at Oxford shortly before 1100. His activity is known from his letters. He seems to have stayed on teaching at the town until the 1120s. Probably he taught secular subjects, for one critic ridiculed him for meddling in theology. Theobald did indeed have some theological interests (in his letters he discusses whether salvation is possible without Christian initiation, whether the sons of priests may be ordained, and whether monks may carry out the role of secular priests), but there is no evidence of his having taught the subject; perhaps he simply could not find enough interested students among the sixty to one hundred he is reputed to have had in his school.

The next teacher we know at Oxford was a capable and ambitious scholar, Robert Pullen, English by birth, who apparently came to Oxford from Exeter in 1133. A chronicler informs us that he spent fifteen years teaching; that he preached each Sunday to the people, to their great profit; and that the schoolmen of his time in England simply did not teach the Scriptures. In other words, he was an innovator. In any event, he was drawn back by the lodestone of Paris, the place of his own former studies, and from there he was called to Rome, in 1144, to become chancellor of the Holy See and cardinal. Although he seems to have left Oxford without having had a successor, he had shown that it was possible to do what had not been done before him, namely, to attract to Oxford sufficient young scholars to hold a school of theology. In other words, in more favorable circumstances a concentration of students could come about there.

During the fifty years following Pullen's departure the circumstances of Oxford were apparently not favorable, and there is no record of scholastic activity there. When evidence begins to appear again that might suggest the presence of schools, it comes not from theology but from the side of law and administration, both ecclesiastical and civil.[2] The lawyer Vacarius of Bologna came to England before 1150, attracted to the service of the archdiocese of Canterbury, and then that of York. It may be that he carried out some instruction (his book, *Liber pauperum*, was a compendium of Roman law suitable for teaching); however, there is no evidence of any Oxford connection.

Evidence of the existence of law courts at Oxford is found (1177–1179) in a letter of Peter of Blois, who accuses a certain Master Robert Blund of making the rounds between Paris, Bologna, and Oxford, taking part in lawsuits, when properly he should have been at Lincoln alongside his bishop.

Oxford had a considerable number of religious houses in its neighborhood, and in the last twenty years of the century these generated their share of litigation. Papal judges delegate were nominated to hear appeals, and each of them must have brought with him his retinue of experts and clerks. Oxford was a convenient, midland center for judicial hearings, both civil and ecclesiastical. Did the increased practice of the law lead to the actual teaching of one or more of its several forms (common, Roman, and ecclesiastical)? It seems likely that this was so, since the principles, in particular of Roman law, could be learned only by guided study, while its practice was mastered by observation of the courts at work; school and court were complementary. By 1190 or so the combination of legal instruction and practice in the courts was beginning to draw students of law to Oxford. From the evidence of the chronicle of Evesham, and from charters, the names of several practicing and teaching lawyers can be recovered. From these modest beginnings to the close of the Middle Ages, canon and civil law would be taught at Oxford.

At this same time Oxford was home to a growing number of clerics. Gerald of Wales tells us why he chose to read there his newly completed *Topographia Hibernica*, in 1177 or 1178: it was because "the clergy of England are in the greatest strength and repute" in that town. The public reading took three days, and Gerald does not lose the opportunity to detail the sumptuousness of his own hospitality and the distinction of a part of the audience he was able to draw. He speaks of the "doctores diversarum facultatum" who assisted, but this piece of self-regarding glorification of the schools, written twenty years after the event, cannot be taken at face value, for university-type organization by faculties was as yet undreamt of in the Oxford of the time of which he is speaking. Nevertheless, Gerald's choice of Oxford as a place to find a literate and clerical audience is significant, especially since it was made for reasons of the maximum of self-glorification.

Oxford was developing on other lines than the purely clerical ones indicated by Gerald's account (and by the fact that it was an archdeaconry of the diocese of Lincoln). Its strategic importance was underlined by the civil strife that characterized the reign of King Stephen, and a military storehouse was installed. Meetings of the royal court were held. Princes Richard and John were born there in the royal residence. In 1199, ten years after its rival Northampton, Oxford received the recognition of a royal charter.

It is from the same Gerald, however, that we have some information indicating that theology was not taught at Oxford in any way comparable to other centers in England. About 1195, Gerald was planning a third visit to

Paris to study theology, but was prevented from doing so by the war between England and France. Gerald chose Lincoln as "the place in England where sound and healthy theology is most flourishing, under the best of teachers, Master William de Monte." We should not give undue weight to Gerald's decision, for he was going to Lincoln, at around fifty years of age, to enjoy the company of someone he knew well, William, the chancellor of Lincoln and the head of its schools. It is worth taking a sidelong glance at what was indeed a successful and well-attended center for the study of theology; we can learn from this that a well-placed observer of circa 1190 would have been rash to predict that Oxford would within thirty years become the dominant theological school of the country, for the evidence would have suggested otherwise.

A contemporary explained William de Monte's name thus: "transiit ad montem Montanus, monte relicto" ("Hill has left a hill for a hill")—for William relinquished his school on the Mont Ste. Geneviève, at Paris, for the hill on which Lincoln's Minster was built. St. Hugh of Avalon, the bishop of Lincoln, recruited William as chancellor, in which office he presided over the cathedral schools there for some twenty-five years, up to his death in 1213. Can we say what kind of theology Gerald of Wales would have found at Lincoln? The answer to this question is supplied by the recent publication of a number of his writings, including works on the sacraments, sermons, and a florilegium on theological, religious, and moral topics, the *Proverbia*.[3] William regarded theology as both a moral and an intellectual discipline for clerics and monks in training. These would learn by following lectures on Scripture, by disputing questions and attending sermons. Many, even the majority, were mature men. Considerable emphasis was laid on versification to aid the memorization of penitential and sacramental practice, the virtues and vices, and proverbs of wisdom. His pedagogical techniques were those of the Parisian schools of his own time and presupposed a sound knowledge of the arts. William was to become, without at all intending it, an important figure in the creation of the new Latin literature popularizing pastoral care, which was aimed at less educated priests as well as at laypeople, and which was soon to be found in the vernacular languages.

The war between the kings of France and England, which intensified from 1193 and lasted until 1204 without much interruption, gave for the first time an advantage to English centers of higher study over continental ones—the decisive though limited advantage of accessibility. Students must for long periods of time have found it as good as impossible to cross the channel to

France, and masters who found themselves in England were precluded from returning there. It is likely that local centers of study knew an immediate benefit in the enrollment of numbers of scholars. Even before the war intensified, however, there was at last a sign of theological life at Oxford, in a cometlike figure from whose brief years of teaching some literary traces have survived. He was called Alexander, and he received the sobriquet of Nequam.

Alexander Nequam

Alexander was born at St. Albans in 1157 and was sent to the Abbey school there.[4] He was to return to his old school, as a teacher, probably in 1183; perhaps he had by then already completed a stay in Paris, where he certainly studied during some part of his early career, attending courses in the arts (at the School of the Petit Pont), in theology, in both laws, and in medicine. The origin of his sobriquet is given anecdotally by the somewhat later chronicler of St. Albans, Matthew Paris. Alexander had asked to have the school at the monastery. The Abbot Garinus replied with the words, "Si bonus es, venias; si nequam, nequaquam." The young scholar replied, equally tersely and wittily, "Si velis, veniam; sin autem, tu autem."[5]

He can first be located at Oxford by means of a sermon preached in 1193 or shortly before then. He lectured for several years before entering the Augustinian monastery at Cirencester, at some date between 1197 and 1202; he was to become abbot there in 1212. He was present at the Fourth Council of the Lateran, in 1215, but he died shortly after returning to England, in 1217, and was buried in the Cathedral of Worcester. His reputation spread to France and even Germany, being carried above all by two of his works in the liberal arts, *De nominibus utensilium* and *Corrogationes Promethei*, and one in theology, *De naturis rerum*. A story he tells about himself was to become celebrated through the later doctrinal controversies over the Immaculate Conception of Mary:

> When I was giving public lectures in theology I was strongly opposed to the observance of the Feast of the Immaculate Conception of the Blessed Virgin, and I announced my intention of lecturing on that day as usual. But every year in Oxford I was ill on that day and unable to carry out my intention.[6]

The value of this reminiscence for our present purposes is twofold: it establishes the fact that Alexander held regular lectures at Oxford over a number of years, and, when taken together with numerous other references he makes to his teaching practice as a theologian, it provides a valuable link enabling us to interrelate the few works that stem directly from his Oxford lectures with the much more abundant writings that survive from his monastic period.[7] Using that connecting link we can perhaps arrive at some idea of the nature of his actual theological lectures.

His achievement in arts and theology may be surveyed under four headings: science, preaching, exegesis, and theology.

Science   Alexander was a representative (along with his friend Alfred of Sareshel, author of *De motu cordis*) of the scientific tradition that was a feature of twelfth-century England. In *De naturis rerum* and *Laus sapientiae divinae*, in particular, he extols "our Aristotle," to praise whom would be like "helping the sun with torches." His grasp of Aristotle is firmest in the new and old logic, but he endeavors to explain many natural phenomena, mineral and animal, through the mixtures of the elements and the humors. He knows many titles of works by Aristotle, including the *Ethica vetus*, but it is difficult most of the time to ascertain how much actual acquaintance with their translations underpinned his enthusiasm. He often did not understand the Philosopher and he added his own to the complaints (which were general in the twelfth century) about the difficulty and obscurity of his thought. He was familiar with the Aristotelian definition of the soul (*De anima*), but it can be shown that he borrowed it from his colleague at Oxford John Blund (q.v.). Other philosophical works known to him were the *Liber de causis* (of Neoplatonic and Arabic origin) and the *Liber XXIV philosophorum*. It has been suggested that much of his knowledge of Aristotle was derived from the Salernitan medical writers, one of whom, Urso, Alexander names, and from whose *Aphorismi* he repeatedly draws information, in *De naturis rerum*. Adelard of Bath (*Quaestiones naturales*) was also one of his sources. Alexander had a good and critical knowledge of the computus. He was cautious about astrology: he accepted the general belief that the planets have an influence on the elements that is given them by God; however, they are incapable of determining our free will, since the soul cannot be subject to the operations of the laws that govern bodies, even if they are the higher bodies. In astrology, he warned, all that is harmful to the Catholic faith must be avoided.

Alexander's wide information and many views on natural phenomena were meant to serve religious and moral ends. In the preface to *De naturis rerum* he warns the reader not to expect a treatise of "philosophica eruditio" ("the golden chain of Homer," as he also puts it). This work illustrates his encyclopedic learning, but receives its biblical structure from the six days of creation. It is itself the preface to a commentary on Ecclesiastes, dealing with religious morality. In short, Alexander was writing with his fellow canons principally in mind, especially such of these as may have had an interest in investigating the natures and causes of things. It is significant, however, that the first theologian to establish himself at Oxford in the years immediately preceding the development of the schools there should have been a professed (even though inevitably an imperfect) Aristotelian, and an enthusiastic reader of medical and naturalist literature.

Preaching   Well over a hundred authentic sermons of Alexander survive, but remain unedited. Most of them belong to his Oxford period. They were preached to a variety of audiences. He evidently preached in a style that was biblical, simple and direct, and full of exempla bearing on life. Most of his sermons would have been delivered in French from his Latin notes.

Exegesis   Alexander employed the scholastic pattern of exegesis that was current: a running commentary on a book of the Bible, read in conjunction with the gloss, to which he added disquisitions on doctrinal points as they arose. He also followed in his monastic commentaries (the majority of his exegetical works) the prototype of St. Gregory's *Moralia in Job*, making long excursions not deriving directly from the text. In both genres he explored the four senses of Scripture. In his commentary on the Psalms he used the "ordinary gloss" (Anselm of Laon) and the gloss of Peter Lombard, and had recourse to *distinctiones*, in order to determine the meanings of words and their metaphorical uses. Alexander evidently held disputations in his school, but these are not represented in his exegetical writings, where only brief questions are raised on the text and answered in a few words. The monastic commentaries, on the other hand, move on a devotional plane, employing allegories and meditations for their spiritual purposes. Although he knew no Greek, he gives evidence of some knowledge (not derived from St. Jerome) of Hebrew terms and talks of his exchanges with *litteratores hebrei*. Five quotations from the Talmud ("scripturae gamalielis") have been found in the homilies. He records that he found the Talmudic explanation of a particular passage from the Canticles to be little short of puerile, the product of foolish hearts. We may speculate that this was because its allegories and spiritual senses seemed to him undeveloped and "infantile," because they failed in Alexander's view to recognize the presence in the text of teachings about Christ and the Church (i.e., allegory) and about the human soul (i.e., morality).

Theology   Alexander composed a structured survey of theology, *Speculum speculationum*.[8] It survives in only one manuscript, where it is incomplete; it may have remained unfinished. In its arrangement of subjects it bears some resemblance to the *Sentences* of the Lombard, but its four books are divided differently. The first and second are devoted entirely to God and the Trinity; the third, to creation and the angels, the soul and its faculties. The fourth discusses grace and free will, but the treatment of the virtues and vices promised in the preface of the *Speculum* is missing, or lacking. No survey of the thought of the *Speculum* exists as yet. The task would not be an easy one, for Alexander's method is to set down definitions or views on a given subject and to discuss some selection of them in detail. Somewhere within this critical survey his own opinion is to be sought, but often it is expressed only incidentally, for his thought is not worked out in questions and determinations. In addition to the usual patristic authorities Alexander draws on the two Anselms (of Laon and Canterbury), but without always distinguishing them clearly. He uses the *Proslogion* approach to God's transcendence (God is "quo maius nihil cogitari potest"—"greater than whom nothing can be thought"), and he may be one of the first theologians to come somewhere close to its sense. He is a pioneer in the part "de viribus animae," for psychology had not been included in twelfth-century theology, and Alexander was conscious here of his own originality. He had read Avicenna's *De anima* and was the first theologian to employ its psychological vocabulary. He was remembered in later times, notably by William of Ware, O.F.M., for his advocacy of the doctrine of the Immaculate Conception and his change of mind on that issue; however, he seems to have admitted the doctrine only in a limited and qualified form.

The manuscript tradition of his theological works points almost exclusively to their use in England. *De naturis rerum* and the comment on Canticles were used and quoted from in the thirteenth and fourteenth centuries, and books of exempla often carry Alexandrian material. It is noteworthy that a copy of *De naturis rerum* was solemnly presented to the university library at Oxford as late as 1452; perhaps we are entitled to interpret this as a late tribute to the earliest, but still well-remembered master of Oxford.

John Blund

When Alexander Nequam quoted Aristotle's definition of the soul as "the perfection of an organic body possessing life in potency," he cited it in the form employed by his younger contemporary, Master John Blund. Blund's *De anima* was likewise his source for the doctrine of sight and the angles of vision, in *De naturis rerum*. Blund is a significant figure in the development of philosophy in England, for his is the first writing we have from a master who was teaching the liberal arts, and Alexander's close acquaintance with it suggests that both men were working at Oxford.

According to the evidence of a contemporary, Henry of Avranches, Blund lectured on Aristotle both at Oxford and at Paris, and was a regent in theology for twelve years. We may suppose that after teaching the arts at Oxford he returned to Paris during the interdict (1208–1214) and the contemporaneous suspension of the schools at Oxford (1209–1214), to study theology. His theological regency should be placed at Paris. From 1227 he was in the service of the king, Henry III. He was elected archbishop of Canterbury in 1232, but the election was set aside, because Blund was considered to be a pluralist. He was chancellor of York from 1234 up until his death, in 1248.

The *Tractatus de anima* is the only writing we have of Blund's; it survives in three manuscripts.[9] It is the work of an artist, not a theologian, but it set an agenda for psychology that within a generation was to be fully taken up into theology. Alexander's paraphrasing of it means it must have been written before 1204 at the very latest. Like all his contemporaries, Blund regarded the *De anima* of Avicenna as a commentary on the homonymous treatise of Aristotle, but, finding the latter obscure and the former clear by comparison, they made it their main inspiration. John refers also to Algazel, to (Pseudo.-) Alexander of Aphrodisias and to many of the physical works of Aristotle. Blund's treatise reflects his teaching method. He expounds the doctrine of Aristotle, offers reasons for each important teaching and objections to it, and in a *solutio* states a reasoned position of his own.

Blund defends the role of the Philosopher in the science of the soul: the natural philosopher has the soul within his domain inasmuch as it is united to the body, imparting life to it. The metaphysician considers the soul in itself as a substance, while the theologian is concerned with the conditions of its salvation or punishment, not its nature. Clearly it is a master of arts, jealous for the territory of his newly discovered discipline of psychology, who pens these words. Broadly speaking, Blund follows throughout his book the plan of Avicenna, but adds a chapter (26) on free will; here he is much indebted to St. Anselm of Canterbury. Like Avicenna (and St. Augustine) he maintains that the soul is immortal because it is a substance existing in and by itself; though united to the body it cannot perish with it. The soul is described, not in Aristotelian terms as the form of the body but as the latter's "perfection" (cf. Avicenna). Blund repudiates the notion of spiritual matter (found in the Jewish philosopher Avicebrol), and hence maintains that neither the angel nor the soul is compounded of matter and form; the soul is a simple substance, the unique source of complex activities: those of life, sensation, and rational thought and action.

Blund's philosophical achievement was considerable. It is a pity that we have none of his theological works and consequently do not know how his thought developed and, in particular, what theological use he later made of psychology. With his treatise a whole block of thinking, Greek and Arabic psychology, arrived at Oxford; it was to maintain its presence there and to undergo development throughout the thirteenth century, just as it did in Paris and elsewhere.

Our evidence for placing Blund's arts teaching at Oxford and around 1200 is circumstantial, depending as it does upon the use made there of his ideas by Alexander Nequam. A more famous man certainly did teach arts and philosophy at Oxford at the same time, Edmund of Abingdon; unfortunately, nothing of his liberal arts teaching has survived.

St. Edmund of Abingdon

If Edmund's career as a teacher of arts and of theology at Oxford emerges with some little clarity, that is due less perhaps to his theological style than to his authorship of a classic work of spirituality (as it would be called nowadays), and to his early canonization as a saint of the Church, which marked him out uniquely among Oxford professors of theology, and occasioned several contemporary hagiographies.[10] The recent biography by C. H. Lawrence gives us the best reconstruction that we are likely to get of the early career of Edmund in the schools. Born at Abingdon about 1174, he was sent to nearby Oxford for grammar, at the school beside St. Mary's Church, before following the arts course at Paris, not long before 1190. He returned as a master to Oxford, where he taught the arts for six years (1195–1201?). Roger Bacon claimed that he was the first to lecture there on the *Sophistici Elenchi* of Aristotle. Warned in a dream to forsake secular learning, he returned to

Paris for theology. There are quite good reasons for thinking that his inception fell in 1214, only a year after his return from Paris upon the resolution of the Great Interdict. He must have begun to teach at Oxford not long after 1214, for Master Robert Bacon, O.P., described himself as Edmund's "most particular scholar, an attender of his lectures, and his assistant";[11] Bacon was a master of theology already in 1219.

During the years between circa 1200 and 1214 Edmund had been a conscientious, beneficed clergyman, who earned (in stages probably) the money required to spend periods of time in study and formation. In 1222 he was appointed treasurer of Salisbury Cathedral, and he may have done some lecturing at its school. In 1234 he became archbishop of Canterbury, after the election of John Blund had been set aside, and he led the Church in England up to his death, which took place at Soisy, near Pontigny, on his way to Rome as it would seem, on 15 November 1240. His former colleague both as master and as bishop, Robert Grosseteste, was to serve on the commission to enquire into his sanctity, convened by the pope at Lyons, in 1245. Another member was Alexander of Hales, O.F.M., formerly Grosseteste's *socius*, or assistant, at Oxford. Obviously these two men were nominated for their personal acquaintance with Edmund.

An anecdote narrated by Matthew Paris, one of his biographers, tells how Edmund was persuaded by a dream apparition of his dead mother, Mabel, to quit the teaching of the arts. On finding him lecturing on arithmetic she took his hand and drew three circles in it, signifiying the Trinity and said: "Henceforth, dear son, make these and no others the subject of your study." It was a commonplace that the liberal arts were valuable purely as equipment for the study of theology. Numerous anecdotes and preachers' stories illustrate this attitude. Matthew Paris suggests to us that Edmund did not find the transition an easy one to make: at the time when he began to study theology, "his palate was still numbed by the bitter sweetness of the liberal arts." Edmund may have undergone the experience described as follows by a Paris preacher, Jacques de Vitry: "Those who have grown old in an alien land, when they come to study theology can scarcely bear to be parted from their Aristotle." Like the Paris masters of around 1200, Edmund shows in his surviving writing that he felt responsible in the classroom for the shaping of future pastors for the Church.

We can learn only a very limited amount from Edmund himself concerning the actual content of his theological teaching at Oxford, for only two writings of his survive. The first of these, *Moralities on the Psalms* (unedited,

one surviving manuscript), was the fruit of his teaching. These glosses contain spiritual exegesis with a strongly moral bent, the style familiar from the
teaching at Paris of Stephen Langton and Peter the Chanter. They represent a well-tried genre and are deliberately devoid of any notable doctrinal
development or personal, individual stamp. The *Speculum*, however, is a
treatise of perfect living, and its success, not only in Latin but in Anglo-
Norman and English versions, bears testimony to the spiritual need that it
answered, as well as to its effectiveness.[12] Edmund's purpose is to show how
the religious may become holy through daily prayer and contemplation. Self-
knowledge is to be acquired by means of the frequent examination of conscience. "Consideration" or "meditation" should range over the miseries of
the human condition and the gifts of God. From that basis the religious can
progress to the knowledge of God, first in creatures, next in the Scriptures,
and lastly in God as He is in his own nature. The points recommended for
meditation are biblical, centering on the mysteries of the life, death, and
resurrection of Christ, and theological, grace and the Trinity; but the goal
of the program is the personal union of the soul with God, in a mystical form
of prayer that seeks to rise beyond all corporeal images and even beyond
reason itself. St. Bernard is invoked on mystical prayer, but by far the greatest debt is owed to Hugh of St. Victor (*Meditatio in moribus; De arrha animae;
De arca morali*). Indeed the *Speculum* can be viewed as a humble but effec-
tive endeavor on Edmund's part to summarize the religious ideal of the first
great representative of the Victorine school; it was composed in all probability
for the use of a religious community. Edmund drew together compendiously
and lent structure to the advice and spiritual encouragement scattered
throughout Hugh's works of theology and spirituality.

It is, I think, legitimate to suppose that the *Speculum*, although intended
for the instruction of the members of a religious community, is capable of
throwing some light upon one component strand of its author's thinking that
was carried over there from his Oxford lectures. His exegetical classes aimed
at expounding the spiritual and practical teaching of the Scriptures, and the
influence of Hugh's *De sacramentis*, and possibly of Richard of St. Victor's
notable work *De Trinitate*, would have been tangible at many important
points in his lectures. Victorine spirituality was a living force in Hugh's
abbey at Paris during the time Edmund spent there. Above all, there is an
anecdote, recounted by Robert Bacon, that records vividly an event that took
place at a lecture of Edmund's and that suggests the spiritual quality of his
teaching. While Edmund was lecturing, the abbot of Quarr entered the

schoolroom and listened to the end of the lesson. At its close, seven of the students, "fired, it may be thought, as much by the master's eloquence as by the presence of the abbot," left with the latter to take the habit in his order.[13]

Edmund was not an innovator in theology and his teaching left little mark on the schools of the succeeding generations, but he was venerated after his death as a holy man. His cult spread rapidly, largely owing to the fact that "he appealed to the popular imagination because he satisfied the profound conviction of simple people that those who ruled the Church should be learned, humble and holy men."[14]

Crisis and Resolution, 1209–1214

According to a leading authority, "During the 1190s the schools of Oxford took a very large step forward towards the range of studies of the later university . . . Taking them as a whole they represent almost the whole field of later studies."[15] As we have seen, the practice and study of law predated the developments we have just surveyed in theology, with Alexander Nequam, and in the advanced study of the arts, with Blund. We can conclude that by around 1200 a range of teaching was already available to students from the island of Britain who could no longer make the traditional passage to Paris. We may not speak as yet of a university, nor even of faculties and curricula. There is no evidence of any corporate organization of masters and scholars. Mention is admittedly made, in 1201, of a "Magister scholarum Oxoniae" (named as John Grim), and a few years later of a certain Alard, who is styled "rector scholarum." This indicates some sense of an at least symbolic unity among the teachers there. We are left to suppose that each master conducted his own school and was responsible only for his own pupils. Any organization that existed was of an informal and pragmatic kind, and dealt probably with the fixing of rents for schoolhouses owned by townsmen. It was out of this inchoate nucleus that the university developed, after 1214. The career of St. Edmund has a notable place in the unfolding story, as representing the only definitely ascertainable link of a personal kind between the embryonic and the fully corporate states of the developing studies, for he taught arts at Oxford before 1209 and theology at the university that was incorporated in 1214. Between these two stages in his career, however, a crisis intervened that placed all higher studies at Oxford at the gravest risk, but whose successful resolution established them on a new, and this time permanent, footing.

Troubles between students and townspeople were a familiar part of life. Toward the end of 1209 an Oxford student killed his mistress and fled. Two of his companions were seized by the officers of the town and hanged as accomplices. This trespass on the immunity of clerics compelled the great majority of the masters and students to leave for other places, such as Paris, Cambridge, or Reading. In normal times the quarrel might have been composed, but from the previous year England had lain under papal interdict, and so the local upset became part of the regional confusion, wherein ecclesiastical authority had no direction to offer apart from that of waiting and hoping for a settlement between the king and the pope. Only within a wider framework of agreement could the townspeople of Oxford still hope to secure the return of those lucrative sources of income, the schools and their scholars. Their commercial interests led them to seek a meeting with the papal legate who was eventually sent to England to bring an end to the interdict. Nicholas, Bishop of Tusculum, arrived in the country as cardinal legate in September 1213, bringing the interdict to an end, and he met the representatives of the town in October. The terms he proposed (20 June 1214) after two visits to Oxford came to be known as the Legatine Ordinance, and they mark the true beginnings of the University of Oxford.

In the briefest possible summary, the decisions of the legate, which were in effect conditions for the return of the scholars, concerned the rents for lodgings, future income to be derived from the townspeople for the benefit of poor scholars, the securing of just prices for scholars' provisions, and the jurisdictional immunity of clerics. In addition, masters who had continued to teach during the period of the withdrawal were suspended for three years, and penance was to be done by all those directly involved in the hanging of the two clerks. The legate had given thought to the continuing supervision of the agreement in order to underwrite authority and secure continuity. Not unexpectedly, he decided to place the bishop of Lincoln in charge of affairs, so that ecclesiastical discipline, in regard to both scholars and townspeople, might be reinstated. He laid down that the bishop should set a chancellor over the scholars. The legate's instrument was a charter of submission issued by the town and handed over to the bishop. This document bound the townspeople to keep faithfully the terms of the settlement. During the summer of 1214 the bishop, Hugh of Wells, took action in the wake of the legate, so that the momentum of events might lead to the rapid reopening of the schools, presumably in the autumn. He laid down detailed arrangements for the swearing of the prescribed oath, and thus reinforced the solemn and permanent nature of the arrangements, as well as his own direct overall responsibility for the successful conduct of the institution that was being brought into existence. It is not known whom the bishop chose as his chancellor "to be set over the scholars," but in 1216 it was Mr. Geoffrey de Lacy who occupied that delicate but unremunerated office.

The long-term effect of the legatine settlement is easy to assess (the institution got under way and began to expand), but the short-term is hard to discern. There is little evidence of scholastic activity at Oxford for ten or more years after 1214. The impetus that had visibly been building up circa 1200 had been completely dissipated. There can have been but little continuity, with the exception of a few masters, of whom Edmund of Abingdon alone is known by name. Academic activity doubtless took place from the autumn of 1214 onward, but the effort must have been an uphill one and little trace of it has survived—unless of course some portion of the large surviving output of that prodigy of the early university, Master Robert Grosseteste, can be assigned to these otherwise silent years.

A LIFE POORLY KNOWN

The First Six Decades

Had Robert Grosseteste not lived to be over eighty, and had he not become bishop of Lincoln, our knowledge of him, as a writer and thinker, and especially as a man, would have been as sketchy as it remains for most of his direct contemporaries, the known facts of whose lives can for the most part be written down on a page or two. As it is, a great deal is known of his activities, journeys, and undertakings from about the year 1230 (when he was already over sixty) onward due to the fact that his fame was growing and his influence spreading. As his activities increased, records relating to him naturally became more numerous. However, despite the redoutable efforts and enterprise shown by modern historians, only a very few certain facts are known about his life, up to the point when he could no longer be overlooked.

Evidence concerning His Early Life

What is actually known with some degree of certainty concerning the first six decades of Grosseteste's life can be set down fairly briefly. The hypotheses suggested by historians to fill in the largest gap in his biography will be outlined subsequently.

Robert Grosseteste was born at Stowe in the county of Suffolk, in the diocese of Norwich. That his parents were of the poorest we know, both through the prominent chronicler Matthew Paris (of St. Alban's Abbey), and because his low birth was an issue when he became bishop, and thereby a *seigneur*. He had a sister named Ivette, who became a nun; but that is all we know of his immediate family. His native language (like his name) was French, or rather the dialect spoken by the descendants of the Normans settled in England. The best argument in favor of the claim that Anglo-Norman was his native tongue is that it was in that dialect that Grosseteste wrote the lengthy religious poem known today as *Château d'Amour*, as well as some prayers; other brief writings are attributed to him. Now, it is notoriously rare to find someone who can write poetry, or even versify well, in any language but his own; daily prayer also comes most easily in the native tongue. Grosseteste's dialect of French also makes an unexpected appearance in one of his Latin writings on the Sacrament of Penance. Suggesting a formula of words to be used by the penitent, he switches to Anglo-Norman, for, as he states, confession should be made in French, or in the other vernacular if it is better known to the penitent:

> Confessio autem facienda est gallice uel ydiomate magis noto. Et est ita incipienda—hec autem sunt prima verba: Io me faz confes a Deu, e a nostre dame seinte Marie, e a tuz seins, e a vus, pere, ke io par ma mauveite ai mut pecchee, e offendu mon creatour, et trespasse ses comaundemenz. Io ai mut pecche en penser, en parole, e en fet.

Grosseteste continues with a lengthy injunction for the priest to use "in English or French" (*ita dicat anglica uel gallica lingua* . . .). He himself gives it in French only.[1]

Growing up as he did in a society where two languages were spoken, Grosseteste evidently could speak some dialect of English, as the following story, recounted by the Franciscan chronicler Thomas of Eccleston, makes clear. Some young Italians had come recommended to the bishop of Lincoln as candidates for benefices in his diocese. Grosseteste, who shared the medieval genius for the eloquent gesture, acted the part of a penitent who failed to make himself understood in English to his confessor:

> He got up and went to confession in English, on bended knees, before the boys presented to him by the cardinals, and beat his breast, and wept and shouted; and they retired in confusion.[2]

Grosseteste's point was that as Italians they in some cases might already have adequate French, but they would experience extreme difficulty with the English dialects of the country. Both languages mattered equally in his eyes as far as the everyday pastoral activities of the Church's ministers were concerned. Grosseteste himself possessed a definite linguistic gift, which he may well have exercised in learning some English even before he began Latin at school. He was, of course, to master ancient Greek, much later in life.

A youthful master Robert Grosseteste is mentioned in a letter of Gerald of Wales, who wrote as follows to the young man's employer, William de Vere, bishop of Hereford, to emphasize his merits:

> I know that he will be a great support to you in various kinds of business and legal decisions, and in providing cures to restore and preserve your health, for he has reliable skill in both these branches of learning, which in these days are most highly rewarded. Besides, he has a solid foundation of the liberal arts and wide reading, which he adorns with the highest standards of conduct.[3]

The young master is associated with Lincoln for the first time in a charter that he signed as a witness, at some point between 1186 and 1189–1190, at the time when the Carthusian Hugh of Avalon was bishop there (1186–1200). If Grosseteste could be styled a master (even in a rather loose and informal sense) by 1189, at the latest, he cannot well have been born after circa 1168. We know from an allusion of Roger Bacon that he attained to a great age, and we are entitled by the evidence to say that he was at least sixty-seven years of age at the time of his elevation to the see of Lincoln (1235). That would make him eighty-five or more at his death, in 1253. It is likely enough that his medical knowledge contributed to the length of his life.

Grosseteste's name appears as a witness to several of Bishop De Vere's charters, but after the death of his patron (1198) we lose sight of him. In the years 1213 and 1216 he was involved as an official in litigation within the diocese of Hereford. Some time later (before 1227) he witnessed a charter of the bishop of Hereford instituting a priest to a church in Shropshire. The next fact we know is that Grosseteste himself was presented by the bishop of Lincoln, Hugh of Wells, to the church of Abbotsley, on 25 April 1225. The charter tells that he was then a deacon. Further eccesiastical promotion marked his rise to prominence, for he was appointed archdeacon of Leicester in 1229, with a prebend in Lincoln Cathedral. And we know that in the year 1229–1230 he accepted the invitation of Br. Agnellus of Pisa, the provincial of the newly arrived Franciscans, to become their teacher. From that point onward documentary evidence for Grosseteste's activites and movements becomes more plentiful. Certain things can even be inferred with probability concerning the time at which some of his most important writings were put into circulation.

So much, then, for what is actually known of his life up to the time when he was over sixty. Where historians are met with documentary silence, they have resorted to hypotheses and conjectures in an attempt to fill up gaps, using such hints as are supplied, mostly very tantalizingly and often problematically, by contemporary or later sources.

It is perhaps of some significance that the later the information we have concerning Grosseteste's career, the greater is the certitude with which it is expressed. A seventeenth-century historian of the university of Paris claimed Grosseteste among the early doctors of theology there. A fifteenth-century chancellor of Oxford, Thomas Gascoigne, an admirer of Grosseteste and an assiduous collector of his theological writings, was convinced that Grosseteste was an M.A. of Oxford and a doctor of theology of the same university. Unfortunately, no documentary evidence was quoted to back up either of these claims, nor has any turned up so far.

Two Rival Hypotheses Considered

What was Grosseteste doing during these twenty or more problematic years, circa 1200 to 1225? Where did he study? How did he support himself? Did he teach? Here we are in the realm of hypotheses and conjectures, where the best we can do, at present, is to outline the salient points first of an older, then of a much more recent reconstruction of his career.

In 1953 the seventh centenary of the death of Grosseteste was marked by the preparation of a volume of essays by distinguished historians.[4] Daniel A. Callus, O.P., the editor of the volume, presented the life and intellectual development of his subject in a learned study, whose influence has been felt ever since. He suggested that the young master, on leaving Hereford after the death of his employer, went to Oxford to teach the arts. His career there would have been interrupted by the dispersion of masters and scholars, which lasted from 1209 to 1214. Callus assumed that, like Edmund of Abingdon, John Blund, and other English masters of arts, Grosseteste emigrated to Paris, there to study theology, as so many from the island of Britain had done before him and were to do after him, the way to that greatest of intellectual centers being for the islanders an easy and obvious one to take. When things were finally straightened out at Oxford by the papal legate sent for that purpose, a charter of 1214 guaranteed the rights of masters and students and instituted the post of chancellor of the new institution. Callus was convinced that Grosseteste was the first chancellor of the university of Oxford, and that he was a regent master in theology from 1214 until he moved to the friars' new schoolhouse (1229), where he continued to lecture until his elevation to the see of Lincoln (1235). The contributors to the centenary volume seem collectively to have regarded Grosseteste as a distinguished product of the nascent university world, a master of arts and of theology, a product of the new Parisian scholastic theology, and a most eminent scholar-bishop—a figure, in short, of European and Catholic dimensions.

In 1986 Sir Richard Southern showed just how much of the evidence used by Callus in his argument could be stood on its head.[5] In Southern's revisionist hypothesis, Grosseteste's mind as it is known to us from his writings was the product not of metropolitan, scholastic Paris but of the provincial setting of the England where he spent probably all his earliest years: years of schooling, of clerking to ecclesiastical patrons, and of occasional teaching in centers whose repute was largely of a local kind. Grosseteste's "English mind" (referred to in Southern's title) could best be understood as a product of the English school system and the native scientific tradition of the twelfth century. His scientific originality was the mark left on him by his insular formation; his individuality flowered into a speculative power that, in attempting to reach beyond the limits of what was known, remained acutely aware of the element of uncertainty in all knowledge. His was an undogmatic temper that expressed itself in a rich variety of tentative initiatives. He lacked the patronage that might have sent him to study at Paris, so that he came very late (only after 1225) to the study and teaching of theology (and likewise to the chancellorship), and his mind remained in a different mold from that of the continentally trained scholastics. His theology was less systematic than theirs, rather more programmatic, more rooted in scientific observation and reasoning, more pastoral in character, and more open to the Greek theological experience. In his old age he, who had sprung from the great mass of the underdogs of this world, came more and more under the influence of the current apocalyptic tendencies, which led him, reluctantly, to identify the papacy with the Antichrist and to descend into despair, prophesying at the last the imminence of bloodshed as a sign that the last times had overtaken the unreformable, papally organized Church. Grosseteste was a radical by virtue of his lowly origins; his actions as a bishop showed him to be a passionately principled but rather violent extremist. He was not, however, a revolutionary, but rather a prophet of the failure of institutional Christianity and of the consequent inbreaking of the eschaton upon a wholly unprepared Church and world.[6]

On what is surely the pivotal issue between these two hypotheses, namely, the question as to when Grosseteste occupied the post of chancellor, Callus argued that Grosseteste was chancellor either immediately after the university was effectively chartered, in 1214, or not long after. Southern argues that even by 1225 Grosseteste was not yet in priest's orders and therefore could not have become chancellor until sometime later; and if that is so, then we simply have to think in terms of a new and very different shape to his career, up to 1229.

The Southern hypothesis has had the effect of forcing each scrap of relevant evidence under the microscope, as never before. Some of the evidence turns out to be truly kaleidoscopic in its effect, as in the case of the well-known Gestalt dot-patterns (a quasi-visual fatigue, induced by seeing the pattern for too long in one way, produces its own click-over effect, and suddenly the rabbit is an elephant—or vice versa).

A critical appraisal of Southern's hypothesis about the unknown part of Grosseteste's career could perhaps place it between two points in time, circa 1214 and circa 1225. A series of questions can be hung on or about the year 1225, when we do at last know something of Grosseteste, that is, that he was beneficed as a deacon. Were deacons in fact not entitled to teach and to exercise other functions in the theological schools of the time? Does Grosseteste's entire professorial career as a theologian, together with his published output in exegesis and theology, have to be squeezed by the historian into the brief span of ten years (or perhaps even less than that) as a priest, between 1225 at the earliest, when he was still a deacon, and 1235, when he was made bishop? Some of the evidence used by Southern to argue his case is ambiguous, and, as I hope to show, open to an entirely different reading.

It is often in the assumptions from which they set out that historians are vulnerable, rather than in their hypothesizing and exploring. It is Southern's assumption that no deacon would have been permitted to teach theology that constrains him to restrict Grosseteste's theological activity to his priestly period and that encourages him to think that Grosseteste's chancellorship must consequently have come late in the day (i.e., after 1225 at the earliest). If, however, we compare the case of Grosseteste with that of William of Auvergne, the Paris theologian and bishop who was his contemporary (ca. 1190–1249), the source of Southern's major difficulty can, I think, be cleared up. Much in William's career is obscure, but it appears certain that he was a master in theology in 1223, was a regent master by 1225, and held a canonry at Notre Dame from 1223, at the latest. Yet when Pope Gregory IX personally nominated him bishop of Paris, in very unusual circumstances, in April 1228, he was ordained both priest and bishop. Now, if a deacon could be a regent in theology at Paris, a deacon could lecture in theology at Oxford; and it was undoubtedly from the ranks of the regent masters that the chancellor was elected or nominated. Perhaps historians should get used to the idea that the secular masters at the universities were, as a rule, not priests. In any case it is no doubt from a modern perspective that we are inclined to say, "he was *only* a deacon." The fact seems to be that no one at present knows exactly what a deacon (as distinct from an archdeacon) actually was, in the Middle Ages. It would appear that the deacon had a status that allowed him to teach theology, to preach, to hold a benefice, and even to be elected pope! It is thought that St. Francis became a deacon in order to preach with legitimacy. Lothar de Segni was a deacon at the time of his election as Pope Innocent III. The well-known Paris theologian Petrus Cantor died in deacon's orders. Even in the late thirteenth century Gerard of Abbéville and Henry of Ghent, two prominent Paris theologians, appear to have been in deacon's orders all their lives.

In terms of Grosseteste's orders nothing we know of precludes his having been a teacher of theology at Oxford from, say, 1214 onward.

Southern has interesting remarks to make about a letter addressed by Grosseteste to Master Adam Rufus, which he assigns to the years 1225–1229. Grosseteste replies there to his former pupil's question as to whether it is orthodox to refer to God as "the form of all things, the first form." Southern relates this epistolary exchange to the condemnation of David of Dinant on grounds of pantheism, in 1210. However, a more economical reading of the evidence would lead us straight to the pantheism imputed to Scottus Eriugena. The masterpiece of Eriugena, the *Periphyseon*, was condemned by Pope Honorius in a letter of 23 January 1225, addressed to all the archbishops and bishops of France and England. Adam presumably wrote to Grosseteste about a question of notable theological actuality, in order to have the core of the issue analyzed for him. That would be in 1225 or 1226, presumably. In all plausibility Adam turned to Grosseteste as an established theologian, and very likely his own teacher, for enlightenment.

A commonsense objection can be mounted against Southern's hypothesis that Grosseteste's theological career and publications must be late; it is simply that no human being, however gifted, could have mastered, taught, and published theology in the way that Grosseteste did, in the space of a mere decade. Grosseteste's theological reading was little short of encyclopedic. Moreover, during the years in question he worked hard at Greek; he read Greek manuscripts (which is slow work!) of writings by Basil, Chrysostom, and Theophylact that were not available in Latin versions, as well as others that were, such as Damascene and the Pseudo-Dionysius. As one takes the measure of Grosseteste's very extensive reading in the Latin and Greek Fathers, the point comes when one is forced to perform too many mental acrobatics in order to accommodate the hypothesis of his late theological development.

The Chancellorship of Oxford

Both Callus and Southern attribute the utmost importance to a recorded statement of Bishop Oliver Sutton of Lincoln, to the effect that Grosseteste had occupied the office of chancellor of the University of Oxford. Once again, their interpretations are widely divergent. Here is what Sutton said, in a literal translation:

> The Bishop added that blessed Robert, the late bishop of Lincoln, who held this office at a time when he was regent in the university, said that at the inception of his creation as bishop the bishop of Lincoln, his immediate predecessor, had not permitted that the said Robert be called chancellor but master of the schools.

Callus preferred to situate this incident in the earliest years of the new institution, arguing that the dispute about the title can best be understood as having taken place at the very beginning, before things had settled down. Southern, on the other hand, understands the problem that arose for Bishop Sutton in 1295 (is the chancellor elected by his peers, or is he nominated by the bishop of Lincoln?) to be the same as the one involving Grosseteste, so many years earlier. He argues that a dispute over the method of appointment was out of the question in 1214, when the legate and the bishop simply decided the terms on which the schools might reopen (i.e., under the supervision of a chancellor appointed by the bishop). Later, however, as the masters gained in collective self-confidence (say, ten or fifteen years after 1214), a dispute between them and the bishop is more likely to have arisen, concerning not only the title of the office but its very nature.

Now it happens that an interpretation different from both Callus's and Southern's is possible. What reason, it may be asked, could have prompted Grosseteste to proffer at the beginning of his episcopacy (1235 or shortly thereafter) the reminiscence reported by Sutton? Michael Haren can see none.[7] Instead he has shown that there is a possible ambiguity in the Latin of Sutton's reported statement. Grosseteste's bishop, in 1214, was Hugh of Wells. Did Grosseteste himself make the statement quoted above at the beginning of his own (*suae*) creation as bishop; or is it not legitimate, on the contrary, to construe the words in question as stating that Wells, "at the beginning of *his* creation as bishop . . . had not permitted that the said Robert be called chancellor but master of the schools"? (If one rereads the English translation while omitting "that" after "said," the ambiguity of the Latin can be recovered.) Of course, the reflexive in Latin (*se, suus*) should not in terms of grammar be used equivocally; the fact remains, however, that it sometimes was.

When did Hugh of Wells's episcopacy begin? He was consecrated in 1209, but because of the papal interdict that lay on England he was not in control of the temporalities of his see until July 1213—which could be regarded as "the inception of his creation as bishop." It remains true, of course, that the traditional reading of the reflexive adjective in the passage is the more obvious and natural one; nevertheless, once the possibility of Haren's reading is acknowledged it exercises a subversive attraction all its own, and it allows the possibility that Grosseteste was the very first occupant of the post whose title was disputed, and which in Sutton's eyes (all those years later) amounted to the chancellorship. The incident would fit quite snugly and naturally into the beginning of Hugh's episcopacy and the creation of the university that followed it within quite a short time. We know that the title of chancellor was in use by 1221. We know likewise that by June of 1216 Master Geoffrey de Lacy had acceded to the office. If Grosseteste was indeed the first chancellor (in all but name), his term was very brief.

If Bishop Sutton's story refers to a decision taken in 1214 about the title, then his attitude to it is quite understandable. St. Hugh of Avalon, Wells's predecessor as bishop of Lincoln, had recruited William de Montibus as his chancellor, in which office the latter presided over the cathedral schools there for some twenty-five years, up to his death in 1213. Now in 1214, would the bishop not have felt some hesitation in conferring the title of chancellor upon the master of the new schools at far-off Oxford, when in fact he already had a chancellor (or at least a vacancy for such) within the diocese, at his own

venerable cathedral school on the hill at Lincoln? The ecclesiastical reorga-
nization of the schools at Oxford in 1214 was presumably not meant to eclipse
or even lessen the bright light of Lincoln.[8] After all, the new scholastic arrangements were an experiment, one whose importance should be viewed
not in proportion to the subsequent illustrious history of Oxford University,
but rather in the much humbler terms of a venture undertaken in the light
of a marginally positive calculation of the probability of a successful outcome
to the undertaking. No one, we may be sure, thought in terms of re-creating
Paris on the island of Britain. The bishop's attitude to the title suggests a
conflict in his own mind between his natural loyalty to his cathedral school,
on the one hand, and his willingness to respect the terms of the Legatine
Ordinance, on the other.

   On these considerations Grosseteste's chancellorship should be placed
between 1214 and 1221, as Callus argued, but not in any case as late as 1225–
1230, as Southern believes.

   A further piece of evidence employed by Southern to argue for the late
dating of Grosseteste's theological regency, and consequently of his chancellorship, is similarly open to more than one construction.[9] In an unedited
sermon Grosseteste requires clerical penitents to avow their status to their
confessor, on the grounds that sin increases in gravity with the responsibility and position of the sinner. He gives an illustration in the first person:
"First I was a cleric, then a master in theology, and a priest, and finally a
bishop." Southern regards it as "very striking that he appears to divide his
own career into three phases," the second of which intimately associates his
lectureship in theology with his priesthood. Taken in its context, however,
is it not more likely that the assertion draws its force from the four distinct
levels of increasing responsibility through which Grosseteste himself (as his
audience would have been well aware) had passed in the Church?

   Grosseteste's life up to 1225 cannot be reconstructed chronologically, yet
several features of his career may be posited with a degree of probability.
Some working hypothesis is required as a provisional framework for our
exploration of his writings.

   At least in the early part of his life Grosseteste had a documented association with Hereford. The scientific tradition of Hereford was strong in the
twelfth century; we may suppose with some confidence that it left an early
mark upon his young mind.[10] Grosseteste certainly taught the liberal arts,
as his mastery of logic and his treatise on the arts sufficiently attest. Several
considerations indicate that he spent a period of theological study at Paris,

which can be set with plausibility in the years of the Interdict in England, at a time when higher scholastic activity was very severely reduced and normal ecclesiastical administration practically suspended. A family of Grossetestes can be located at Paris who were acquainted with William of Auvergne, Grosseteste's friend; they may have been relations. Grosseteste had other acquaintances in Paris, and he was approvingly familiar with the course of study that prevailed at Paris during the earlier part of the century. Besides, in later life he showed no reluctance to cross the channel, and he was intimately acquainted with a precious Greek manuscript conserved as a relic at St. Denis, containing the writings of the Pseudo-Areopagite. On the other hand, his theological teaching seems to have been confined to England, and probably to Oxford, for no trace of theological influence on his part can be found at Paris. He cannot be linked to the pre-1209 Oxford by any document. Thomas Gascoigne, in the fifteenth century, asserted as a fact that he was a Master of Arts and a Doctor of Theology of Oxford. His theological career there very likely covered the entire period from circa 1214 to 1235.

The Public Life

Robert Grosseteste was presented as deacon to the Church of Abbotsley by the bishop of Lincoln, on 25 April 1225. From this point onward many aspects of his life are well known, as he lived increasingly a public life. He was archdeacon of Leicester from 1229 to 1231, with a prebend in Lincoln Cathedral that seems to have been the Church of St. Margaret, Leicester. This prebend he retained (minus the cure of souls) when, in 1231, in the wake of a serious illness, he resigned his other benefices, judging in conscience that he could not discharge his responsibilities. His adoption of voluntary poverty reflects a growing spiritual affinity with the Franciscans, to whom he lectured from 1229/30 until 1235. He remained attached to their humble school until on 27 March 1235 he was elected bishop of Lincoln. Matthew Paris records the death of Bishop Hugh of Wells on 7 February 1235 and continues:

> After his burial, when the canons had to elect someone to succeed him, a division manifested itself among them; this one could not bear that so-and-so should be appointed, no more could that one suffer the other candidate, all from jealousy and resentment. At last, after many disputes

among themselves, the canons voted unanimously for Master Robert, *cognomen* Grosseteste, to the surprise of all, even though it was being said that he was bound to the Franciscans.

In other words, Grosseteste was elected as a compromise candidate. He was consecrated bishop of Lincoln, the largest diocese in England, at Reading, on 2 June 1235, by Edmund of Abingdon, his old colleague at Oxford.

The central motif of his episcopate was the personal responsibility of the bishop for the pastoral care of every soul in his diocese, to be discharged through every means at his disposal: the education and appointment of worthy pastors; the conscientious correction of abuses; the pastoral visitation of the cathedral chapter, as well as of the monasteries and the deaneries of his diocese; the encouragement and the pastoral employment of the mendicant orders of Dominicans and Franciscans; the publication of numerous pastoral writings; and the example of his own preaching. His fervent attachment to the reforming measures decreed by the Fourth Council of the Lateran is reflected in the influential set of statutes he promulgated (before 1240) as a guide to the priests of his diocese. He took part in the General Council of Lyons (1245). Disappointed by the failure of the council to give new impetus to pastoral activity, he returned to Lyons to present to Pope Innocent IV, on 13 May 1250 and subsequent days, a memorandum severely critical of the archbishop of Canterbury and of the provision to English benefices by the Roman curia of candidates unworthy or incapable of the pastoral charge. God had granted to the successors of Peter the *plenitudo potestatis* in view of the edification of his Church; abuse of that divinely given power was a grave and unforgivable scandal, he argued. In his last year of life (1253) he vehemently rejected the nomination of a nephew of Pope Innocent to a canonry at Lincoln. He died in the night of the eighth to the ninth of October in the year 1253. Several attempts made in the course of the century following his death to secure his canonization remained unsuccessful, despite the reputation for sanctity that he left among the faithful. His tomb is in Lincoln Cathedral. At it a moving service is held annually on the anniversary of his death.

THE COUNCIL OF LYONS
AND ITS AFTERMATH,
THROUGH GROSSETESTE'S EYES

Grosseteste's participation in the First Council of Lyons is one of the least researched aspects of his career as bishop. There can be little doubt, however, that it was in his own eyes the most important moment in the ten years that had intervened since his consecration. For a Catholic bishop, to take part in a general council should be a high moment of the experience of ecclesial unity with the pope, the patriarchs, and many other bishops and dignitaries of the Church. I will attempt in what follows to bring out the preoccupations that accompanied Grosseteste both as a Council Father and as a visitor to the curia in its exile at Lyons. Some of his activities there can be discerned clearly enough, even though none of them can be reconstructed in any great detail on the basis of our present knowledge.

Grosseteste at Lyons, 1245

In the Latin Christian consciousness of the year 1245 the memory of the Fourth Council of the Lateran (convened in 1215 by Pope Innocent III) would have remained sufficiently strong to arouse considerable expectations regarding its successor, and also to present a model for what was about to happen under the new Pope Innocent.[1] There can be no doubt that Grosseteste shared the widely felt veneration for Innocent III. As bishop he modeled his pastoral strategy upon that of the council of 1215; as a pastoral theologian he endeavored to meet its recommendations regarding both clergy and laity. It was no doubt with a considerable sense of privilege, as well as in anticipation of another notable event in the life of the Church, that he attended the gathering at Lyons.

In fact, the notion of a council had been bruited for several years under Pope Gregory IX, who saw in it the only way of getting out of the impasse at which empire and papacy had arrived in their bloody conflict on the Italian peninsula. Gregory regarded the occupation of the papal states as an attack not only upon the Patrimony of Peter but on the papacy itself in its international role of leadership and care for all the Churches. He issued a bull of excommunication of Emperor Frederick II in 1239. He wished to convene an ecumenical council at Rome before the Easter of 1241. However, his plans were upset when on 3 May 1241 the forces of the emperor captured the Genoese fleet carrying a large number of the intending participants from the East to Rome. Just at that time the Mongol attacks had produced ravages in Hungary and Eastern Europe, occasioning a preoccupation of the popes that would last until the sudden, unexpected withdrawal of the invaders, which still left uncertainty behind it. Things were going badly in the Holy Land also, for in 1239 Jerusalem fell to the sultan of Damascus. At the same time pressure was growing upon the Latin empire of Constantinople, which was rapidly being reduced merely to the city itself and its immediate environs. The initiatives undertaken by the papacy in regard to these crises sharply increased its own need for money. In short, it was an exceptionally heavy burden that Gregory IX passed on to his successor when he died on August 21, 1241.

After a lengthy period of *sede vacante*, Sinibaldo Fieschi, a native of Genoa, a distinguished lawyer and an experienced member of the curia, was unanimously elected pope, on 25 June 1243.[2] He chose the motto "*Sedens ago*" ("Even while resting I am active"), and he lived up to it throughout the eleven years of his papacy. Forced to flee Rome and Italy for fear of falling into the hands of his enemy, the emperor, he passed through Savoy and came to Lyons (12 December 1244) where, against all expectation, he was to reside until April 1251. He was by then determined to bypass all negotiations with the emperor, in whose personal trustworthiness Innocent reposed no confidence whatsoever, and to summon an ecumenical council, thus fulfilling the project of his predecessor. At the end of December he convoked the council for the Feast of St. John the Baptist (24 June) of the following year. Bulls were sent to bishops, princes, and cities on 3 January 1245. The news of the council must have met Grosseteste already on his way to Rome (as he expected), for in fact he had left England on 19 November. There is not much mystery about his desire to pay a visit to the curia, for he had long been at loggerheads with the dean and chapter of Lincoln over his right to carry out official visitation of the chapter, that is, to oversee its affairs. As it turned out, Grosseteste's business was to keep him at Lyons far beyond the end of the council; in fact, he did not return to England until the month of October. Most English bishops were represented at the assembly by procurators, but Grosseteste was present in person throughout its three weeks duration, accompanied by Adam Marsh as his advisor.

A general council of the Church had a well-established form to follow. At Lyons, a preparatory session was held on 26 June and was attended by all the important figures. The agenda seems to have taken the following shape. First came discussion of the empire of Roumania; then came the situation in Greece and Constantinople. There followed in third place a request from the English representatives, reinforced by eight archbishops and twenty bishops, for the canonization of the late archbishop of Canterbury, Edmund of Abingdon (d. 1240). Innocent said that there were more urgent matters to be attended to, but promised to respond to the request within a short time. Following hard upon that matter came a speech by the lawyer Thaddeus of Suessia, the delegate of the emperor, opening the subject that was to dominate the three sessions of the council. The pope replied to the protestations of Thaddeus. Toward the close of the session, Bishop Valerian of Beirut read a letter from the bishops of Palestine concerning the situation in the Holy Land. To have managed to get the canonization of Edmund placed third on the initial agenda was a major achievement, one in which Grosseteste no doubt played a prominent part.

Grosseteste and Edmund Rich (Edmund of Abingdon) were colleagues at Oxford for some time during the years between 1214 and 1222. It was to be Edmund who, as archbishop of Canterbury, would consecrate Grosseteste bishop, on 17 June 1235, at Reading Abbey. To do this he overrode the prohibition of the monks of Canterbury that forbade episcopal consecrations to take place outside of Canterbury Cathedral, unless with their permission. Grosseteste made several attempts to push the archbishop into action concerning various manifestations of royal encroachment upon the liberties of the Church. The first matter concerned the employment of clergy and heads of religious houses as royal judges, but he had to complain later that in this regard he had found his senior colleague unhelpful. In or around 1237 Grosseteste wrote a long letter to Edmund concerning the encroachment by the royal courts upon the jurisdiction of the Church. Edmund was prodded into action by the bishop of Lincoln, but one feels instinctively that he was by temperament more of a conciliator than a challenger. Grosseteste wrote another letter to Edmund, this time to complain about the bribery and intimidation being applied by the king in favor of his own candidate for the diocese of Hereford. The two bishops differed in temperament, but of Grosseteste's sincere admiration for Edmund even in life, there can be no doubt. Once his friend was dead, he simply regarded him as a saint and tried to have him canonized as quickly as possible.

Innocent IV issued mandates for an inquiry into the case of Edmund on 23 April 1244.[3] Two commissions were appointed in the matter, one in France and the other in England, consisting of the bishops of London (Fulk Bassett) and of course Lincoln. The French inquiry was held at Pontigny Abbey, where Edmund had been buried less than four years previously. Witnesses were summoned and depositions were taken, which were then forwarded to the pope. The same procedure was followed by the English commissioners. These submissions met with a cautious response, for the procedure in canonization causes was continually being tightened by the curia. New commissions were established. The one in England was conducted by Richard de Wych (formerly Edmund's chancellor), who was by then bishop of Chichester, assisted by Robert Bacon, O.P. (a former colleague of Edmund and Grosseteste at Oxford), together with the prior of Canons Ashby. (Some years before then the two friends, Edmund and Robert, had been in competition for the services of de Wych in their respective dioceses.) The new French commission returned its documents in May 1245, before the opening of the council, but the arrival of those from England was delayed until the following November.

It was the fact that not all the requisite testimonies were available that allowed the pope to exercise caution a second time at the council itself (as we have seen). The task of inquiring into the French dossier was delegated to a committee of seven, including three cardinals. One of these was Hugh of Santa Sabina (Hugh of St. Cher), whom Grosseteste would certainly have known by reputation at least (he had been the occupant of the Dominican chair at the University of Paris) and whom he was to meet again in 1250. The second was the English Cistercian scholar John of Toledo. The other four members were Grosseteste himself, Fulk Bassett, the canonist Vincentius Hispanus, and the English Franciscan scholar Master Alexander of Hales, who at some much earlier period in his career had (according to the chronicler Salimbene) been Grosseteste's university *socius*, or junior fellow and assistant. This was an extremely impressive commission, three of whose members were among the most eminent theologians and scholars of their generation. The commission declared itself in favor of Edmund's canonization. However, the pope was still unwilling to pronounce sentence; it would seem that he was not impressed by the large number of miracles that were claimed and wanted a new investigation to be carried out on the basis of the interrogation of witnesses. The procurement of witnesses from England caused further delay, but proved to be of decisive value. On Sunday, 16 December, a consistory met in the Lyons Cathedral of St. Jean. Cardinal Hugh of Santa Sabina delivered an address on Edmund's sanctity and miracles, at the conclusion of which the pope pronounced sentence and proclaimed Edmund a saint. Grosseteste would not have learned of this happy outcome until well into 1247, when the bull *Novum matris ecclesiae*, promulgated on 11 January 1247, would have reached him, naming 16 November as the feast day of the new saint. With that there concluded one of Grosseteste's major pieces of business at Lyons, and probably one of his several motives for setting out for the curia even before the promulgation of the council was made. More than almost anything he had achieved up to then, it must have given him deep satisfaction to see his friend and former colleague raised to the altars of the Church.[4]

But let us return to the council. Official business was transacted in three sessions: 28 June, 5 July, and 17 July, the closing session. Pope Innocent inaugurated the council by addressing to the impressive assembly filling the cathedral a discourse on Psalm 93 [94]: "According to the multitude of my sorrows in my heart, thy comforts have given joy to my soul." The sermon, which proved to be about the five sorrows of the pope, signaled the principal preoccupations of the council. According to the order he laid down, these were corruption in the behavior of clergy and laity at all levels; the distress of the Holy Land at the hands of the Saracens; the division of the Church through the schism of the Greeks; the threat of the Mongols or Tartars; and, finally, the persecution of the Church by the emperor. We cannot here trace even in outline the unfolding of the council, but it is worth noting that the reform of the Church was placed first in its program, as had been the case with its predecessor at Rome, in 1215. The pope illustrated his theme of laxity at every level, including that of the hierarchy, with a series of examples.

It would appear that the final point (concerning the emperor) was developed in somewhat more detail than the three preceding ones. Much of the remainder of this first session was occupied by a point-by-point defense made by the procurator of the emperor on behalf of his master. The pope replied in equally great detail, addressing all the litigious matters, which included the repeated violation of oaths, the suspicion of heresy, and sacrilege. The session of 5 July saw the continuation of these discussions. The pope received notable support in his case against the emperor from the bishops of Spain. Innocent agreed to a delay in fixing the third session in order to permit the emperor to fulfill his proclaimed desire to attend it.

The third session was finally held on 17 July; the emperor had not turned up. The resolutions of the council were given a formal reading: twenty-two decrees, mostly of a juridical nature, and five constitutions concerning the principal issues that had been referred to in the pope's initial discourse. According to Matthew Paris, the delegation from England entered a protest against the reading (among other privileges) of the document of King John, placing his kingdom in vassalage to the Apostolic See. The English representatives protested that this surrender had never received the assent of the nobility. The memorandum read out by Guillaume de Powicke had in addition a financial grievance to declare against the different levies that the Holy See had imposed on England. The protest extended to the collation of benefices upon foreigners and the collection of the taxes that the papacy had recently imposed. In answer the pope could do little else but temporize, because a plenary session of the council could scarcely be expected to get to the bottom of these points. The undertaking was given to the delegates that the curia would accord due examination to the matter and would make an end of the excesses that had been the object of the protest. The attention of the council was turned once again to the clash between the emperor and the pope. After several exchanges, Innocent read the bull of deposition of the emperor, who in any case had already been excommunicated by Pope Gregory IX. This appears to have been the very last act of the final session.

Even though we cannot trace the part that the bishop of Lincoln played as a representative of the clergy of his nation, the attitude of the English delegation is of importance in view of Grosseteste's own well-thought-out position on the matters raised, especially regarding the appointment of pastors at every level. He was to give very public expression to his ideas five years after the council, when he returned to Lyons in 1250.

Months before the opening of the council Grosseteste took part in the consecration of his friend Roger de Weseham as bishop of Coventry and Lichfield, which took place on 19 February 1245 at Lyons. Weseham had been the third lector at the Franciscan school at Oxford and had been chosen by Grosseteste to be dean of his cathedral. His election to the episcopate doubtless owed something to his bishop's constant preoccupation with identifying suitable candidates for the highest office, but it may also have been motivated by a desire on Grosseteste's part to smooth the very strained relations between the chapter and him in advance of the settlement of differences which his visit to the curia aimed at achieving: the removal of the dean formerly selected by the bishop would in turn allow the canons to elect to the vacant office someone more acceptable to themselves. If Grosseteste himself preached at the consecration, which may have emanated in the presence of the pope, that would account for a report which is to be found in the *Lambeth Palace MS 499*, a source of much diverse and worthwhile material on Grosseteste, some of which appears to have emanated from his own household. Preceding the titles of the canons of the council of 1245 in the codex, the following rubric was inserted:

> These new constitutions which follow were made law by Pope Innocent IV at Lyons in the General Council. Robert Grosseteste bishop of Lincoln was present and preached there, taking his theme from the Gospel verse, "A very great multitude spread their garments in the way" [Mt 21:8].[5]

No such sermon has been identified. Yet the claim advanced is a definite one and should not lightly be set aside. The word "there" is of course ambiguous: does it mean at the council, or simply at Lyons? Grosseteste would certainly not have been chosen to preach at one of the solemn sessions of the council, granted the precedence over him of patriarchs and curial cardinals, but on the other hand he would have been the most natural and obvious choice as preacher (as well as co-consecrator) at the Mass on 19 February during which his close associate was raised to the episcopate.

How did the bishop of Lincoln spend his time at Lyons, and in particular the crowded three weeks of the council itself? In the first place, just like all his fellow bishops, he would have spent the interval between the official assemblies in attending consistories, consecrations and other liturgies, commission meetings, and numerous discussion groups. This was a privileged moment for the more than 150 bishops who, together with abbots, deans of chapters and other dignitaries, in addition to numerous lay delegations sent by kingdoms and cities, assisted at Lyons. Each of the representatives was able to extend his acquaintanceship within the Church, at its largest gathering for a generation. Their presence at Lyons also allowed the participants to take the measure of the pope and his principal officials at close quarters. It is known that an opportunity was given to each bishop to meet the pope personally (Grosseteste and his party had months before, on their arrival, been received with courtesy and honor by the pope himself; see *Ep.* 113). Innocent, taking the hands of each bishop into his own, asked him to pledge support for the papacy, in the face of the ravages made by the emperor and his army throughout Italy. Grosseteste, just like any other Council Father, would have given his undertaking face-to-face in this manner to the supreme pontiff. One may suppose that regarding the consideration accorded by the council to the Greek territories, the Holy Land, and the Tartar threat, the bishops of the Latin Church can only have been impressed by the quality and the extent of the information that had been assembled by the curia, through legations sent as far as the Baltic missions and embassies to the sultans of Egypt and the Levant. (Commissioners were shortly to be sent to make contact with the Mongol princes.) It is worth noting that Adam Marsh, who was present in the capacity of counselor to his friend the bishop of Lincoln, took an active part in the discussions of the Mongol problem conducted at the council itself. He later followed this up with a treatise, *Ad Dominum Papam*, concerning the possibility of a mission for the conversion of the Asian raiders. There can be little doubt that Grosseteste joined with him in attending informative discussions bearing on this missionary problem in particular. For them and the many others coming, like them, from far-flung and even marginal provinces of the Church, the sense of being able to influence the uniquely supraregional agency of the Christian world must have been impressive indeed.

The design of Frederick II was to reduce the papacy from territorial independence to subjection under him and his heirs. There was in the thirteenth century a long-standing and still-prevailing agreement among Latin Christians to the effect that the spiritual independence of the papacy could be exercised effectively only on the basis of territorial autonomy. The pope seized the occasion presented by the council, meeting in exile from Rome, to reaffirm the rights and privileges of the successors of Peter over the papal states, which were known as the "Donation of Constantine." A very lengthy document, which has survived in great part, was drawn up. Known to historians as the *Transsumpta of Lyons*, it reaffirmed the privileges of the Holy See, detailing its temporalities. Like every other bishop, Grosseteste would have been closely informed about what was going forward. He was even asked, as a bishop of great standing, to be one of the forty leading personalities present at the council who applied their seals to the compilation. The exemplar of the document that has survived in the Vatican Archives carries the name "Robertus Lincolniensis," placed in the upper half of the list of dignitaries; his seal is still attached to the document.

Among the constitutions of the council the one that doubtlessly possessed most interest in the eyes of the bishop of Lincoln was entitled "Cura Nos Pastoralis," on pastoral care. It addressed itself to the reform of the Church. During the deliberations of the council the economic plight of numerous dioceses, chapters, abbeys, and collegiates was discussed. The economy was undergoing change from an agrarian civilization in the direction of a new dominance of urban and commercial centers, while the Church continued to depend essentially upon revenue coming from land and from tithes. Many dioceses had contracted enormous debts and were repaying them at usurious rates. The conciliar constitution laid down with the full approbation of the Fathers the detailed basis for the responsible and healthy financial administration of all ecclesiastical communities. It instituted annual accounting of revenue and debts, and decreed the regular and systematic verification of financial records, measures from which not even bishops were exempted. Grosseteste was no doubt in agreement with the document, but he may well have felt at the same time that the reform of abuses ought to go a good way beyond legislation for the prudent and accountable material administration of the various institutions of the Church.

Grosseteste's own major administrative preoccupation during the six years preceding the council, one that he prosecuted with zeal while present at the curia, was the outcome of his sense of pastoral responsibility. The refusal of the dean and chapter of Lincoln Cathedral to submit their affairs to his pastoral and administrative oversight filled him with dismay. His side of the dispute can be found in a series of his letters, the longest of which is a treatise on pastoral responsibility.[6] Grosseteste was determined to uphold this reforming measure and to secure for the entire English episcopate a lapsed right. This was probably foremost among the affairs that had prompted him to set out for the curia well before the promulgation of the council. The acrimonious dispute was settled in his favor by a papal decision of 25 August 1245, which put an end to it. He seems to have remained on at Lyons until the document was published and in his actual possession. Evidently, he was determined not to return home without it.

It would be false to history to present the Council of Lyons in a one-sided light, as though the issue concerning the emperor monopolized it completely. This was certainly the principal object of its deliberations, but these extended far and wide beyond it, and the constitutions on the Holy Land, the Greek territories, and the Mongol threat are a testimony to the breadth of outlook of the pope. But the five years following the council, right up to the death of the emperor (which occurred on 13 December 1250), were filled with efforts to implement the deposition of Frederick.

The council decreed measures for the reform of the Church. However, its legislation dealt with symptoms without going to the root of the evil. Pope Innocent deplored the pastoral neglect and the prevailing abuses in the most public way, when opening the council. It is a tragedy in the history of the Church that, far from being able to heal the existing ills, he in fact allowed them to continue, and even multiplied them as years went on by resorting to the very expedients that he had himself condemned. His constant need for money to finance his unrelenting struggle with the emperor produced vexatious effects that were resented almost everywhere, and with particular vehemence in France and England. To finance successive diplomatic and military campaigns, benefices were granted wholesale to servants and supporters of the papal policy (including close relatives of the pope), in order to mobilize their aid or retain their loyalty. The impression was given that under this pope the will to reform the Church was weakened. The complaints of the English representatives during the council itself and of the French king in 1246 suggest that this impression became firmly rooted. Among the critical reactions fomented by the continuance of abuses would in due course be found Grosseteste's own. It is no doubt an exaggeration to see (as some have claimed to do) in Innocent the prototype of a secularized papacy, but one may legitimately regard him as the last of the series of popes whose guiding aims in religion and politics were so intertwined as to become almost indistinguishable.[7]

As he left the city of Lyons in the late autumn of 1245 Grosseteste must have felt tolerably certain that he would not see it again. In fact he was to return there within five years, to protest against the abuse being made of the pastoral ministry.

The Protest of St. Louis of France (1246)

It is worth recalling that Grosseteste's visit of 1250 was not the only, nor the first, public sequel to the recently held council. If England felt it was suffering a severe financial drain in the matter of benefices and collations, France was the other territory of Christendom where resentment against the curia was at its height. Now it is well known to French historians that Louis IX, that king who was to be held up by the papacy itself as a model monarch and who was scrupulous in observing his royal promise "to honour and protect the Church, its personnel and its goods," made his own very serious protest to the pope. Innocent and Louis met in several sessions at Cluny, in 1246, and seem to have had a stormy and rather inconclusive encounter. In the following year the king wrote in protest against the attitude of the papacy with regard to the Church in France. Louis put forward essentially two complaints, and he did so in terms that were close to sounding abrasive. The first was a denunciation of the financial exactions being imposed in the form of taxes on the clergy. The second grievance concerned the conferring of benefices, for the pope had taken upon himself (the king complained) the collation of most of these, thus usurping the rightful place of the king himself, the nobles, and the bishops, all of whom had long-established rights in such matters. The papacy preferred to nominate nonresident foreigners, with the result that the financial aid due from the benefices in question, to the poor, on the one hand, and to the king, on the other, were simply not respected, according to the monarch. In other words, money was being extracted from the royal territories without regard to the king's own responsibilities or his subjects' benefit.

The most recent biographer of St. Louis, Jacques Le Goff, sees in this criticism not so much a movement of laicization as a form of proto-Gallicanism, which he describes as a transfer to the state of the sacredness that is at work in the Church, and an appropriation by the monarchical state of a part of the temporal power in the name of the king's service.[8] Be that as it may, what interests us here is the very close parallel that exists between the criticism urged by the future Saint Louis of France, whose loyalty to the papacy was never placed in the slightest doubt, and that launched by Grosseteste three years later, when he made the journey to Lyons for the second time.

The Consistorial Protest of Friar Hugh
of Digne (Lyons, 1245–1248)

It is through the chronicle of Adam de Salimbene of Parma that we are informed about another voice that was raised loudly in protest against curial appointments to benefices.[9] Hugh of Digne (alias Hugues de Digne; de Barjol; de Montpellier) was a Franciscan spiritual, one of the best-known friars in Provence, indeed in the entire order. He wrote a commentary on the Rule, upholding a strict "spiritual" interpretation of radical community poverty. He was (like Salimbene) a convinced follower of Joachim of Fiore; he has been called "the Father of the Spirituals." He enjoyed a great reputation as a preacher and preached by invitation before King Louis. Salimbene tells us that his voice was "like a trumpet," and so moving that when people listened to it they shook "like rushes in the water." Hugh died about 1257.

The Franciscan was twice invited to address consistories, the first at Rome, the second at Lyons (after the council but sometime before 1248). Salimbene accords several pages to his second discourse. We should not of course assume that we have the wording of the address as it was actually delivered, but there is, on the other hand, no reason to doubt that the substance of it is repeated by the chronicler, and even many of the actual scriptural references that the eloquent speaker invoked. Hugh denounced the nepotism of leading curial figures, who regularly selected candidates for the episcopacy among their own relations instead of inquiring widely after worthy appointees, and who went abroad showing off the red hats of cardinals (the privilege granted them at the recent council), in order to get preferential service. In Salimbene's account great fun is made of the pomp and comfort in which some leading churchmen at the curia lived. The discourse, on the other hand, is in no way anti-papal; on the contrary, the pope's administrators are accused of locking him away and keeping him out of things. The cardinals listened "stupefied" to this audacious speech (they had expected instead to learn from this Joachite prophet what the future had in store), but Innocent IV gave Hugh his blessing together with an encouraging word at its close. Salimbene concludes by stating that he has written down the account just as he had it from the lips of Hugh himself, who confided to his fellow Franciscan that he had relied throughout upon the guarantee given him by the sovereign pontiff that he could speak with complete freedom at the consistory. One has the impression that Pope Innocent was not sorry to have his closest collaborators learn (and learn the hard way) what a low opinion was being formed by outsiders to the administration itself of their practices and their attitudes.

Interestingly, Salimbene recounts that Hugh claimed to have four close friends: John of Parma, the Franciscan Minister General; Jean I, archbishop of Vienne; Robert Grosseteste, bishop of Lincoln, and Friar Adam Marsh. (He informs us, by the way, that these two great friends, Robert and Adam, were both buried in the cathedral of Lincoln.) Grosseteste's long sojourn at Lyons must have provided the occasion for his meeting Hugh and for the rapid blossoming of their friendship. The bishop doubtless spent a good deal of time in the company of Franciscans in the area of Lyons.

It would not be long before Grosseteste would stand where his friend had stood, to say similar things.

Return to Lyons (1250)

Until fairly recent times our knowledge of Grosseteste's appearance at the papal court in 1250 depended primarily upon Matthew Paris's imaginative account, some information in the bishops' letters to Adam Marsh, and the so-called sermon that he was thought to have delivered there. Today that picture has been considerably altered: there exists a fully critical edition of the documents, and recently a diplomatic study has been made of their contents.[10]

Grosseteste was accompanied by Richard Gravesend, an archdeacon, and it was the latter who supplied rich information concerning the dossier of eight texts that Grosseteste, after returning to England, set down as a record of what had transpired and sent to "some of his friends among the cardinals, lest the great labours of his travels be forgotten, or neglected." In other words, the dossier is a memorandum of both the oral and the written arguments that Grosseteste had put forward at the curia and that he endeavored to keep fresh in the minds of the cardinals. The record seems to suggest that after waiting a number of weeks for an audience he was received four times in private by the pope, the first meeting taking place on 13 May 1250, and that he returned a fifth time, to the curia, in order to defend himself against malicious stories that were circulating about him. The documentation is quite exceptionally informative, making up the most detailed record of any private consistory held in the entire period to which it belongs.

Gravesend recounts in the following terms the circumstances surrounding the first appearance of his bishop in semiprivate audience with the pope:

> In the year of the Lord 1250, the Friday after the Ascension (which in that year occurred on the third Ides of May), at Lyons, the venerable Father Robert, Bishop of Lincoln, in the presence of the Lord Pope Innocent IV and the venerable cardinals, accompanied only by me, Richard, his Archdeacon of Oxford, having first captured their good will and made them attentive to those things which he was about to present, handed to the pope a roll in which was written the following. Another roll he handed to William, cardinal bishop of Sabina, a third to Hugh [of St. Cher], cardinal priest of Santa Sabina, and a fourth to John, cardinal deacon of S. Nicola in Carcere Tulliano, saying that each of these contained what he wished to declare to them. This text was then read out by the aforesaid John, cardinal deacon, in the hearing of the pope and the cardinals alone.

At the outset of his first audience Grosseteste underlined the vast areas of common ground that he and his four listeners shared. He began with a sketch of the history of the Church and of its pastoral ministry. The latter was handed down from the Apostles and entrusted in a very special way to the papacy. What he said was clearly intended to capture the goodwill of his audience. From there he turned to the pitiful state of the Church in their own times, as he perceived it:

> But, alas! this great expansion, achieved at the cost of immense toil, has been squeezed as it were into the confines of an acute angle. For unfaithfulness has taken over the greater part of the world and removed it from Christ, while schism has separated from Christ a large section of that part which goes by the name of Christian. A considerable portion of what remains—which I take to be small and limited by comparison with the two areas referred to—has moreover been taken away from Christ by the evil of heresy. Almost the entirety of the remainder has been bodily joined to the devil and removed from Christ by the seven deadly sins.

All this was common ground; indeed its tenor recalled in a general way the bleak picture painted by the opening discourse of Innocent IV at the council of 1245, concerning the five wounds of the pope. The cause of the dramatic contraction of the Church is then identified: it lies in the failure of pastoral activity. Grosseteste does not spare negligent and unworthy bishops, calling them "antichrists, satans, thieves and robbers, and murderers of the souls entrusted to them." However, he points to where the ultimate responsibility for these evils lies, and that is in the papacy and its curia, which have together both the power and the duty to foster pastoral care. Not only have they failed to correct the negligent among the Church's pastors but they have themselves stood in the way of the pastorate, by failing to support bishops who are attempting to remedy abuses and to restore pastoral discipline.

Regarding England, Grosseteste made the claim that patrons of parochial benefices were finding encouragement in the bad example of the central authority in promoting unworthy candidates, often their own relatives and friends, to pastoral office. He deplored the appointment by English patrons of nonresident priests to parish charges. He supplied examples of the ways in which the pastoral power of the bishops was being restricted by the archbishop of Canterbury, Boniface of Savoy. In his concluding argument he pleaded for central action to be taken to remedy abuses, such as favoritism and the acceptance of gifts in return for judicial decisions. He then touched on a point where he very likely represented a general episcopal resentment against Canterbury, to whom the fruits of all vacant benefices in the whole province for one year following vacancy had been granted by the papacy. This complaint was, as it turns out, very close to the center of Grosseteste's preoccupations during his visit to the curia. His *Memorandum* concluded with a plea to the pope and cardinals not to misunderstand the nature and tenor of the submission he had just made, and not to regard him as presumptuous in the views he had expressed.

It would be for the remaining documents to take up the specific issues for which the *Memorandum* provided the framework. In the second and third statements one can sense some continuity with the grievances that the English representatives at the Council of Lyons had originally publicized. The first issue to be developed concerns the apprehensions on the part of the clergy that the archbishop will receive procuration (i.e., payments and hospitality for his retinue) when he carries out visitations in the provinces. At the same time, the clergy are worried that the pope will compel them to pay the king a heavy crusading subsidy. Grosseteste warns that this is the way resentment can build up against the central agency of the Church. Together these two documents are the record of his second appearance before the pope. The counterargument, that procuration was countenanced by common law, was the occasion of a written response by the bishop in which he unfolded his deepest convictions concerning the hierarchical government of the Church. He relied here upon two works he himself had translated from the Greek, namely, the *Ethics* of Aristotle and the two *Hierarchies* of the Pseudo-Areopagite. He contrasted tyrannical with legitimate government and transferred Aristotle's idea of good monarchical rule to the prelates of the hierarchy.

In his written presentation accompanying his fourth appearance the bishop argued that the divine and natural law is to be preferred to positive human law and its glosses, and applied his considerations to the question of procuration. It is evident from these elements of the dossier what a degree of preponderance was accorded to this matter during these encounters. Following the last audience an incident occurred that jeopardized Grosseteste's standing in the eyes of the curia. In the introduction to the final document Gravesend informs us that the bishop had been pressed repeatedly by a Roman nobleman for a benefice in his diocese, claiming the pope's authority for its conferral. Grosseteste, as we might expect of him, refused— just as he had done already in other similar circumstances, and as he would famously do again. A malicious version of the story reached the curia, and he asked permisson to return "in order to declare his manifest innocence and mitigate the aforesaid offence, and in order to instruct his listeners." He put in an honest but diplomatic way before the cardinals what he had said and done, and why, and concluded by expressing, once again, his great love for the Roman see and his exalted view of its unique responsibilities within the ecclesiastical hierarchy.

What was the outcome of Grosseteste's prosecution of his arguments? Joseph Goering considers that regarding the issue dominating the documentation (the threatened procurations by Boniface of Savoy) Grosseteste and his fellow bishops were vindicated entirely: papal letters were issued during the following year that severely restricted the archbishop's power of visitation. Grosseteste was successful also regarding some other matters; for instance, a papal letter gave him greater power of control over vicarages in parishes held by monastic patrons, as well as authority to curb appeals and opposition to his actions. In the matter of the annates of vacant benefices and the crusading tithe for King Henry III Grosseteste was admittedly less successful, but far from declining into despair, as has sometimes been thought, he took an active part right up to his final year of life in the ecclesiastical meetings that were held in England to determine policy and action in these matters. Regarding papal and curial appointments to benefices out-side of Italy, he was to prove successful in the pursuit of his argument, but his success came too late for him to know of it. This question became the object of a very famous letter written in the year of his death, to which I shall shortly turn. In the meantime it should be noted that Grosseteste's speeches at Lyons were intended as arguments, not denunciations. He was concerned primarily with particular matters of English interest that required redress. The pope and cardinals, for their part, showed themselves capable of listen-ing to what a very respected and very senior member of the hierarchy had to say. In the judgment of their most recent student, Joseph Goering, Grosseteste's dossier and the arguments it contains reveal "both his practi-cal skills in political wrangling and his inimitable manner of placing reform-ing ideals within an overarching conception."

The Final Letter (1253)

Very few bishops had ideas on the pastoral care as clear as were those of the bishop of Lincoln; fewer still were prepared to apply them, as he was, with-out respect of persons. Grosseteste held that the bishop carries direct, per-sonal responsibility before God for every soul in his diocese.[11] This respon-sibility extends to the appointment of good pastors and the exclusion of candidates who are unqualified or who have disqualified themselves by the nature of their behavior. He thought of his own relationship to his diocese in terms of hallowed images: watchman in the vineyard of the Lord; shep-herd feeding his sheep with justice and doctrine; steersman of the ship; hus-band faithfully married to his Church. His correspondence, from the very first year of office onward, documents the struggles he had with patrons (and even with the papal legate Otto) to ensure that the candidates they presented to him as bishop would make worthy pastors, on penalty of being simply turned down. He applied the same principles throughout his time as bishop. In this regard Leonard Boyle commented, "It is a lengthy step from attack-ing noblemen, canons, archbishops, papal legates, and a king to reprimand-ing the papacy itself in the interests of the *cura animarum*, but Robert Grosseteste eventually took it. Given his obsession with the pastoral care and his horror at the evils of presentation and provision, it was inevitable."[12]

The final letter in which he declared his refusal to confer a benefice at Lincoln upon a nephew of Pope Innocent has received many interpretations.[13] The following account is deeply indebted to the ideas published by Boyle in his diplomatic analysis of this, the one and only document in the case. The letter was sent by Bishop Grosseteste to the two provisors who had been appointed by papal mandate to implement the appointment; one of these was Stephen de Montival and the other, Master Innocenzo, a papal scriptor who was resident in Yorkshire. Grosseteste received a document from them, and he began his response by summarizing it. (It contained the papal confirmation of the nomination that had already been made without reference to him.) His personal response follows. It is much too long to be quoted here in full.[14]

The letter is very angry in tone. Grosseteste must have been infuriated to learn that a benefice had been conferred without any consultation with its patron, for that offended against one of his own principles, as well as against the best practice of the time. A further source of dismay was the series of "notwithstanding" clauses (Latin, *nonobstante*): these were designed to lead directly to the implementation of the nomination by setting aside any existing legal arrangements, entitlements, or exemptions affecting the patron. Grosseteste insisted that his rebellion was made against "the things contained in this letter"—principally the *nonobstante* clauses. The fact is that he had sought and obtained from Pope Gregory IX, in 1239, a special privilege whereby he would not be bound to respect any papal provision unless it made full mention of the privilege in question. This, in Boyle's opinion, was the root of his rebellion, for he saw in it a grievously sinful abuse of power. He found his own pastoral ministry "cheated and defrauded"; he felt betrayed in the trust he had placed in the Church's law and administration. He complained in bitter language that he had been hurt by "his father and mother," namely the papacy, and he uttered severe condemnations of the evil nature of what had been attempted. The letter of confirmation sent by the provisors to Grosseteste had invoked the sentence of excommunication against "those who oppose and rebel against" the command it contained. At the close of his response Grosseteste took up these very words:

> For these reasons, reverend lords, because of my obligation to be obedient and loyal, an obligation that binds me, as to both my parents, to the most holy Apostolic See, and because of my love of union with it in the body of Christ, as a Catholic, a proper son, and one who owes obedience, I disobey, I oppose, and I rebel against the things contained in that letter, chiefly because they so clearly verge upon the sin I mentioned, so abominable to our Lord Jesus Christ and utterly destructive to the human race,

and also because they are in every way opposed and contrary to the sanctity of the Apostolic See. Your considered judgment can recommend no harsh measures against me because of my stand, for my every word and deed in this matter is neither opposition nor rebellion, but rather the filial respect due by God's command to one's father and mother.

And he concludes regarding the papacy:

To sum up briefly, I say that the Apostolic See in its sanctity "cannot destroy, it can only build." For this is its fullness of power, to be able to do all things for building up. Those so-called provisions, however, have nothing to do with building but rather with the most obvious destruction. They cannot therefore be the work of the blessed Apostolic See. For "flesh and blood," which will not possess the kingdom of God, have revealed them, and not "the Father" of Our Lord Jesus Christ "who is in Heaven."

May the most high God ever watch over and defend you.

Given at Lincoln, etc.

The distinction drawn here between the office and its occupant for the time being could not be more clear.

What effect did this letter have when (according to the Burton annals) it was sent on by the provisors to the curia? Fr. Boyle was the first to take seriously a remarkable letter, *Postquam regimini*, which was sent out by the pope to prelates, and in many copies to England. The letter effectively restored the rights of patrons over benefices and instructed them in the future to tear up any mandate that infringed those rights. What is remarkable about it is the "frank, uncurial language" of this *proprio motu* (or personal-initiative) letter. Innocent admitted that mistakes had been made in the system of provison of foreigners, because petitioners had been dishonest and because the pope himself had sometimes been forced, against his better judgment, to grant certain provisons. Boyle comments, "A papal letter that allows that there have been mistakes in policy or in practice is a rare event, but for a pope to admit to having had his arm twisted on occasion is quite unusual, if not a landmark in the history of the papacy" (p. 35). The Burton annalist makes the claim that this letter was a direct result of Grosseteste's criticism. Boyle draws the conclusion that Innocent was not always in complete control of all documents issued from his chancery and suggests that the pope's reaction to the ineptitude of a chancery that allowed a letter of that kind to be sent, at the expense of such a conscientious and respected bishop, one personally well known to him, was probably one of shock. Referring to the papal letter, he concludes as follows:

> With its clean sweep of many grievances at the provision of foreigners, its frank admissions, and its complete lack of recrimination, it is as eloquent a testimony, short of a personal letter of apology, as one could wish for, both to the effect of Grosseteste's letter and to the respect which Innocent came to have for him. (p. 38)

RELATIONSHIP WITH THE MENDICANTS

The relationship of Grosseteste with the two mendicant orders of Dominicans and Franciscans, and especially with the latter, is an obligatory chapter in even the briefest life of the bishop.

When Grosseteste's friendship with the friars is mentioned, people think in the first place of the Franciscans and forget too easily his friendships with Jordan of Saxony, O.P. (the successor of St. Dominic), John of St. Giles, O.P., whom he wanted at his side at Lincoln, and Robert Bacon, his theological colleague at Oxford who joined the Dominicans. As bishop, Grosseteste had both Dominicans and Franciscans living at the palace at Lincoln. The Br. Hubert (otherwise unknown) who wrote a Latin verse lament for him during the vacancy following his death was probably one of the former. He regarded the late bishop as a saint. The following short extract portrays the relationship between the friars and their episcopal patron.

> Two orders mourn the loss of a father, the Preachers of the Word and the Minors.
> He was the father and protector of them both, and won their undying gratitude.
> He loved to have friars by him, loved to see them come;
> the greater their numbers and the more frequent their talks with him, the more pleased he was.

He determined to have the friars as partners in his task, to lighten his
  burden of work.
With the tenderness of a mother for her offspring he favored, loved,
  protected, cherished and valued them.
He could not live without friars in his household and outside; he kept
  them right through, and his devotion to them was lasting.
Who now will be the protector of his wards the friars? To whom shall
  they fly, who will be their support?
Their stronghold is now gone, with Robert's death; their helper is
  powerless, their spokesman is silenced.

As a matter of fact a great deal more is known from various sources
(including his own writings) about Grosseteste's dealings with the Franciscans than about his relationship with the Dominicans. His association
with the Franciscans, in particular, supplies a vital clue to the nature of
his own religious idealism, for as he grew older in faith he saw more and
more clearly that the stricter, more evangelical following of Christ implies
the renunciation of possessions, of egoism, and of worldliness of all kinds.
The Benedictine chronicler Matthew Paris reports the reaction of certain
commentators who were taken by surprise by his election to the see of
Lincoln, because many expected him to join the Franciscans. A number
of his friends and former pupils did so: we know of Alexander of Hales,
Adam Marsh, and Adam Rufus of Exeter, but there probably were others
besides these. Indeed it is difficult to know why Grosseteste, who evidently
felt a profound affinity with the Franciscan life, did not follow them; that
he thought seriously about doing so there can be little doubt. At all events,
the influence he exerted upon the Franciscans had its counterpart in the
impact that their movement, their idealism, and their friendship came to
have upon him.

A *dictum* (or personal note) of Grosseteste's makes a brief but unmistak-
able allusion to the stigmata of "blessed Francis," drawing a likeness between
an iron-shod horse and a man strengthened and protected by the iron in-
struments of the passion of Christ.[1]

A horse shod with iron can run unhurt along a rough road, even though
its hooves be tender. In the same way a man, even though a tender and
delicate one, should it occur that he is made into iron through the lance
of the Savior in his heart, and pierced in hands and feet by the nails of
Christ, is able to walk manfully on the hard road of penance.

The "delicate man" is of course Francis, and the hard penitential road is the life he chose to live for Christ.

We do not have to search very far to identify definite sources of Grosseteste's information about St. Francis. Agnellus of Pisa and Albert of Pisa, the first two provincials in England, were formed in the religious life by the immediate companions of Francis, and both men had known the saint personally. A later provincial, Peter of Tewkesbury, the friend of Grosseteste, was also a friend of Br. Leo, one of the most intimate companions of the Poverello. In addition, Laurence of Beauvais and Martin of Barton, both of the English province, had met Francis repeatedly. It is clear that Grosseteste had ample opportunity to question immediate followers of the saintly founder of the order, and through them to acquire a thorough appreciation not only of the origins of the movement but of the character and mind of the saint.

From the time of Francis's death onward his movement was traversed from end to end by internal tensions and debates. Francis had insisted that all his followers embrace complete personal as well as communal poverty. However, within a few years sharp divisions appeared, as the initial fervor waned and thousands joined who had not known the saint in person. Other aspects of these debates concerned the place of learning and preaching, and the clericalization of the order. How much do we know of Grosseteste's attitudes toward these matters, which so agitated and divided the friars?

On the focal issue, poverty, Grosseteste expressed his views on a number of occasions. For instance, in a sermon delivered (he tells us) in the presence of Franciscans and in one of their houses,[2] he claims that the mere matter of possessing or not possessing things is in itself indifferent; what makes it good or bad is the state of mind that accompanies it. A rich man may be poor in virtue of his detachment, and equally a poor man may in fact think like a rich one, through attachment to the little he possesses. Coming to religious, voluntary poverty, Bishop Grosseteste contrasts the Benedictine vow of personal poverty with the Franciscan renunciation of even common possessions: the Franciscan attitude, he maintains, comes closer to the nakedness of Christ. Besides, it recalls paradise and anticipates heaven on earth, for if Adam had not fallen into sin private ownership would never have been there to subvert the "common possession of all things by all"; and of course in heaven God will be "all in all."

In another sermon, preached probably before a Franciscan chapter, Grosseteste reflects on poverty, using the image of a ladder. Humility, contempt for the world, and the embracing of everlasting goods form its rungs. Humility is founded on the conviction that of ourselves we are and have nothing; we must treasure the thought that all we are and all we have comes from the giver of all good gifts (Jas. 1:17). Poverty and humility overlap each other completely. To think of oneself as the least of all is the first step on the ladder. The next step raises one above the love of worldly goods to indifference regarding their loss or their possession, and preparedness to sacrifice them. The highest degree of poverty is to regard oneself as being here entirely for God's service. Even if it should happen that one be deprived of the use of a faculty, or lose a limb, one should accept the loss gratefully and with inner, spiritual joy.

In these convictions Grosseteste was undeniably close to the mind of St. Francis, whose ideal of poverty he both understood and forcefully defended. Again, like Francis, he believed that the friars should beg alms only when the work they did was not rewarded. Other evidence of his affinity with Francis can be found. In a brief meditation, for instance, Grosseteste indicates the outlook from which generous almsgiving comes, in terms of a paradox of loss and gain:

> You should meditate that you will die inevitably; that you cannot put off your death; that you cannot prolong your life against the will of God; *that of what you own you can take nothing with you, unless what for God's sake you gave away.*[3]

This thought accords perfectly with the teaching of Francis in the *Letter to All the Faithful*:

> Men lose everything that they leave behind in this world; but they carry with them the right to be repaid for their charity and almsgiving, and they will receive a reward and generous repayment from the Lord.

Like Francis, Grosseteste was convinced that truth is more easily recognized by the experiencing of what is actually done than by verbal explanation. In addition, there is a perceptible Franciscan overtone to the following remark:

> Note that when you see somebody doing wrong, you should not immediately judge him but regard him with compassion, considering that if you were to have such temptations, you might fear you would do even worse.[4]

Grosseteste intervened directly in the most public and divisive aspect of the dispute about poverty. Elias of Cortona, the third minister general of the Franciscans, conceived a grandiose and correspondingly expensive project to commemorate the saint by building a monumental church at Assisi. Grosseteste, apparently at the behest of the friars of England, addressed a letter to the cardinal protector of the order, protesting against the betrayal of poverty involved in the scheme, and the divisive nature of Elias's decision.

If Grosseteste really did understand so well the mind of St. Francis, why then did he encourage the friars toward learning, by becoming their teacher? The late Bishop J. R. H. Moorman argued that Grosseteste did serious damage to their movement, and claimed he would have done better to devote his academic attention to the Dominicans rather than deflect the Franciscans from their original ideal of absolute poverty and renunciation. It can be said in response to this verdict, however, that Francis himself gave permission to Anthony of Padua, who had been a doctor of theology before taking the habit, to lecture. In a similar way, Grosseteste thought of theology as essentially a preparation for the apostolic ministry, and in particular for preaching. One of his contemporaries, the strictly Franciscan Thomas of Eccleston, saw no conflict in his attitude, as the following story reveals.

> Friar Peter of Tewkesbury was worthily favored by the special love of the bishop of Lincoln, and more than once did he hear from him many secrets of his wisdom. For he remarked once to him, that unless the friars cultivated study and applied themselves studiously to the law of God, we would certainly end up in the same state as other religious, whom we see, alas! walking in the darkness of ignorance.

Servus Gieben has expressed the view that Grosseteste and St. Francis were in agreement about the use and the abuse of learning:

> I am inclined to believe that regarding learning and preaching Grosseteste was, once again, perfectly in line with the views of St. Francis . . . Grosseteste's views on learning and preaching agree with what Francis himself urged upon his friars in his Admonitions, his Rule, his Letter to St. Anthony [of Padua] and his Testament. In these personal writings Francis does not show himself any more worried about learning than about manual labour.[5]

Both believed, in short, that learning should be placed at the service of evangelization. Moreover, like any gift, learning, and even preaching, is open to abuse by the self-seeking and the ambitious. Again it is Eccleston who, in an anecdote, has supplied us with a key to Grosseteste's attitude:

He said that he rejoiced when his students were not paying attention to his lecture, even though he had prepared it very carefully; because, of course, he would have no occasion for vainglory—and also would not lose any of his merit!

Gieben draws a general conclusion, one that deserves to be quoted:

> If the Order in any way departed from its original inspiration it was not because the friars followed Grosseteste's line of thought but rather because they did not follow it.[6]

Grosseteste's views on the clericalization of the order have not yet been brought to light. We might recall in this respect that he regarded Holy Orders and ecclesiastical office as making those who received them, or exercised them, into servants, not masters. St. Francis said as much in the Rule:

> That is the way it ought to be: the ministers should be the servants of all the friars.

In what way did Bishop Grosseteste involve the mendicants in the pastoral mission? He himself gives us an example of his practice regarding the visitation of rural deaneries. In a personal statement written out for reading before the pope, in 1250, he has this to say:

> When I became a bishop I believed it to be necessary to be a shepherd of the souls committed to me, whose blood would be required of me at the Last Judgement unless I used all diligence in visiting them as Scripture requires. So I began to perambulate my bishopric, archdeaconry by archdeaconry and rural deanery by rural deanery, requiring the clergy of each deanery to bring together their people, along with their children, at a fixed place and time, in order to have their children confirmed, to hear the Word of God, and to make their confessions. When the clergy and people were assembled, I myself frequently preached to the clergy, a Friar Preacher or Minor preached to the people, and four friars heard confessions and imposed penances. Then, having confirmed the children on two days, I and my clerks gave our attention to enquiring into things which needed correction or reform, so far as they lay within our power.[7]

The fact that Grosseteste was the first teacher of the Franciscans at Oxford has led some scholars to describe him as the founder of a school of thought among them. That he exerted a degree of intellectual influence upon individual Oxford friars is beyond doubt, and has been established in the cases of Richard Rufus, O.F.M., and Richard Fishacre, O.P.[8] Much more piecemeal research is required before anything like an overall view can emerge. The Franciscan Roger Bacon, who praised Grosseteste to the skies for promoting the study of the Bible, mathematics, natural science, and ancient Greek, was probably correct in claiming that no school of thought was created by his teaching. Such intellectual influence as Grosseteste did have upon individual friars in subsequent generations came about partly as the result of his own generosity in bequeathing his library to the Oxford convent, where it remained until that house was suppressed at the Reformation. Perhaps in three theological issues positions favored by him did exert a certain influence upon some later Franciscan theologians at Oxford. Grosseteste roundly denounced as a dangerous error the ancient Greek belief that the cosmos has neither beginning nor end, and he insisted that any compromise with it would end by endangering the Christian faith. He argued, though without the support of any authority, that even if the Fall had not taken place the Incarnation would have come about, since it must have been at the center of God's plan and not simply a kind of afterthought occasioned by something that might not have happened. Finally, it was believed among the Oxford Franciscans that Grosseteste had taught the Immaculate Conception, or the belief that Mary was conceived without stain of sin by a preventive grace, in view of her unique role as the future mother of Jesus Christ. It looks as though Duns Scotus was indebted (at least indirectly) to Grosseteste's position concerning the Incarnation. In the present state of scholarship, however, few reliable generalizations can be made about Grosseteste's intellectual influence, even at Oxford, during the century following his death.

If Grosseteste did not have a school of Franciscan disciples, he did at least have a like-minded colleague who became a Franciscan. His name was Adam Marsh. Readers of Roger Bacon will recollect that the intellectual achievements of the two men were inseparable in his eyes, and were such as to elevate them far above all of their contemporaries and successors in the schools. They were united, he tells us, for over thirty years in their joint study of Greek, mathematics, and natural science. According to the South Italian Franciscan chronicler Salimbene, Marsh was a productive writer; unfortunately, everything of his except a large collection of letters has been lost, so that we are in no position to verify Bacon's claim. It must be taken seriously for all that, for Bacon, though cantankerous, was perceptive, and he was eminently well disposed to both men. Though the letters of Marsh betray nothing at all of the speculative ability attributed to him by Bacon, they do reveal the profound agreement that existed between him and Grosseteste on pastoral and political affairs, as well as in doctrinal belief.

Marsh loved Grosseteste and admired in him the gifts of leadership he himself did not possess. Marsh had a genius for friendship, and regarding Grosseteste he exercised it in all the ways the friend of a lifetime does—in continual concern for his health as he aged, in warning him that he was overdoing it, in recommending physicians to him, and in exercising the friend's privilege of forthright speech—to save him from the severe side of a temperament Marsh knew better than did any other. Marsh professed gratitude to him for the kindness he had shown him "ever since his youth." Although our knowledge of their relationship is very unequal (sixty-two letters from Marsh to Grosseteste survive, as against only two letters from Grosseteste to Marsh), it is plain that their friendship overcame the inequality of its beginnings. "Nothing in human affairs," he wrote to Marsh (who had expressed the fear that his frequent letters might be a burden to answer), "save only your holy conversation when we are together, causes me such joy as the consolation I get from your letters." When he resigned his supernumerary benefices, in 1231, he confessed to Marsh that until receiving a letter from him he had found no understanding of his actions from any single soul, but had had to endure nothing but obloquy and contempt, even from his kindred. During his tenure as a bishop, his lonely command was many times made bearable by his confidence that at least one person would understand him. Although he had a number of friends (including those among his correspondents whom he addressed using the familiar Latin *tu*-form), it was Marsh who was, and who remained, "My beloved in Christ"; Grosseteste remained "Your Robert," sending Marsh in his valedictories "health, and himself."

It was undoubtedly with the Franciscans that Grosseteste felt most at home among men. With them he worked hardest and relaxed most completely, and by them he was very kindly remembered. Many of the more intimate insights we can gain into his character come from the memories of friars. The warmest illustrations of his friendship with them are to be found in Thomas of Eccleston's account of the coming of the Friars Minor to England, a chronicle written around 1250 by a man who, though not himself a scholar, in all probability had a personal memory of the former lector. Eccleston first tells how Grosseteste came, by invitation, to the friars' school, and in a much later chapter he records a medley of anecdotes about the bishop that brings us closer to his warm, wise, and humorous personality than does any other source.

Grosseteste had a sharp eye for anything resembling a bribe:

> And the same Friar Peter [of Tewkesbury] told how, when the Lord
> Robert, the Bishop of Lincoln, was in great need of horses at the time of
> his elevation, his seneschal came to him, found him seated at his books,
> and announced to him that two white [i.e., Cistercian] monks had come
> to present him with two lovely palfreys. And when he pressed him to
> receive them and pointed out that they were exempt, he would not agree,
> nor even rise from his place, but said, "If I took them, they would drag
> me by their tails down to hell."

Cistercian monks were exempt from episcopal jurisdiction. The seneschal
was implying that no strings were attached to the gift, but the bishop-elect
was not naive enough to behave as though episcopal influence ended at the
limits of the actual jurisdiction of his diocese.

The bishop was particular in matters of money when there was any likelihood of usurious practice. Eccleston approved:

> Moreover, when the chamberlain of the Lord Pope asked him for a thou-
> sand pounds due on the occasion of his visit to the Curia, wishing him to
> raise them from merchants, he replied that he did not want to give the
> people in question the occasion of sinning mortally; if, however, he got
> safely back to England he would deposit the required sum with the
> Templars in London; otherwise not a halfpenny would be forthcoming.[9]

Eccleston was a simple man, yet he understood admirably Grosseteste's
central objection against harmful provisions:

> Again, he said to Friar John de Dya to look out for six or seven suitable
> clerics from his parts [France] whom he might appoint to offices in his
> Church. Even if they did not know English they could preach by their
> example.[10] It is evident from this that it was not for their ignorance of
> English that he refused the Pope's candidates and the nephews of cardi-
> nals, but because they were only out for temporal ends. In the same spirit,
> when a lawyer in the curia said to him, "The canons [canones] require
> this," his answer was, "Exactly, the canines [canes, lit. 'dogs'] want it."

Grosseteste's attitude to poverty was remembered:

> The aforementioned friar, William [of Nottingham], once said that when
> the Lord Bishop of Lincoln of holy memory, at the time when he was the
> official lector to the Friars Minor at Oxford, was preaching on poverty
> at a chapter of the friars, and placed the mendicant state at the next rung
> on the ladder of poverty to the embrace of heavenly things, he yet re-

marked to him in private that there was a still higher grade, namely to live from the rewards of one's own labor; whence he said that the Béghards have the most perfect and holy religious order, because they live by their own work and do not burden all and sundry with exactions.[11]

He was ready also with practical advice and encouragement:

He remarked to him [Peter] that houses (*loca*) above water are not healthy unless placed well up. Again, he said that it pleased him greatly when he saw the sleeves of the friars patched. Again, he said that pure pepper was better than salted ginger [as a preservative of food, presumably].

Eccleston tells us that St. Francis once forced Br. Albert of Pisa, when they were staying together at a hospice, to eat twice as much as usual, for his health's sake. In a similar vein Grosseteste gave unexpected advice to a scrupulous Dominican (most likely a priest) and to a Franciscan, in the following terms:

Moreover, he said to a friar preacher, "Three things are necessary for temporal well-being: food, sleep and jest." Again, he enjoined upon a certain friar who was melancholic to drink a cupful of the best wine for his penance; and when he had drained it, albeit with much aversion, he told him, "Dear brother, if you had that penance a few times you would end up with a better conscience."

There is also an amusing and very human story of the bishop in a huff.

The Lord Robert Grosseteste, the Bishop of Lincoln, was once so badly vexed that the Minister [Provincial] did not permit a certain friar whom he had once had with him, to remain in his guest house, that he refused to talk to any friar at all, even to his confessor. And on that occasion Brother Peter declared to him that if he were to give all his goods to the friars but would not give them the affection of his heart, the friars would not care for them. And the bishop began to weep and said, "In truth it is you [the Franciscans] who are at fault, in that you cause me too much pain, for I cannot not love you, even if I show you the face I do." Yet the friars ate at his own table beside him, and still he would not talk to them.

Finally, it is from the Chronicle of Lanercost that a very well authenticated Franciscan story comes, of the bishop's falling asleep during ordinations held on *Gaudete* Sunday:

It happened that Bishop Robert Grosseteste of Lincoln, [a man] beloved of God, was to perform solemn ordinations at Huntingdon during Lent.

One of the Minorite Order, who still survives, though greatly aged, living at Doncaster, was present there. He received ordination and witnessed the course of events. He describes what took place in the following manner:

"After Mass began," said he, "and the bishop was seated on his throne, the one who had to read out the names of those who were to be ordained and presented to the bishop came forward with the roll. And since he was very slow in reading out the list, the bishop leaned his head upon the side of his seat and fell asleep. After the clergy had hesitated for some time, wondering what to do, he was gently awakened by one of his secretaries."[12]

These stories recorded by Franciscan chroniclers speak to us eloquently of the love the friars had for Bishop Grosseteste and the respect in which they held him. Through the oral tradition that the stories reflect we have a memorable access to a personality who is known to us not only better than any other of the great academic figures of the time but differently than the others: we feel we know him somewhat from within, even down to his human qualities and his foibles.

THE MYTH OF THE
PROTO-REFORMER

Grosseteste was remembered in the England of after 1500 or so in two lights, which were not unrelated to each other: as a powerful preacher of the word and as a critic of papal provisions to English benefices. This dyptych represents the most enduring strand of the English historical memory concerning his life and achievements. The conviction that he had taken a bold stance in defense of the liberties of the English Church against Roman interference and curial venality may be said to have become, as a recent writer has put it, "a standard part of the repertory of English ecclesiastical and national history."[1] The historiographical examination of the growth of this myth shows how, upon a medieval substrate contemporary with Grosseteste himself (the chronicle of Matthew Paris, essentially), layer after layer of significance was in succeeding centuries heaped upon his *Memorandum* of 1250 and his Letter to Master Innocent (Ep. 128; 1253). These overlaid meanings can be peeled off again one by one, by the application of the historian's tools, in the interests of an unbiased assessment of what Grosseteste actually thought, said, wrote, and did. The gain to the study of his life and activities promises to be a considerable one. The same exercise may prove to be of indirect benefit to the assessment of his academic and literary achievements, since for too long now the red herring of myth has unduly diverted attention from his stature within the intellectual movement of his own times and made him appear in an unfairly marginal or even eccentric light.

The Rediscovery of Grosseteste
in the Nineteenth Century

The second half of the nineteenth century witnessed a fresh interest in the Middle Ages, which came about largely as a sequel to the Romantic movement. The by then almost forgotten figure of Robert Grosseteste began to be recovered by historians and theologians in Germany and England. The stages of that rediscovery were marked by numerous publications, some highlights of which can be briefly recapitulated as follows. (It should be remarked at once that the then prevalent atmosphere of controversial opposition between Catholics and Protestants marked that historical rediscovery, and even hastened it on its path.)

The Evangelical theologian Gotthard Victor Lechler published (Leipzig, 1873) a monograph on John Wyclif, including in it a chapter on Grosseteste, considered as the precursor and inspirer of the English theologian. This work appeared in English translation in 1878.[2] A decidedly Protestant viewpoint was put forward by a canon of Lincoln, George Gresley Perry, in a popular work.[3] The Protestant case was based by both writers upon the antipapal attitude they attributed to Grosseteste, something that, together with his direct influence on Wyclif, allowed him to be claimed as a far-off precursor of the sixteenth-century Reformers (*"ein Vorgänger der Reformation"*). It was held that his belief in the *plenitudo potestatis* of the papacy was in explicit contradiction to his severe criticism, not to say denunciation, of the pope and curia. The assertion and rebuttal of precisely this alleged contradiction was to prove influential for a century and more after it was first launched. A riposte to the Protestant adoption of Bishop Grosseteste was made by a German Catholic Church historian, Josef Felten, in a monograph of 1887.[4]

The controversy thus initiated did in fact produce some positive effects. It awoke the interest of the Catholic philosophers Clemens Baeumker and Ludwig Baur in the unedited writings of Grosseteste and helped in this way to bring about their valuable explorations of his thought, especially in its philosophical dimension. A second beneficial effect was to ensue: the attention of a notable archival researcher, the American Samuel Harrison Thomson, was drawn to the literary heritage of the medieval bishop. Thomson, who was working on the Wyclif edition, diverted fruitful years of research to Grosseteste, whom he always looked upon in a double light: as an author of formidable learning and originality in his own right, and as a forerunner and source of Wyclif and thus a harbinger of the Reformation.

It must be emphasized from the point of view of historiography that the age of methodical history-writing rediscovered the bishop of Lincoln by the route of confessional rivalry, together with its atmosphere of claim and indignant counterclaim. Until quite recent times, Grosseteste studies still labored to some extent under the burden laid upon them at their very beginnings.

Matthew Paris, Progenitor of the Myth

Three writers of very different character, each one of whom had a direct acquaintance with some aspect of Grosseteste's activity during his lifetime, wrote about him: Thomas of Eccleston, Friar Roger Bacon, and Matthew Paris. From these three, as from three separate fountainheads, different (though not wholly separate) historiographical traditions have flowed. Thomas portrayed a learned and devout master of theology who took charge of the friars' schooling, to their great benefit. This conscientious chronicler became the source of the Franciscan tradition of writing concerning Grosseteste and his influence on the mendicant order. Bacon penned a number of appreciations of Grosseteste, laying emphasis upon his originality in the study of mathematics and the sciences and his proficiency in the ancient languages. In terms of character and interest, the third source, Paris, the Benedictine chronicler of St. Alban's Abbey, is, broadly speaking, political. Paris certainly met Grosseteste, no doubt on occasions when the latter stayed at St. Albans on his way to and from London, while bishop. Although he was critical of the bishop's reforming zeal insofar as it affected the monasteries, he laid down all the elements of a view that saw in the bishop of Lincoln a redoubtable, even an implacable, opponent of central (and centralizing) papal policies and a declared enemy (in death as in life) of Pope Innocent IV. Each of these three strands has produced its own historiographical tradition, but it is the last-named that has been most, and most continuously, adverted to in England, down the centuries.

Under the year 1250 the St. Alban's chronicler records that the bishop of Lincoln crossed the sea to Lyons. Paris tells a story, the gist of which is that Grosseteste became angry at the abuse of money at the curia, and said, "Oh money! money! What power you have, especially in the Roman Curia!" However, he was overheard by the pope, who replied in exasperation that the English (bishops) were greedier still, laying tax burdens on the poor monks "tyrannically and greedily," and thus impeding them in their provi-

sion for the poor. Paris evidently enjoyed the thought of the bishop's embarrassment; he also claimed that he achieved nothing of any value by his
trip to France.

Paris's dislike of tax-imposing bishops, however, was matched by his
resolute disapproval of the pope and the curia, as rapacious foreigners who
drained money out of England. He recounted a long speech that Grosseteste
is supposed to have made on his deathbed, calling the pope a heretic and the
Antichrist, and denouncing a series of other troublemakers. Paris also told
the story that after Grosseteste's death the specter of the bishop appeard to
Innocent in the night and attacked him with his episcopal staff, stabbing him
in the side and bringing on a pleurisy from which the pope eventually died.

One should bear in mind that Matthew Paris was an extremely important source of information for his times, regarding England especially, but
also Western Europe. However, information is so mixed with prejudice in
his work that the two can scarcely be disentangled. At many points Paris is
a cross between a journalist and a gossip columnist. He was an angry man,
resenting all those who threatened Benedictine privileges, all foreigners (such
as the queen and her courtiers), all taxation and levies of royal or papal origin, and all visitations of monasteries by bishops. He was a hard man to
please! His cantankerous nature, his acidulous observations, and his unin-
hibited sarcasms, when taken together with his incessant gossip, would have
completely discredited any chronicler who lacked his positive qualities—for
he was possessed of wide information and a treasury of contemporary documents, and he had considerable narrative and artistic (as a sketcher) gifts.
These attributes have ensured him a readership throughout the centuries.
Most English historians of a hundred years ago would have thought of him
as a trustworthy source of knowledge for his period, an unrivalled medieval
documentary historian and a reporter generally worth heeding. A perceptive English critic of Paris, A. L. Smith, remarked (in 1913), with reference
to the "last discourse" of Bishop Grosseteste as the chronicler spun it out,
that all those things and persons are attacked in it who were the objects of
Paris's own perennial animosity; he added, shrewdly, "The modern historian is often faced by the demoralising alternative, whether he will be critical, cautious and dull; or will accept Matthew Paris and make a good story."[5]
Richard Vaughn, in his monograph on Paris, warned repeatedly that while
his information is most useful, his judgments are full of prejudice;[6] one might
add that the constant difficulty is to distinguish between them. The debate
about the reliability of his witness is not over, however, because Paris has

found a recent defender in R. W. Southern, who argues that he has been too severely handled in more recent decades, and who sets out in his book on Grosseteste to reassess and to upgrade the value of the chronicle.[7]

Reducing things to their essentials, we may say that Paris depicted Grosseteste's relations with the papacy in a way that is unrecognizable from the documentary record itself as it has come down to us. The chronicler managed to put poison into the well from which, century by century, writers on the English past have slaked their thirst. In what follows the attempt will be made to show how, century by century, the myth of Robert Grosseteste grew by gradual (but still traceable) accretion, as supplementary layers of meaning were added to the account given by Paris. Our examination must limit itself, at the risk of appearing cursory, to writings that appeared before 1800.

Thirteenth-Century Elaborations

During the years following Paris, stories proliferated in England, portraying a conflict between the courageous and independent English bishop and the proud Roman pontiff. It is certain that not all of these went back to Paris himself, but they all have a broadly similar character to his. A number of them relate that Grosseteste appeared after his death to rebuke the pope. One of the earliest of these tales is to be found in *Lambeth Palace MS 499*. It recounts that when some of the cardinals reported Grosseteste's death to Innocent, the pope's response was that the bishop of Lincoln was both dead and buried in hell; the following night Grosseteste appeared to the pontiff in a dream, to announce that he was not dead but living with Christ; he foretold that Innocent himself would shortly be dead and buried in hell; the next morning the pope was indeed found dead, and the stench of his body was scarcely bearable.

The Lanercost Chronicle, which was influenced by Franciscan spirituals (and was thus favorable to Grosseteste but not to the papacy), asserted that the bishop was actually excommunicated by the pope. It thus outdid Paris himself, who claimed that the pope wished to excommunicate his critic but, being restrained by the cardinals, contented himself with suspending him instead. The legend of Grosseteste's excommunication was thus launched. Neither story was to die an easy death, or to be exempt, after being killed off by criticism, from resurrection.

From William of Occam to John Wyclif,
via Provisors and Praemunire

During the first half of the fourteenth century reinforcement was given to the growing myth, through a version of the May 1250 audience set down by William of Occam in his *Dialogus* (ch. 9). It is argued there that the theologian, or the philosopher, is a better and more reliable judge of the moral principles contained in the canon law than is the canonist himself. In the dialogue the master defends this view with arguments and recounts a story in its support. The story clearly concerns Grosseteste at Lyons. Since this passage has apparently not been noticed up to now, I reproduce it here in full.

> Secondly (principally), they try to make their assertion known by an example, recounting that when a commentator on blessed Dionysius, having been accused in connection with many [legal] articles by his rivals, who had corrupted the pope and cardinals with gifts, was forced to reply in consistory, he, as a pure philosopher and theologian, completely ignorant of the law, asked the pope for an attorney. The pope replied to him, "Let us not create for you, who regard yourself as more learned than all the other clerics in the world, the embarrassment that another should speak for you. Speak for yourself." Perceiving the [pope's] malice, he took a copy of the objections and received a recess of three days for deliberation. On the fourth day he replied from the resources of theology and natural reason to all the objections raised against him from the civil law and many [clauses] of the canon law, on which his adversaries had, unanswerably as they thought, based their accusation. He clearly assigned them such a meaning in his favor, that all the laws and legal considerations that had been alleged against him were in the judgment of all who understood the matter plainly conclusive for him. Whence the cardinals who had been opposed to him, it is reported, afterwards accused his rivals, saying, "You said that the bishop does not know the laws and canons: he knows the principles, roots and causes of all laws and canons." From this they conclude that a theologian who is also a great philosopher judged more certainly, deeply and clearly about the meaning of laws, of which he had absolutely no knowledge beforehand, than people who were ignorant of theology and natural reason, but who had nevertheless been nourished from their infancy in those matters.[8]

This version of what took place at Lyons in 1250 evidently reached William through proponents of the argument he himself expounded, but there is no knowing whence they derived it; no written source for it has as yet been identified. The story, which pits the bishop against the "malice" of the pope, against a background of curial venality and corruption, turns out to his credit. We may note, however, that with a change in the emotional charge of only a word or two in the narrative, the pope would actually have been portrayed as paying a sincere tribute to Grosseteste's intellectual eminence within the Church. As it stands, the tale makes up one more strand in the English view of Grosseteste as the target and the adversary of the pope and curia.

The mid-fourteenth century witnessed the passing of the first laws of the English Parliament against papal provisions. The first Statute of Provisors (1351) upheld the freedom of ecclesiastical patrons in England and decreed that if the Roman curia made provision to a benefice then the presentation was to fall to the king. The Statute of Treasons (1352) included a clause declaring that all who procured from the papal curia any provision to a benefice should fall outside the king's protection and be regarded thenceforth as outlaws. The First Statute of Praemunire (1353) defended the authority of the king's court and of the common law against any appeal to "another court," on pain of contempt of the royal jurisdiction; French popes were evidently suffering from a loss of insular confidence, as the war with France continued and Englishmen grew to fear that monies drawn from their own country, by way of the papal provision of foreigners to benefices, might be used in the form of loans to finance the war. The radicalization of antipapal sentiment that is attested to by the passing of these unprecedented statutes was no doubt in part responsible for the revival of interest in Grosseteste's attitude to provisions and the pastoral care, an attitude to which Higden and Wyclif, each in his own way, were to bear witness. It is to them that I now turn.

Ranulf Higden, who died in 1364, was a Benedictine monk of St. Warburg's, Chester. His fame rests on his *Polychronicon*, the most far-reaching chronicle that had yet appeared. That it enjoyed unprecedented popularity in the country of its origin for nearly two centuries after its compilation is evident from the fact that it is extant in over a hundred manuscripts. It was translated into Middle English in 1387 by John Trevisa and again in the following century by an anonymous translator. Printed by Caxton in 1482, it was issued by Wynkyn de Worde in 1495 and by Peter Treveris in 1527. It enjoyed, in other words, an enviably wide readership, both up to and long after the invention of the printing press.

Recording the death of the bishop on 9 October 1253, Higden refers to his "noisy" letter to Innocent IV, condemning the exactions he laid on the churches of England and refusing to appoint his nephew. He may have known something of the *Memorandum* of 1250, but if he did then he understood it only imperfectly. Robert, asserts the chronicler, was called to the curia and excommunicated, but he appealed from the court of Innocent to the tribunal of Christ. A version of the story of the dead bishop's apparition to the pope is retailed, and the conclusion is drawn that canonization was unfairly refused him by the curia, despite his real holiness and the miracles he worked. The notion of an appeal from the curia to the court of heaven, together with the refusal of canonization, constitutes the new element introduced by the monastic chronicler into the growing myth.

John Wyclif grew to admire Grosseteste above all other thinkers of the more recent centuries.[9] He acquired an extensive knowledge of a whole range of his writings, and quoted from him frequently and at great length, always with approbation. After 1370 or so he began to repeat the accounts of Grosseteste's relationship with the pope and curia given by Paris and Higden. He invoked the authority of *Lincolniensis* in support of his personal positions in theology, in particular on the papacy as the cause of the decline of the Church. He employed the singular epithet *archidoctor* in connection with Grosseteste's refusal of the papal mandate of 1253. Wyclif's writings from *De Civili Dominio* (1376) up to his death (1384) had the effect of reinforcing the beliefs that Grosseteste had been the enemy of the papacy and of the worldliness of the Church, that he had died excommunicated and persecuted, and that, though a saint, he had been refused canonization. The extreme nature of these claims evoked a reaction at Oxford that was to last for over forty years: in Wyclif's own time John Tissington, O.F.M., and following him Thomas Netter, O. Carm., reclaimed the bishop of Lincoln for orthodoxy.[10] Wyclif's effect was to give wide currency to the name of Grosseteste among Lollard preachers, who had access to some extracts in English versions from the bishop's writings. They found great comfort in the belief that this holy man and great writer had suffered at the hands of the magnates of the Church, in order to bring the truth of Christ to the simple and the powerless—in other words, to people just like themselves.

Two Elizabethans: Foxe and Holinshed

In the sixteenth century two Englishmen wrote of Grosseteste, to somewhat different effect. Raphael Holinshed, that well-read and industrious chronicler, selected some salacious details from Paris's account of the visitation by Bishop Grosseteste of monasteries and (especially) of convents, and repeated his statement that the bishop was suspended by the pope, for refusing a benefice to an Italian "that had no skill of the English toong." Grosseteste was (among many other things) "a manifest blamer of pope and king . . . a contemnor and a verie mallet of such strangers as sought preferment in this realme by the popes prouisions." (This eulogy is, of course, wholly indebted to Paris.) The entry in the *Dictionary of National Biography (DNB)* recognizes Holinshed's accomplishments as a narrator (William Shakespeare had paid a still higher tribute in the form of several of his history plays, in addition to *Macbeth* and *King Lear*), but its author justifiably adds that "his protestant bias is very marked throughout."

Elizabethan Protestantism was characterized quite centrally by apocalypticism and by the search to identify the presence of Antichrist, both throughout history and in the present age. John Foxe, in his *Book of Martyrs*, traced the continuity of the true, persecuted Church of Christ from the Donatists of antiquity through the Poor Men of Lyons and the Waldensians of the Middle Ages, and also the Hussites and Lollards nearer to his own times when, by divine Providence, the papal Antichrist had been fundamentally challenged and overthrown in wide areas of Christendom by the Reformers. Grosseteste he placed among those who had stood for Christ against the corrupt papal thraldom of the Christian body.[11]

As part of his extensive account of Grosseteste's relationship with the papacy, Foxe translated both "The Pope's unreasonable Letter to his Factors in England" and "The Answer of Bishop Grosthead to the Pope." Although he had seen "works and sermons" of the bishop in the Royal Library at Westminster, Foxe had no firsthand knowledge of Grosseteste's writings but relied for his narrative upon the familiar medieval chronicle sources. His appreciation of the bishop's attributes is prefaced by a portrait drawn from the resources provided by Nicholas Trivet, O.P., whose chronicle entry on the bishop was entirely laudatory of the philosopher, the master of all three ancient tongues, the translator from the Greek, and the man of virtue. Paris's various accounts were pressed into service by the Elizabethan chronicler, and they lost nothing in the telling: Foxe refers, for instance, to the pope's "cousin or nephew—so popes were wont to call their sons." In responding so vigorously as he did to the papal warrant, Grosseteste, concludes Foxe, "deserveth herein a double commendation, not only that he so wisely did discern error from sincerity and truth; but also that he was so hardy and constant to stand to the defense thereof against the pope." He appends to that the famous letter of 1253, in his own vernacular version. As a punishment for the bishop's offense (relates Foxe, following Paris), the pope "willed to have the bones of this bishop of Lincoln cast out of the church, and, to bring him into disgrace with the people, that he should be counted an ethnic [i.e., a heathen], a rebel, and a disobedient person, throughout the whole world; and thereupon caused he a letter to that effect to be written and transmitted to the king of England." However, the following night the bishop appeared to reproach Innocent and, losing his ghostly temper, attacked the pope with his staff as he lay in bed; "for Robert of Lincoln, saith the story, did not spare Sinibald of Genoa; who, for that he would not hear the other's gentle reproofs being alive, did feel his stripes when he was dead; so that he never after that enjoyed one good day or night"—and died shortly thereafter! Conscientiously Protestant as ever, Foxe reminded his "gentle reader" that God has no need, for the punishing of his enemies, to raise any man "materially" from the dead, "with his staff or without his staff, to work any feat, after he have once departed this life."

Grosseteste and the Glorious
Revolution: Edward Brown (1690)

It was in the fateful year of 1690 that the next stage in the mythologizing of Grosseteste was reached. The rector of the parish of Sundridge in Kent republished in that year a work of religious controversy that had originally appeared at Cologne in 1535, compiled by a pro-reform priest of Deventer, Orthuinus Gratius (in German, probably Ortwin von Graz).[12] The rector, Edward Brown, added a second volume of his own compilation, in which Grosseteste figured largely, and dedicated the entire work to the archbishop of Canterbury and the bishop of London. In a lengthy preface, composed in florid, baroque Latin, Brown presented his project: to put before their lordships and the English public certain writings, "condemned by the Roman Church," of Robert Grosseteste, bishop of Lincoln (i.e., the "Sermon" before Innocent IV), of Johannes Huss (*De Ecclesia*), and of Richard Fitzralph of Armagh (sermons and tracts against the friars). In this work there appeared in print for the first time (pp. 244–415) a considerable number of Grosseteste's sermons (especially those concerning the clergy) and *Dicta*, and in addition his constitutions (*Statuta*) for his diocese and his famous letter to

Master Innocent (1253). The editor made a spirited defense of the inalienable freedoms of the Anglican Church, denouncing King John for having become a vassal of the papacy and lauding his successors for having progressively reversed that national calamity. The foreign power, asserted the rector of Sundridge, never at any stage ruled the *Ecclesia anglicana* by right, but only insofar as the native laws freely permitted it. The conventional baroque linkage of throne and altar was naturally upheld by the patriotic rector. Stern warnings were issued concerning the conspiracies of the Jesuits and the other Romanists, who would reduce the land and its Church once again to vile servitude, by reintroducing the frivolous captivity that characterized the Dark Ages. The prefatory letter concluded with a resounding prayer to the Almighty for the continued flourishing of the Reformation Churches, the Christian peace and welfare of the world, and the safety of the two prelates who were its addressees.

The learned and industrious compiler exercised the freedom of the editor to address here and there, as occasion seemed to require it, an *admonitio* or a *censura* to his Esteemed Reader, by way of assisting the latter at once to appreciate the exceptional greatness of Robert of Lincoln, and to excuse those tarnishes that his doctrine (on the angels, for instance, or on faith and good works) inevitably contracted from that superstitious corruption of the Church that was prevalent in the former age. How could one possibly expect (asks the Reverend Brown) that a bishop of those times, moving as he must do in the midst of papal darkness, should have been a Protestant? Corruption, tyranny, and thraldom had continued their sway for so long that they had penetrated into the sanctuary of even Robert of Lincoln's great soul. Despite that, one must understand the bishop of Lincoln, and learn to excuse in him such blemishes as marred his otherwise sincere love of God and his undeniable zeal for the salvation of souls. The editor of the collection acknowledged the benefit, as well as the documentary help, he had derived from "that royal and faithful historiographer," Matthew Paris, as well as from none other than John Foxe. With the resounding achievements of the bishop—his sermon before the pope; his denunciation of the evil ways of clerical concubinage; his learning, so singular for the times; his condemnation of the pope for acting like Antichrist in offending against the doctrine of God's word—with all of these, Edward Brown confidently pronounced, Englishmen would be more than satisfied.

Brown had his work ready by 1689. His warnings concerning the dangers of the times can only be construed as referring to the Catholic King

James II, who had by then a son and heir. The two volumes were delivered to the public, perhaps just in time to play their part in the religious controversies and the constitutional debates that within a short time succeeded in bringing about the Williamite and Glorious Revolution.

Thus it came about that Grosseteste, quondam bishop of Lincoln, was enlisted as propaganda for the Orange cause.

The Antiquarian's Anglican Bishop:
Samuel Pegge (1793)

The parish of Sundridge was to form a link (was it a wholly accidental one?) between Edward Brown and one Samuel Pegge, who served briefly as curate there in 1730–1731. Pegge (1704–1796) was (according to the *DNB* entry) in his youth a fellow of St. John's College, Cambridge. Ordained in 1729, he rose eventually to be a canon of Lincoln Cathedral. He was a fellow of the Society of Antiquaries and an LL.D. of Oxford (1791). His writings reflected a wide variety of interests, but his life of Grosseteste, which appeared in London in 1793, is acknowledged to be his principal claim to fame.[13] Justice has never been done to it, and it cannot be done in the space available here. Despite its merits and its charm, it belongs to the age of antiquarian writing that continued to flourish in an Enlightened sort of way, not long before the exploration of the human past was to be placed on a properly scientific footing, notably through the genius of Leopold von Ranke. Pegge drew learnedly upon the medieval past of his country, accepting all (and rejecting nothing) that the chroniclers of medieval and Elizabethan England could supply. He acknowledged, for instance, Foxe, who very usefully drew to his attention that it was foreseen by many in Grosseteste's own time that "some time there would be a falling away from them [the Roman authorities], in other words, a Reformation" (p. 197n.). Pegge translated his Latin sources for his readers' benefit, including, of course, the letter of 1253, "a most celebrated performance [that] has both immortalized the bishop's memory, and endeared it to all generations" (p. 196). The biographer believed (on the authority of Tanner) that Grosseteste was excommunicated and that a successor for him at Lincoln was named by the pope, but that "on his part, [he] appealed from the sentence to the tribunal of Christ, after which he troubled himself no more about it, but died composedly in his bed."

Some Modest Conclusions

What results can we garner from this summary inquiry?

In the first place, the historiography of Grosseteste, right from its medieval elements up to 1800, was insular to an extent that one could scarcely exaggerate; indeed, instead of "insular" one might well say "English." Adam de Salimbene apart, it is hard to think of any writer from the European continent who figured in the elaboration of the Grosseteste story. To this day, monographs on Grosseteste's life and thought are few and far between in any other tongue but English. Even in medieval studies, which are in theory interdisciplinary, one is forced to conclude that national tradition and native language remain something of a force.

A strong and continuous English tradition, whose successive layers have been distinguished in this chapter, regards Grosseteste (especially from the times of Wyclif onward) as being recognizably English in his attitudes and in the temper of his mind. It should be borne in mind that Grosseteste, though born in England, was in reality French (or Anglo-Norman) by language, family, and culture. While there is no documentary evidence that he studied or taught at the university of Paris, there are ample grounds for believing that he was no stranger to France.

It emerges also from our inquiry that the medieval sources for Bishop Grosseteste's life and activities are not unproblematic, to say the least of it, above all when they handle his relationship with the pope and curia. Those wellsprings, the chronicles, have colored much of the later historiography, through a mixture of exaggeration, imaginative decoration, and outright distortion. All the elements of what I have called "the myth of Robert Grosseteste" are to be found already present in the thirteenth-century chronicle sources. Does it not appear to be very desirable indeed that all the relevant sources, from the bishop's own time right down to circa 1700, should be assembled, in good texts and in their original languages, and analyzed individually? I believe that no one has yet managed to see them all, or at least not all together, for purposes of comparison and critical analysis (some of them are in fact very hard to come by). Only upon the entirety of this material could a thoroughly critical study of the historiographical tradition be constructed, of the kind that has been only adumbrated here.

Attention has been drawn to the strength and continuity of the "political" strand of historiography that goes back in its essentials to Matthew Paris. The incidents concerning the bishop's relationship with the pope and the curia were embellished by stories, and were distorted right from the start. I leave with my readership the invitation to stroll at leisure through the historical hall of mirrors that houses the historiographical tradition concerning the medieval bishop of Lincoln, and to identify in the numerous, prismatic reflections of his exceptional personality the various stages in the elaboration of a purely English myth. This was made up of reflections of reflections of the historical figure, who was remodeled in succeeding eras to become, successively, the persecuted critic of a worldly Church leadership (Wyclif and the Lollards); the apocalyptic witness against Antichrist (Foxe); the medieval proto-Protestant, the English national hero, and the whig *avant la lettre* (Brown); and the Anglo-Catholic defender of liberty (Pegge). The myth of Robert Grosseteste, the antipapalist who died excommunicate, secured its hold in times when the past was regarded as a cupboard filled with objects that, though aging and in some respects antique, could still be made to serve the purposes of the current mentality or of the present controversy.

CONTRIBUTION TO PHILOSOPHY

Grosseteste's output was vast and diversified; it has not been completely edited as yet. It is difficult to construct an overview of it, and the chronology of his writings still remains subject to disagreement among scholars. Only occasionally can we glimpse a classroom setting behind a page of his writings. His intellectual life was marked by rich development, as new books (or translations of books) arrived to add interests that supervened upon his thought, without obliterating what they covered. So far as we know, his major publications appeared late in his academic career and followed each other into circulation in quick succession. The further back we go in his life, in consequence, the less we can say with certainty concerning his intellectual activities. His mental life cannot be divided into watertight periods (e.g., philosopher, exegete, pastoral theologian), nor can the strands that made up its rich texture be separated out without an unacceptable degree of artificiality. However, it is impossible to talk about everything at once. For purposes of exposition I will say something about Grosseteste's philosophical interests, beginning with his numerous contributions to the liberal arts.

Treatises on the Liberal Arts and Related Topics

In Grosseteste's day there were no professors of philosophy; there existed as yet no scholastic discipline known as philosophy. The seven liberal arts, however, contained much that can be labeled philosophical: logic and dia-lectic within the *trivium*; geometry and arithmetic, together with astronomy and theoretical music, making up the *quadrivium*. The model books of the *artes* that were received texts in the medieval schools went back to the culture of late antiquity, notably to the pagan Martianus Capella and the Christian Boethius. In particular, the logic of Boethius was the basis of all rational knowledge, and it was to remain prominent in medical, legal, and theological science up to the close of the Middle Ages. From about 1150 onward logicians began to study works of Aristotle in translation, and they were thus enabled go back to the historical foundations of the science. In Grosseteste's younger days the *Posterior Analytics* represented the ultimate challenge to the teacher of the *trivium*. In his mature years he himself was to write the first Latin elucidation of that notoriously difficult work on general rational methodology.

The teaching of the *quadrivium* offered a challenge of another sort. In particular, the subject of astronomy had undergone developments at the hands of Arabic thinkers, who relied principally upon the classic work of Ptolemy, the *Almagest*. The Latins were aware that they had much to learn from the Arabs, and we find in Grosseteste a dedicated and curious student of their writings in Latin translations. Interest in science was not confined to the study of the heavenly bodies, however; it extended to the world of nature with the rediscovery of the physical writings of Aristotle, notably the *Physics*, the *Meteorology*, and the psychological works. Grosseteste was at the forefront of the contemporary Latin interest in all of these fields and he left behind him a substantial body of writings.[1] Something of the depth and breadth of his philosophical interests (in the widest sense of the term) must be sketched out here.

This brief survey of the philosophical and scientific writings may conveniently begin with *De artibus liberalibus*, one of the earliest writings of Grosseteste to have come down to us.[2] The nature of its doctrine would seem to place the work very early in his career. Its psychological teaching, based largely on the *De musica* of Augustine, is purely traditional and lacks any trace of Aristotelian or Avicennian infiltrations. Mathematics is treated very briefly and is, moreover, the traditional mathematical science of the Latins, being based principally on Boethius. Music and astronomy are the two privileged sciences, music for the universal harmony it uncovers in the universe, and astronomy for the practical guidance it offers to medicine and agriculture. Astronomy is held to be inseparable from astrology.

Grosseteste distinguishes between the *affectus* and *aspectus* of the soul, or its will and intelligence, claiming that we cannot purify the latter from error so long as the former is wrongly inclined. This idea of Augustinian character was to prove a theme song of his life.

The *De generatione sonorum* betrays the influence of Aristotelian psychology: it uses the triple division of souls into vegetative, sensitive, and rational parts. The interests it manifests in language and phonetics are those of an arts master. When we come to *De sphaera*, on the other hand, we find a natural philosopher at work. The deduction of the spherical shape of the universe (as defined by Euclid) is made from reason with an appeal to *experimentum*, the appearances. The results fit the biblical picture quite well, with the sphere of earth at the center of the universe and the waters withdrawing to the areas of its indentations, leaving the dry land distinct as a habitable place for animals. Grosseteste relies on the *De caelo* of Aristotle, but he is still far from being the complete Aristotelian scholar, for he states his view that the motion of the entire heavens, with all their stars and planets, has as its efficient cause the *Anima Mundi* or World-Soul—that very non-Aristotelian agent. Evidently in *De sphaera* we are dealing still with an early work; in later writings we shall be able to register additions made to the information contained in it, and to witness the questioning of some of its basic assumptions and positions.

Of the three treatises on the calendar that have been attributed to Grosseteste, the *Computus correctorius* is the only one of certain authenticity.[3] It contains advanced scientific material not suitable for an elementary book intended for the ordinary arts student (aged on average sixteen or under). A theological interest, something altogether lacking in the earlier works, is present in the *Computus* and supports a dating later than the writings mentioned up to now; it may suitably be placed toward 1230. Grosseteste wished to found the numeration of time upon nature and reason, and to place all human and ecclesiastical divisions of time upon the solid foundation of natural time, in other words of God's own creation. He felt he could not but criticize the pagans, "from whom we have taken the calendar," for the ignorance of creation that underlay their work. His suggestion for reform rested on the premise of a temporal act of creation, so that, in accordance with reason and nature, there had to be a first leap year, the fourth year after the beginning of the world—a consideration that, he tells us, upsets the basis of the pagans' assumption that any given time was always preceded by other time. This criticism rejoins the many denunciations of the doctrine of the eternity of the world to be found in Grosseteste's mature writings.

Grosseteste wrote about comets (*De cometis*), a work he may have revised more than once. His argument is that the comet cannot be a star but must be a phenomenon of the sublunary world. It consists of fire sublimated from the earth to the sky, where it obeys the diurnal motion caused by the first sphere. When Grosseteste enlarges upon the process of the generation of comets, bits and pieces of astrology and alchemy appear, notions that are of Arabic derivation but of course quite foreign to pure Aristotelianism. The presence of these ideas suggests that this treatise should be located early in his development, for they do not recur in his mature work.

The reform of the calendar represented in Grosseteste's eyes the chief practical application of the science of astronomy; he thought of it as a service to the Church and the proper conduct of its liturgy. Hand in hand with his interest in astronomy there went a fascination with another kind of application of the science, namely, astrology. The high point of his astrological explorations was the treatise *De impressionibus aeris* (also named *De prognosticatione*). Here Grosseteste attempted to predict the state of the weather on 15 April 1249 from the position and the qualities of the planets, and concluded that the day would be temperate. The autumn of 1255, he predicted, would see a bad wine and fruit harvest. Grosseteste was later to become a severe critic of astrology, fearing that its widely diffused influence undermined belief in the freedom of the will. On the other hand, he most likely continued to accept the conviction generally held in his time to the effect that the heavenly bodies and constellations exert a physical influence on earth, in ways that may be predictable.

In *De impressionibus elementorum* Grosseteste argues that the light rays of the heavenly bodies are the most potent cause of terrestrial mutations. Light works geometrically to produce differentiated effects; at the same time it is a numinous creature, at least in its associations—a symbol of every good and perfect gift that descends from the Father of lights (Jas. 1:17). The aim of this opuscule is to account for meteorological phenomena (the warmth of the air, the formation of clouds, and precipitation) in terms of their cause, which is the heat of the sun. The idea that all forms of precipitation come from condensation and the raising of vapors by the sun's heat from water and land is, of course, an Aristotelian one. Grosseteste specifies that the sun heats by means of the reflection and condensation of its rays. From optics we know that focused rays burn, and we find in the reflection and condensation of rays the reason that valleys, though further from the sun, are warmer than mountaintops. This is very likely the earliest work in which Grosseteste discusses a favorite topic of his, namely, the causes of heat, applying to its exploration the Aristotelian method of *resolutio* and *compositio* (analysis and composition).

Grosseteste's profound interest in the nature of light and the phenomena associated with it is present in a series of interlocking writings that bear the mark of maturity and were probably written during his final years in the schools, circa 1230–1235.

He read Al-Kindi's book on burning glasses, and he tried to apply to the rainbow (*De iride*) its theory of the refraction of light. Aristotle held that the rainbow is produced by the reflection of light from drops of water in the cloud. Grosseteste corrected him by attributing the phenomenon to refraction, but wrongly thought that the refraction is caused by the whole cloud acting as a great lens. He attempted to treat refraction quantitatively, but without decisive success. He thought of color (*De colore*) as light incorporated into a material medium. Like all light, it seeks to multiply its form into a sphere. Its incorporation, however, prevents its connatural action of self-generation from taking place, so that it requires further light to be shone upon it from outside in order to be made actually visible, or capable of affecting the eye.

De calore solis is perhaps the best example of Grosseteste's scientific reasoning, based upon the method developed in the *Posterior Analytics* of Aristotle.[4] How does the sun generate heat? Three possibilities are explored. The sun does not generate heat as a hot body does, by being in actual contact with other bodies, nor by its motion, for circular motion contains no intrinsic cause of heat. Heat can be produced only by the concentration of the sun's rays. Grosseteste proceeds to demonstrate that the rays that fall perpendicularly upon a portion of the earth's surface are reflected back upon their path at ninety degrees and so produce the maximum scattering of particles, and hence heat. However, the farther outside the tropics of Cancer and Capricorn the rays fall, the more obtuse are the angles of incidence and reflection from the earth; hence less heat is produced because the scattering is lesser.

Grosseteste's interest in natural questions was both genuine and deep. Part of his motivation for inquiry undoubtedly lay in his religious faith. This comes out at its clearest in a brief (and probably fragmentary) commentary of his on an Old Testament book, Ecclesiasticus (43:1–5).[5] (The theme of chapters 42 and 43 is the power and glory of God as revealed in nature, especially in the activity of the sun, moon, and stars, and of the rainbow, clouds, winds, snow, mist, etc.) He evidently felt that an exegete who (like himself) was a scientist was best placed to illustrate the utility of natural philosophy as a key to the understanding of the literal sense of the word of God. In approaching the sacred text Grosseteste fully expected that whatever was true and certain in philosophy or astronomy was already present, implicitly at least, in the text whose chief Author is also the Writer of the book of nature. The commentary opens with a condensed evocation of the cosmogonical action of simple light (i.e., the form of corporeity) upon simple primordial matter, before moving along, with the drift of the biblical text, to the works of the sun. The sun theory traces the action of the world's "heart" upon its "body." The sun is presented as the chief activating cause of all natural phenomena: it educes all corporeal forms of earthly things from potency to act; it regulates the seasons and the annual cycle of generation and corruption in nature; it is the cause (or "heart") of heat universally, the producer of differences of climate and temperature; it is the giver of light and influence to the stars and the moon; it is the chief cause of geological phenomena, and therefore the shaper of the ceaselessly changing surface of the earth; it is the producer of all motion through its light rays and is the uniquely privileged one among the planets. Grosseteste's universe, in short, is heliocentric in every respect save the cosmographical. This commentary should be placed in the last part of his theological regency, circa 1230–1235.

It seems certain that Grosseteste taught the liberal arts, but where (Hereford? Oxford? Paris?) we do not know; nor can we say for how long. It may be that he combined (or alternated) his teaching with other kinds of employment, such as diocesan administration or work for patrons, as R. W. Southern has suggested. In any case, the grasp of logic he was to display in his mature years, as well as that of geometry and astronomy, gives the strong impression of a teacher of wide and lengthy experience. In particular, it stretches the imagination too much to see in the *Commentary on the Posterior Analytics* anything other than the published outcome, no doubt long delayed, of earlier teaching activity.

Aristotelian Developments

In his works of natural philosophy Grosseteste showed an ever-increasing knowledge of writings by Aristotle. Before exchanging the professorial chair for the episcopal cathedra he circulated a literal and continuous commentary on the *Posterior Analytics*. A couple of generations after his death an unknown hand copied out glosses from the margins of his copy of the *Physics*, one of the many books Grosseteste bequeathed to the Franciscan friars at Oxford. Something must be said here about his Aristotelian scholarship.

What is knowledge (*scientia*) in the strictest and highest sense of the term, and how can it be securely attained? The question is Aristotle's. In trying to discern the meaning of the inquiry conducted with such great intensity in the *Posterior Analytics* Grosseteste got some help from a version of the *Paraphrasis* (or summary) of the work made by Themistius.[6] The aim at truth is pursued in an indeterminate way already in the opinions and beliefs we hold. Science in the proper sense of the word begins with our efforts to grasp the truth of what is always or nearly always the case with regard to a particular kind of being. A higher form of scientific knowledge takes geometrical demonstration as its model and aims at knowledge of what is always the case. Demonstration consists in the logical exhibition of the properties that invariably accompany an unchanging essence, which is itself their productive cause. Like Aristotle, Grosseteste maintained that demonstrative science consists in the grasp of principles, that is, of propositions that are true and underived, prior to and explanatory of the conclusions that are logically deduced from them.

Demonstration has as its object, Grosseteste affirms, "universals located in singular corruptible things." In what sense, however, can universals be incorruptible, given that singular things are corruptible? Grosseteste's very way of addressing this *aporia* is strongly conditioned by Neoplatonic influences. Plato, he recalls, named the universals in various ways: ideas, archetypes, genera, and species. However, he unfortunately did not regard them as being the contents of the divine mind, where of course they are the ultimate, universal, creative source of both being and knowledge. The universal ideas are replicated in the angelic intelligences, as the created formal or exemplary causes of things of a lower kind of existence; there likewise they are incorruptible. Universals are also present in the heavenly bodies, as the causal reasons of earthly species; they are incorruptible in the heavens but corruptible in the individuals that exemplify them on earth. The Aristotelian universal occupies the lowest space in this entire ideational hierarchy, as the formal cause of the singular, composite being and the principle of its intelligibility. Now, it is upon formal causes that demonstrations and essential definitions are founded. Of course, the singulars of natural species are supposed to maintain a rough numerical constancy. It is in this sense that the Aristotelian universal is incorruptible: it never ceases to be instantiated in nature.

We can easily recognize here Grosseteste's adhesion to the general scheme of the Aristotelian theory of science: knowledge is not innate; it differs both from opinion and from intuition, and it connotes demonstrative knowledge founded on true principles. On the other hand, his position on universals betrays the clear influence of the Boethian distinction of universals *ante res*, *in rebus*, *et post res* (literally, before the things, in them, and after them)—the distinction that transmitted in Latin terms Proclus's mediation between Plato and Aristotle. Thus it can be seen that Grosseteste in fact followed one strand of the exegetical tradition of Aristotle, in interpreting the universal as a trace of the first, creative light.

For the thinkers of ancient and medieval times Aristotle stood for empirical inquiry into the physical world and its phenomena. Opposed to Platonic idealism, the philosopher stressed the inductive basis of all knowledge, a truth that Grosseteste presented in the following terms:

> The proof of this is as follows. Sense apprehends singulars, wherefore the lack of a given sense means the incapacity to apprehend certain singulars. Now since induction is made from singulars, the defect of a sense necessitates the impossibility of induction from the singulars which are the objects of the missing sense. When, in turn, induction from such singulars is ruled out, so also is the intellect's universal knowledge of them, since the universal idea can only be arrived at by way of induction. The absence of the universal in the understanding removes the possibility of demonstration, which can only begin from universals; and if there can be no demonstration, it follows that there can be no scientific knowledge. *Ergo*, the basic lack of a given sense means the absence of the corresponding science.[7]

Without in any way wishing to deny the basic truth that knowledge takes its origin from sense experience and proceeds through induction from observed singular occurences, Grosseteste chose to widen the discussion, spreading before his reader the entire Christian metaphysics (as we may term it) of knowledge and being. All knowledge is to be found in the divine mind from eternity, not of universals only but of singulars as well, the latter being known abstractly and without material accidents. How different this knowledge is from ours, which cannot know individuals in the purity of their essence but only as mingled with accidents! The highest capacity of the human soul, the *intelligentia*, which functions without a corporeal instrument, would have complete knowledge by illumination and without recourse to the aid of the senses, were it not encumbered and darkened by the conditions that are normal for fallen man. Indeed, some men do perhaps enjoy such illumination as the souls of the blessed receive, but only to the extent that those men are absolved from the ordinary human lot. In the normal case the higher human powers are "lulled to sleep" (in the Boethian metaphor) by the weight of the flesh.

Granted these conditions, the awakening of reason can take place only through sense experience. The senses' repeated meeting with their objects stirs the reason and ferries it down to join the sensible things. Reason has the capacity to discriminate among the objects perceived only in a confused way by the senses. Abstraction is made from the repeated experience of singulars, one and the same thing being judged by reason to be present in many instances. Thus both the abstraction of simple, universal ideas and the perception of universal relations of cause and effect arrived at by, for instance, medical science, can be reached only by the aid of the senses, granted the actual fallen condition of human nature. Grosseteste expresses his own conviction that knowledge, though it begins in sensation, must not end there but must rise to the spiritual level. But why is the mind so easily clouded over? The commentator explains that its capacity to understand (*aspectus*) is inseparable from its loves (*affectus*) and cannot transcend them. When the latter are turned toward the body and the seductions of matter that surround us, they entice the capacity for truth to dally with them and they distract it from its true light, the sun of the intelligible world, leaving the mind in a darkness and idleness that only begin to be relieved when it issues through the external senses into a light, which is a reminder (*vestigium*) of that other Light, its own birthright. The measure of the mind's success in finding and following the pathway of light is the degree to which the soul's love can transcend purely ephemeral objects. In these and like ways Grosseteste effectively reaffirms Aristotle's adage, "one less sense, one less science," and with that the necessity for sense knowledge as the foundation of all higher knowing dimensions. However, he puts all this into a Christian perspective, which shows it to be a partial and limited truth rather than the whole.

The commentary contains a wealth of scientific knowledge derived from Aristotle, as well as from Arabic and other sources. Grosseteste examines a wide range of natural phenomena (e.g., color and vision, the rainbow, the tides, the flow of the Nile, thunder) and does so for the most part to illustrate scientific method. One very influential reading of the work maintains that its author broke new ground by professing a methodology of scientific knowledge that included the experimental verification of hypotheses and the resort to geometrical explanations of phenomena.[8] Most present-day students would find that view exaggerated. A very different interpretation of Grosseteste's scientific achievement has been advanced: Grosseteste made the metaphysics of light into the foundation of geometrical optics and thereby took the first step toward the establishment of a mathematical science of nature.[9] On a balanced view it appears that there is some truth in both evaluations. Grosseteste's logical theory was fully Aristotelian. He was neither an experimenter nor an observer of great distinction. Yet he took a decisive step in the direction of mathematical science, and thus merits a niche all to himself in the history of science. His intuition led him to the conviction that mathematics, far from being merely an abstraction from aspects of physical bodies, makes up the very internal texture of the natural world and presides over its functioning.[10] What this metaphysical faith afforded Grosseteste himself was not so much scientific results in the modern understanding of the term, as delight in the pure understanding of the essences of things, and, what he valued perhaps most of all, a glimpse beyond the beauty of the harmonious texture of things into the mind of the divine mathematician, who dwells in light inaccessible (I Tim. 6: 16).[11]

Grosseteste was a pioneer in introducing to his Latin contemporaries the challenging work that crowned Aristotle's logic. His commentary had a widespread and enduring success up to and even somewhat beyond the close of the Middle Ages, as the history of its copying, quotations from it in later writers, and the existence of several printed editions eloquently attest. In contrast to that, the glosses he made on the *Physics* were not finalized by him nor were they circulated until long after his death.[12] Only three manuscripts witness the text. In glossing book 7 he began to use Averroës's commentary, which first reached a Latin readership circa 1225. Grosseteste's thoughts on physical light appear to have been fully formed at the time when he glossed the first book of the *Physics*. His struggle to understand that work resulted in several short studies that may be taken together here. He wrote on the boundedness of time and motion (*De finitate motus et temporis*), denouncing the implausibility of the Aristotelian (and general ancient) assumption that the world had no beginning in time. (This argument was to be taken up again, very forcibly, in his *Hexaëmeron*, I.viii.) A brief work, *De differentiis localibus*, addresses a number of difficulties arising from the *Physics* concerning the nature and objectivity of place. It manifests considerable interest in geometry, and especially in the properties of the sphere. The suggestion is put forward that the Prime Mover acts upon the heavens by means of light. *De motu supercelestium* examines the nature and cause of circular movement. By the time Grosseteste wrote it (presumably between 1230 and 1235) he was able to compare the doctrine of the *Physics* with that of the *Metaphysics* about the motions of the heavens. The sparing use he made of the *Metaphysics* of Aristotle suggests that he did not get very far toward mastering that difficult work; it may have come into his hands too late to challenge him. However, his interest in Aristotle was by no means exhausted with the penning of the studies mentioned, for he translated the *De caelo* together with the commentary of Simplicius, and he also produced a complete, annotated version of the *Nicomachean Ethics* and its Greek commentators. The evaluation of this aspect of his Aristotelian scholarship, however, is still under way, for the evidence is not all in yet.

Grosseteste's philosophical preoccupations were not limited to the themes of psychology, ethics, and physical science, which reached him through Aristotle and such Arabic thinkers as had been translated into Latin. "Philosophy" seems to have meant in his eyes principally the ancient, pre-Christian heritage of ideas about the world and natural phenomena, together with the Stoic morality that he found in Cicero and Seneca, which is to say that, logic apart (since most aspects of logic have a timeless air about them), its historical origins and dress were an important part of the meaning he attached to "philosophy." He regularly opposed the terms "sapientes huius mundi"("the wise of this world," cf. I Cor. 1:20; 2:6) and "sapientia nostra" ("our wisdom")—a designation that has its primary focus in biblical revelation but is wide enough to include tradition, in the shape of the Fathers of the Church.

Grosseteste had a distinctly philosophical turn of mind, however, which carried him easily beyond the assimilation and discussion of the ancient philosophical heritage, often in ways and directions that had been charted by St. Augustine, Boethius, and St. Anselm of Canterbury. In a whole series of studies he used a speculative philosophical approach in order to explore a variety of themes coming out of the long tradition of Christian reflection—which had itself drawn inspiration (mostly with discernment and selectivity) from the Greek Neoplatonists. Since several prominent Islamic and Jewish thinkers had chosen to pursue somewhat similar paths, it was natural for Grosseteste, as indeed it was for many of his contemporaries, to refer to such parallel developments as Avicenna's ideas on the spirituality and immortality of the soul, and to consult the *Fons vitae* (Avicebrol) and the *Liber de causis* on emanation and transcendental causality. On the other hand, the treatises I have in mind here can be regarded as theological because the themes discussed in them are principally related to Christian faith. *De ordine emanandi*, for instance, discusses the eternal production of the Word by the Father. The examplar causality of the divine creative ideas is focused upon in *De veritate*, *De subsistencia rei*, and *De prima forma omnium*. The divine knowledge of human action is the theme of *De scientia Dei*, *De veritate propositionis*, and *De libero arbitrio*. The work on the freedom of the will is the tribute of a distinguished logician to the Christian tradition, which counted notable probings by St. Augustine and Boethius, and then later by St. Anselm and St. Bernard, into the compatibility of human freedom with divine knowledge and action.[13] All of these thinkers figure prominently among the sources of the treatise. Its author devoted considerable care to its composition and revision, and in fact three recensions of it can be distinguished. The work must have originated in disputations, but its final form was probably fixed about 1230. It is in two parts: arguments against free choice (including so-called divine foreknowledge, statements about the future, prophecy, predestination, fate, grace, force used against freedom, and sin) and a defense of free will together with a positive account of its nature. This work reveals its author as a master of the logic of his day; for instance, he developed modal logic with reference to the different kinds of necessary proposition (absolute and simple necessity). Recent research has shown that the ideas expressed in *De libero arbitrio* exerted considerable influence on Oxford thinkers for a century or more after his death.

It is convenient at this point to outline Grosseteste's principal ideas concerning light, since these are both philosophical and theological in character, and the constellation of themes that is often referred to as "the metaphysics of light" is wholly characteristic of his thought.

The Metaphysics of Light

The term "metaphysics of light" was coined by Clemens Baeumker in 1916 and has been employed widely, though not uncontroversially, ever since. It designates a whole circle of themes, a current of philosophical and religious thought that runs right through European culture from ancient times down to the Renaissance.[14] This current includes the idea that the physical universe is made up of light, so that all its features, including space, time, non-living and living things, spheres, and stars, are different forms taken by a single fundamental energy.

This philosophical intuition inspired the composition of the *Tractatus de luce* (*Treatise on Light*) of Grosseteste.[15] This short work contains a cosmogony, that is, a theoretical account of how the physical universe came into existence and took the form it actually takes, or at least that Grosseteste thought it takes. I do not know of any other work of the same character dating from medieval times, and I regard it as the original creation of a bold and powerful mind that had arrived at its fullest maturity (ca. 1225–1230).

Out of nothing preexisting, that is, not time or space or any material, God created a single point from which the entire physical order was to derive by way of extension or expansion. That first, dimensionless point was light; it was one and simple, containing matter implicitly within its light-form. Light, of course, expands by self-propagation. In its expansion that primordial light created space and extended the matter that it precontained into the three dimensions of a vast sphere. The multiplication or self-propagation of light can, Grosseteste argues, be understood only on the mathematical model of infinity, since the unit that at the start occupied no spatial dimensions could create tri-dimensionality only by an infinite self-generation. The outcome of this infinite auto-propagation, however, must itself be finite, since the power of light enters matter and so determines quantitatively the infinite propagation. Now nature abhors a vacuum; like other medieval philosophers who shared similar interests, Grosseteste is fond of quoting ancient, teleologically colored adages on nature, such as "nature does nothing in vain," and "nature does not do by many means what she can do by few." The world-sphere, therefore, must be a continuum of informed matter, for the radiation of light finds a natural boundary at the point where light and matter are perfectly balanced and where any further expansion would begin to produce a vacuum among the particles of the continuum. The activity of light does not, however, exhaust its energy at the surface of the sphere, but begins to make a sort of bellows movement between circumference and center, for light (*lumen*, the product of *lux*) is reflected back toward the initial point of expansion, and the *lumen*, rushing towards the center of the system, condenses matter to form the sphere of earth. Light continues to work by alternating movements of expansion and contraction, to form, one by one, the celestial spheres and the concentric globes of the three remaining elements. By comparison with the first sphere, in which the simplest and fullest realization of the possibilities of form and matter is to be found, each lower sphere in the sequence is less simple, less unified, more multiple and corporeal. The cosmogony closes with the universe's being set in motion around its center, and the differentiation being established of the circular heavenly motion from the rectilinear movement of the upper elements, namely fire and air.

We should see in Grosseteste's cosmogony of light a speculative interpretation of the biblical account of creation: "Let there be light; and light was made" (Gen. 1:3). In *De luce*, light is described as the first corporeal form. The inner relationship between *De luce* and the light of Genesis (which is assigned to the first day in the biblical account of the world) is evident: Grosseteste himself identifies the sphere formed by the first expanding movement of light in terms of "the firmament," deliberately invoking the biblical term so that the reader may understand that *De luce* presents a theoretical account of the formation of the heavens and the earth, in other words of the creative work of God during the first three days of creation, before the making of the sun, the moon, and the other luminaries.

Like the other theological scholars of his time, Grosseteste studied Genesis through the tradition of commentaries on the work of the Six Days—the hexaëmeral commentaries produced by the Fathers of the Church. We can easily enough trace the influence of St. Augustine and St. Basil, in particular, upon his thinking. Augustine had concluded that the light that God created is present in the work of all six days—hence the repetition by the biblical account of the word "day," which is the time of light. The light first created can be interpreted as a material light, and this may have differentiated day and night by rotation, or by contraction and emission, even before sun and moon were made. In Basil's view, the first word of God produced light, which shone, however, only to illuminate the heavens already formed; it was not actually itself the first thing made. Once created, light diffused itself instantaneously to fill the ether and the heavens. The primordial light of the first three days divided day from night, and for Basil the periods in question were a rhythm of effusion and contraction, an alternation, as it were, of dawn and dusk but without a sun. There is no reason to see here anything more than a verbal analogy with the process of condensation and rarefaction described in *De luce*. Moreover, even when Basil declares light to be a simple and homogeneous body, it is evident that he is thinking still of physical light, not of any kind of dynamic energy. The combined influence of these two authorities encouraged Grosseteste to apply the command *fiat lux* to the conception of a pure light that preceded the sun's creation and suggested to him the notion of a substance, simple and homogeneous, diffusing itself instantaneously through space, uniquely active, transcending the other elements in the direction of spiritual being, and conferring beauty upon the entire "world-machine." All this, however, falls far short of the *prima forma* and its mathematical behavior, as Grosseteste was to conceive of it.

The first corporeal form and matter of *De luce* have immediate roots in Arabic and Jewish speculation. Avicenna, Algazel, and Averroës all developed a theory of common corporeity as the active generator of tri-dimensionality, to which *forma specialis* remains still to be added. The influence of Ibn Gebirol (Avicebrol) upon Grosseteste is probably even stronger than that of Avicenna. In his voluminous treatise *Fons vitae*, universal form and universal matter are represented as two substances differing in essence: "The One" (an echo of Plotinus) causes universal form to be diffused like light over the matter in which form becomes corporeal, the *prima forma substantialis*. Like Ibn Gebirol, Avicenna considered that the first corporeal form extends matter into three dimensions; this view, adopted by Grosseteste, offered the possibility of envisaging the most universal aspect of material beings—pure extension—in geometrical terms. There can be little doubt but that the Neoplatonic theme of emanation conceived of as a cascade of light descending from the One—a theme or scheme that finds a general parallel in *De luce*—reached Grosseteste through Avicebrol, Avicenna, and the *Liber de causis*. The entire conception of the derivation of the visible world from simple light echoes Plotinus or Proclus. Grosseteste emphasized that the origin is something simple; that multiplicity is unified by the first form; that the cosmos is therefore hierarchical; and that the perfection of the first sphere is reproduced in some way in each of the lower ones, just as unity is in every number. It would appear, however, that Grosseteste's identification of light with *prima corporeitas* was quite original. Likewise his argument invoking mathematical infinity (and relative infinities) seems to have been his own invention, at least so far as our present knowledge goes.

If *De luce* and the various treatises on light phenomena (color; the behavior of rays; the rainbow; the heat of the sun; the climates) to which it stands as a sort of framework-theory contained all of Grosseteste's thoughts on light, there would, of course, be no reason whatsoever to apply the term "metaphysics of light" to his thought. Grosseteste did in fact invoke the notion of light in areas of his thinking other than cosmology or the philosophy of nature—which surely provides some justification for speaking of the metaphysics of light rather than of the physics of light. Along with St. Augustine and

St. Anselm, he thought of the human intellect as a created spiritual light, and he employed the optical model in his analysis of the act of knowledge, a model that Augustine had taken over from Greek Neoplatonism. The Oxford philosopher shared Augustine's conviction that certainty in knowing depends upon the illumination of the created mind by the uncreated light, God. However, even if we take Grosseteste's light cosmology and his theory of knowledge together, as a sort of dyptych, by juxtaposing them we still do not have anything we could reasonably call a *metaphysics* of light. As it happens, Grosseteste did not himself gather into one systematic treatise the various strands of his thinking about light. Yet upon closer scrutiny many of his writings yield up thoughts that do indeed give the framework for an overarching metaphysical view.

What is no doubt the central theme of the metaphysics of light is well developed, for instance, in the *Hexaëmeron*: it is that God is light (I John 1:5). If God is truly (and not merely in some metaphorical or poetical sense) light, then clearly all that is made in his likeness, and more especially in his image, must be light of one kind or another. The whole of being, then, is light, since absolute Being and absolute Light coincide and are but one. Grosseteste held firmly to the Augustinian conviction that God is light, not merely in a metaphorical but in an essential sense. Influenced by the transcendental tendency of especially Christian Neoplatonic thought, he regarded the reversal of conceptual direction as something strictly required in order to express the ontological difference between the universal, originating value of the act of creation and the creature understood in its radical dependence upon the absolute principle of all existence. In a dialectic of an idealist or Platonic kind where thinking moves from the *sensibilia* to the *intelligibilia*, a reversal of the initial, experiential concept or metaphor is necessitated. Viewed in this fundamental perspective, each creature bears an intrinsic reference and likeness to the creator, whose infinite, true, and essential light it mirrors or symbolizes in its own finite form. It follows from this that the *lux prima* is incomparably more truly *lux* than is, for example, the sun or its light. If we are to do credit to the deepest dimensions of Grosseteste's thinking, then the metaphorics of light must be thought of as receiving a decisive ontological underwriting in the form of the metaphysics of light; in other words, the latter overtakes the former and gives it its grounding.

In a very notable discussion of light in his *Hexaëmeron* Grosseteste makes the claim that every form that exists is *aliquod genus lucis*, "some kind of light."[16] The reason he gives for this assertion is that the nature of light includes lighting things up (*manifestativa*). Becoming and change result from the generative power of light acting upon matter. Light (or form) has power and energy latent within it. We can observe this in the case of visible light, which as soon as it appears propagates itself into a sphere. Grosseteste calls that power *generativitas* and its exercise *replicatio*, the power to propagate, generate, or replicate itself. I think we can best understand this metaphor, which of course is taken from the propagation of living beings, if we think of light as instantaneously (for the speed of light is considered to be infinite) filling a space, a room, say: for Grosseteste, this happens because the light taken at any given point must, to move beyond that point, be able to bring forth from itself the light that goes out beyond it spatially, and that light in its turn repeats the propagation, and so on. This process can be termed generation or propagation on the analogy of life, insofar as something new is brought into being at each phase and the new is of exactly the same nature as its parent. Dialectically speaking, the light newly generated both is and is not the light from which it comes: it is, because it shares fully in the one nature of light; it is not, however, identically the same light but is a new expression of it. Light, in other words, naturally multiplies its own being; as soon as it is there it unfolds itself (*se replicat*). Beginning from a point, it radiates all around itself in a sphere. In its own very nature, therefore, light can be defined as the power to generate itself. The effect of self-generation, namely, making shapes and colors manifest, follows upon the nature of light as accident follows upon substance. Moreover, the light that constitutes the universe is the source of all perceptible beauty. It has a natural beauty roughly in the way that the sun has, for, like the visible sun, invisible light is simple, being one thing or essence without parts or internal differentiation of any kind. Grosseteste concludes his discussion with the words, "Among corporeal things it is light which provides the most evident demonstration, through an example, of the Most High Trinity."

Like every other Christian theologian, Grosseteste was obliged to make the attempt to think together, in a single rich dialectical concept, the thought that God is one in essence or nature and three in persons. Grosseteste supposed from the very outset that God is in himself absolute being. In God there is no otherness; even though God is other, wholly other, than all that is not God, nevertheless in the Godhead itself there is no *aliud aliquid*, or internal difference of nature, or negation of self. Hence God must be simple, that is to say, wholly equal to himself in all of what he is (*sui ad se omnimoda similitudo*).[17] How better to think this unique self-identity along with the differences of the three persons, in a single thought, than through the mediation of the concept of light?

Light, as Grosseteste thought of it, is perfectly simple and incomposite, yet purely and simply by being what it is it generates something of like nature to itself, by way of replication; and it remains one in nature with its equal, which is *lumen de lumine*, light from light. Furthermore, the presence all together in visible light of three factors, namely, light, splendor, and heat (which are all one in essence but are distinguishable by thought), offers us a model (*demonstratio per exemplum*, to keep to Grosseteste's expression) for thinking the Trinity of God. The generation of the second person from the absolute, beginningless origin of the Godhead ("Father") can be thought out in some degree on the model of the radiation and reflection of light. Here is a compressed, dialectical expression of the intratrinitarian relations:

> The one expresses from out of himself a second; but the second reflects himself back into the first and expresses his own reflection out of himself [back] into the first. Or rather, the first is reflected through the second [back] into himself, and this reflection proceeds at once from the first and from the second.[18]

As he remarks at one point, if God is Trinity, God is light. What is reflected back into the primordial, infinite radiation is its very own nature, a nature that has never left it in order to acquire something additional that was not there at the beginning—for the image reflected back must be a faithful image. The unity and identity of what is radiated forth, received, and then reflected back by the combined radiating action of source and image, is in turn a third factor or aspect of the infinitely dynamic nature of God. The divine dynamic is not to be thought of as the completion of God by some addition (for properly speaking the Trinity is not a number) but as the inexhaustible intelligibility of the plenitude of being—an intelligibility that is at once the action of manifesting all that is in the Godhead and the state of its being manifested and fully expressed, plus the inseparable unity of both of these.

Grosseteste was fully alive to the need to complement this light model of the divine dynamic with a mental one, for the former remains too attached to a nonpersonal nature to be satisfactory in every respect. He considered it to be secondary in richness with regard to the classical trinitarian model, based upon the psychological richness of our mental life, which represents a higher kind of "reflection" than that of physical light, that is, that of our self-consciousness in the triune form of intelligence, will, and memory. But here he did no more than to take up a well-known Augustinian thought, one that cannot be explored in the present context.

Light, being, and form are drawn by Grosseteste into a rich and complex unity of meaning. His doctrine of creation leads back to the exemplaristic conception of God as first universal form (*forma omnium et prima forma*). "Every form draws towards unity and tends towards it (*omnis forma trahit et tendit ad unitatem*)," thus relating every being to the essential Light, the unique and beginningless origin of creatures. Just as unity is present in each number, though without losing its simplicity, so the *lux prima* manifests itself in every finite form. Grosseteste generalizes the equation between light and being: "[A]ll light is manifestation, or manifesting, or manifested, or the receptive subject of manifestation."[19] This fourfold division has implications for every dimension of being.

1. The visible sun is the most expressive example of a light that both manifests itself and makes material objects visible, while not being manifest to itself but only to a higher light.

2. Color is simply light incorporated into matter and made manifest by light. The eye that perceives color is itself active and radiating, in virtue of the light that constitutes its energy. Each of the senses is active through the light that infuses them, but none of them is manifest to itself, though each in its own way receives the manifestations of its object.

3. Intelligence is a light to which both other things and itself are manifest, but which still requires a higher light of manifestation: the mind, whether of angel or of man, requires to be illuminated by the primordial light in which every creature partakes. The intelligence is spiritual light and is "in some way all things" (cf. Aristotle, *De anima*), since the illumination it receives from God opens up all realities to its comprehension.

4. The supreme and essential light, finally, is described as "light which manifests itself to itself, while within itself all other things are manifest to it." In other words, in the perfect simplicity of the first light the principles of knowing (*principia cognoscendi*) and the principles of being (*principia essendi*) coincide.

The metaphysics of light is intimately associated with the theory of beauty. Grosseteste's age was aware of two different aesthetics. Boethius transmitted to it the Pythagorean "musical" equation of beauty and harmony: beauty consists in the agreement of different but complementary elements governed by an arithmetical proportion. To this strongly intellectualist conception another stood opposed, which located the essence of beauty in the simplic-

ity of light. The heritage of Plotinus made of light both the substance of color
and the condition of its visibility. This more sensuous idea of beauty was
transmitted to the high Middle Ages through Basil, Ambrose, Augustine,
the Pseudo-Dionysius, and Scottus Eriugena. According to this tradition
light is beautiful of its very nature and is the source of beauty in all material
things, which it informs. The more noble a thing is, the more beautiful it is.

In three of his mature works Grosseteste developed aspects of the philosophy of beauty (*De operationibus solis*, 1230–1235; *Hexaëmeron*, 1235–1236;
and the commentary on the *Divine Names*, 1239–1243). Although he invoked
the aesthetics of proportion, the triumph of the aesthetics of light is evident
in his reduction of the equality of proportion to unity and simplicity. In a
way harmony is reduced to unity, being no longer conceived of as the con-
cord of differing elements but as agreement between the form of a thing and
its matter. In the *Hexaëmeron* he quoted Basil to the effect that the simple
self-identity of beauty delights the eyes even in the absence of harmonious
bodily proportion: gold is the same throughout its substance, and the stars
are lovely by their light alone, without any differentiation of part and whole.
He invoked Ambrose to the same effect: light is pleasing from any point of
view and not merely in number, weight, and measure (cf. Wis. 11:21) like
other things. The objectivism of this theory should not blind us to an important subjective component, which consists in the intellectual grasp of the
beautiful geometry that characterizes the action of light in nature.

Grosseteste's philosophy of light was never set down by him in a fully
worked-out way or placed within the covers of a single book, but has to be
reconstructed from various writings and contexts of thought. Yet it forms a
fairly coherent whole, and though it owed much to Christian Platonism (to
St. Augustine and the Pseudo-Dionysius, in particular) it has a manifestly
original quality, especially in the cosmogony of *De luce*. The essential scheme
of the philosophy of light was known to St. Bonaventure through a summary of it that Adam Marsh, Grosseteste's collaborator, appears to have
drawn up. Here the endeavor was made to systematize the metaphysics of
light by interrelating the different regions of thought that Grosseteste himself had never drawn together into a unified discussion.[20] A manifest anticipation of Huyghens's ideas on the propagation of light is to be found in the
relevant notions developed by the medieval philosopher of light. Indeed,
Grosseteste's account of absolute cosmic origins from a nondimensional point
of infinitely compressed energy makes the contemporary reader think quite
spontaneously of the Big Bang theory of the universe's beginnings.

EXEGETICAL WRITINGS

Origins are for the most part the obscurest things in history. Pitifully little is known with any certainty of the Oxford in which Grosseteste taught, of the curriculum in arts and theology, the length of courses, and the other structures of academic life that contribute so largely to the shape of a scholar's day-by-day and year-by-year existence, and that even help to set the lines on which he will write. This inability of ours to relate Grosseteste institutionally and imaginatively to a scholastic setting that remains almost impenetrably obscure is the source of the great difficulties we experience in trying to locate his writings in time and to place them in relation to the historical context of his teaching.

Despite the obscurity referred to, I think it is a fair assumption that a master brought his students through the Gospels and the Epistles (especially those of St. Paul), thus preparing them for ministry in the Church, or for teaching at episcopal and other schools. Gospel and Epistle, read in an annual cycle, constituted essentially the first part of the Sunday Mass. It may also be assumed that the teacher covered a fair bit of the Old Testament in cycles of two or three years, commenting with particular care on the opening chapters of Genesis, the major prophets, and the Psalms. He would have to have had at his disposal his own copy of the Vulgate and a copy, owned outright or shared (if he lived in a community), of the Ordinary Gloss. That, at any rate, is how I imagine in the broadest outline Grosseteste's conduct of the theological course at his school to have been.

What survives of his lectures on books of the Old Testament is almost certainly fragmentary, but there is sufficient of it to give a good idea of his method and of his characteristic turn of mind. The most impressive work by far, and the only complete and finished example of his Old Testament exegesis, is of course the *Hexaëmeron*, the commentary on the creation narrative of Genesis. The extensive commentary on Psalms 1–100, which has not been edited as yet, is particularly important in view of the light it helps to shed on Grosseteste's learning of Greek, for in his study of Psalms 80–100 he shows an acquaintance with the language, and his exposition is much fuller and more consecutive than in the earlier part. A comment on Ecclesiasticus 43:1–5 (probably fragmentary) throws into relief an aspect of his interest in the Wisdom literature, an interest that is noticeable in other writings of his.[1] As further evidence for his exegesis of the Old Testament we have two treatises dealing with biblical matters, which incorporate portions of commentary. *De cessatione legalium* contains a verse-by-verse study of Isaiah 52:13–53:12, on the Suffering Servant of Jahweh and the realization of this prophecy in the Passion of Jesus Christ. This is followed immediately by the exegesis of Daniel 9:24–27, the prophecy concerning the time of the passion of the Messiah. And we may not forget that *De decem mandatis* is intended to be a commentary on the literal (and in some chosen places the spiritual) sense of Exodus 20:1–17. The Ten Commandments clearly occupied an important place in the education imparted by Grosseteste. If we include the directly exegetical studies contained in these passages of the two biblical treatises, we have a more substantial and representative body of Old Testament commentary from his hand than is often appreciated. We should, however, suppose that he wrote works that have either been lost or remain unidentified.

Much less evidence has survived of his exegesis of the New Testament than of the Old. All that remains relates to the Pauline corpus: a commentary on Galatians and fragmentary glosses (some of them quite extensive) on all the other elements of the traditional Pauline writings. These were preserved from oblivion by Thomas Gascoigne, the fifteenth-century theologian and chancellor of Oxford, who made extensive extracts from a lost codex of Grosseteste. The most striking gap in Grosseteste's surviving exegetical works relates, of course, to the four Gospels, no trace of his teaching on which has ever been found. We can only suppose that his notes and glosses were used in delivering lectures but were left in a state that did not make them good candidates for survival.

The duties of a master of theology were to "read" the Bible to his students, to conduct disputations, and to preach. Grosseteste certainly must have held disputations on the literal sense and on questions arising from it; Thomas of Eccleston says as much. Grosseteste himself refers to themes of disputations in his commentary on Galatians, and when concluding his treatise *De libero arbitrio* he refers obliquely to its origin in disputations. The Parisian practice of recording such discussions and writing them up for circulation as *quaestiones* was evidently not yet in vogue in the Oxford of his day. His theological writings were composed in such a way as to satisfy chiefly his own requirements; only very occasionally do they betray their origins in actual teaching.

Grosseteste's books were the result of lengthy preparation on his part. He was an inveterate scribbler on scraps of parchment and a habitual glossator of the books he possessed, with the result that when it came to writing he could always begin from preexistent materials. At a disputation held at Oxford in 1316–1317 William of Alnwick, regent master of the Franciscans, countered an argument based on an idea of Grosseteste's by claiming it was nothing more than a marginal note in his copy of the *Physics:*

> It should be acknowledged that the bishop wrote these words with his own hand in the margin of his copy of the *Physics*, which he did not comment on systematically or completely, as he did on the *Posterior Analytics*. But when some noteworthy thought occurred to him he wrote it down there so that it should not escape his memory, just as he also wrote many slips of parchment which are not all authentic. What he wrote disconnectedly in the margin of his copy of the *Physics* is of no greater authority than the other slips of parchment he wrote, which are all kept in the library of the Friars Minor at Oxford, as I have seen with my own eyes.

A good example of his writing method can be found in the case of his commentary on Galatians. Between 1433 and 1456, Thomas Gascoigne was allowed access to the priests' library at the Franciscan Convent of Oxford. There he consulted Grosseteste's copy of St. Paul, which had the Ordinary Gloss written around the text, and the margins crammed with Grosseteste's own notes. (It must have been from this book that Grosseteste gave his classes on the Epistles.) Among the many glosses of the bishop that he chose to copy are thirteen on the Letter to the Galatians.[2] Subsequent to writing these glosses Grosseteste composed a continuous commentary on the Epistle, for which the glosses can be regarded as representing a preparatory stage. Only the general sense of the substrate is taken up in his exegesis.

Grosseteste was an inventive scholar: where aids to composition were not yet available, he produced them. A surviving example is his *Tabula*. As his library and his scholarship grew, he developed a system of reference, evidence of which has fortunately been preserved in a single manuscript, recently edited.[3]

The *Tabula* is an index of the Bible, the Church fathers, and some pagan and Islamic writers. It consists of topics arranged under nine different headings, or "distinctions" (in scholastic jargon): *de Deo*, *de verbo*, *de creaturis*, and so on. It gives references to a wide range of unexcerpted texts and employs a unique system of logographic signs, devised for the gathering of references in view of inclusion in the index, under a multiplicity of headings for theological and moral topics. The *Tabula* is incomplete in the manuscript. Its editor concludes that the project must have been discontinued about the year 1230, while Grosseteste was still a regent master. Its interest is evident. It allows its reader to find, under each of the headings he assigned, all the scriptural references and *auctoritates* that its compiler considered important. Each of his theological writings should be examined on its basis; this kind of work has barely gotten off the ground as yet. It can be of help in dating some of his writings. It even enables us to discern the drift of his mind concerning topics on which he did not publish his thoughts, such as the correct Christian attitude to philosophy. Finally, the logographic signs it utilizes systematically can be followed up in a number of the surviving books that were once in Grosseteste's ownership, and in which these symbols are placed in the margins as reference marks.

Commentary on Psalms 1–100

Grosseteste's hitherto unedited commentary on the Psalms is known in six copies, three of which extend from Psalm 1 to Psalm 100, the point at which he apparently left off. Teaching the Psalter was required of theologians, because of its central importance in the Mass and in the Sacred Office chanted by monks and read by clergy. It was moreover the first book that many children got to know, for they commonly learned to read Latin from it. In the prologue to his commentary Grosseteste praised the excellence of the Psalter:

> The Psalms express the various holy affections of the soul more repeatedly and more expressively than any of the other parts of Scripture, whence in the Psalter the soul in which the meaning of its words has been

engraved with deep effect on the feelings, sings that prayer of praise in a kind of transport.

Furthermore, he allegorized the harp in a way that showed a debt to St. Augustine, who thought of the "ten-stringed harp" (Ps. 91:1–3) as the Ten Commandments, the instrument of the music of charity:

> The three sides of the sacred harp on which you (whoever you are) are to sing the Psalms are, the love of God with which He loves you and your neighbor, the love with which you love God and your neighbor, and the love with which your neighbor loves you and God. Now just as on the harp one end of a string is tied to the lower member and the other end goes up to the head post, while the string itself runs parallel to the resonating chamber, the third member: so in you, as you love God and your neighbor, each of the ten commandments is tied down like a string . . . This is the spiritual harp which we are to carry not as a burden merely, but singing to lighten the weight and the labor.

It has recently been suggested that Grosseteste compiled lecture notes on the Psalter that he later expanded into a longer form, and that each of these autographs survived only in part (Ps. 1–81 and Ps. 80–100, respectively— there are two comments on Ps. 80). According to this hypothesis, the two originals were conflated to form the exemplar that was conserved at the Franciscan library up to the Reformation, and that engendered the existing copies. In other words, an editor intervened who fused the two authentic sources, and furthermore expanded the commentary by drawing in extraneous material from the *Dicta* and the sermons of Grosseteste. Both of these works lent themselves to the compiler's art, particularly the former, which Grosseteste characterized in the following terms:

> In this little book there are one hundred and forty-seven chapters. Some of them are short words which I wrote down briefly and in rough form while I was in the schools. They are not all about one subject, nor are they in a continuous order. I have given each of them a title so that the reader can very easily find what he wants; thus it comes about that some of the titles promise the reader far more than the chapter may fulfill. Others are sermons which I preached to either the clergy or the laity during the same period.

It was commonly held that the Psalms, rightly understood, contained in some way the whole of Scripture. Their essential reference point was understood to be Christ, prophetically foreseen. Commentaries on the Psalms commonly had the Church as a topic of central importance: the Church, that is, understood in its mystery, as the body of Christ and as the spouse of Christ. It has recently been shown that Grosseteste's commentary is rich in ec-clesiological themes.[4] These were the fruit of the spiritual reading of the Psalms, which came about when the mind passed through and beyond the literal sense toward allegory. Light, as Grosseteste remarked revealingly in his work on the creation, "comes when the carnal meaning of Scripture bursts forth into the spiritual sense."

The comments up to Psalm 78 are a haphazard affair, being far from continuous, skipping some Psalms altogether and having much material in common with the *Dicta* and sermons.

In the comment on Psalm 79 a new source suddenly appears, Gregory of Nazianzen. From Psalms 80 to 100 every Psalm is extensively dealt with, in its structure, content, and relation to other Psalms. Gregory is joined as a source by Athanasius, Basil, Gregory of Nyssa, Eusebius, Theodoret and, above all, Cyril of Alexandria, to supplement the usual range of Latin au-thorities. Grosseteste was evidently drawing upon a Greek catena on the Psalms; he was likewise using the Septuagint text. His increasing reliance on Greek authorities is the sign of a new start in his intellectual life, and the linguistic notes he included show that he was proficient in the language. The commentary contains passages that introduce some of the themes that were—or were to become—established favorites of his. As it progresses, we can see "a growing confidence, a widening range of theological speculation, and a new mastery in handling his sources."[5] It is not known why its author discontinued the work.

Trilogy on the Old and New Dispensations

Three writings of Grosseteste closely related to the Scriptures are themselves thematically and doctrinally interrelated. The three can be considered as making up something like a trilogy that sprang from a unitary inspiration in the mind of their author. The commentary on St. Paul's letter to the Galatians was written before the other two. The Apostle vigorously attacked the countermovement of some Jewish members of the Church who had seized upon the rite of circumcision as their test case for the continuity of the covenant, which they regarded as one and indivisible. Paul argued that there had in reality been two covenants and two Israels, and that the Torah had already served its pedagogical function of bringing the human child to the school of Christ. In the treatise *De decem mandatis* ("On the Ten Commandments"), Grosseteste examined the relationship between the Decalogue and the command of Christ to love God and the neighbor and insisted that the Mosaic Law looked forward already to its own fulfillment in Christ. *De cessatione legalium* ("On the Cessation of the Ritual Torah") is a treatise on salvation history. Beginning from his reconstruction of the Judaizing movement within the primitive Church, he studied the interrelationship of the Old and New Testaments. He showed how the prophecies were fulfilled in the paschal events. He defended the value of the moral precepts of the Mosaic code (as distinct from its ritual and ceremonial law), since none of these is abolished but rather subsumed and manifested as an expression of true, redeemed love. He extended his reflections magnificently to the unity and harmony of the entire divine plan of redemption, attempting to show that providence, far from being frustrated by the Fall of Adam, worked in and through the long preparation of the covenanted people toward the Incarnation, an event that, he argues, would have taken place even if man had not sinned.

Of course, a project of the sort we have here may have taken a considerable time to realize. Precise dates for the three works are not available. *De cessatione* was written in the 1230s (as Grosseteste tells us incidentally) and may have been completed just before he became bishop (1235). It refers back to the commentary on Galatians, which is likewise presupposed by *De decem mandatis*. Grosseteste may well have spent a considerable portion of his time during the last decade or so of his teaching life in preparing these three writings, which, when taken all together, represent the realization of a major preoccupation of the mature scholar and teacher.

The Commentary on Galatians

Galatians, along with the Acts of the Apostles, is the primary historical witness concerning the tension generated by the detachment of the Christian *ecclesia* from the Jewish nation.[6] Grosseteste's fascination with the mentality of the Judaizing section within primitive Christianity is a notable aspect of the close interest he displayed in every dimension of the life of the early Church, and in the literature either stemming from or attributed in his day to the origins of Christianity. He seems to have made a deliberate decision to study this Epistle in depth. His option bears significantly upon the theme of Christian liberty. The fruit of the indwelling Spirit of God, liberty may not be spied upon or enslaved anew in the name of ethnicity, for it is the source of spiritual love of God and of the neighbor as such.

Grosseteste prepared himself diligently and thoroughly for his task by reading all the commentaries available to him, both Greek and Latin, beginning with the quotations from Origen's homilies preserved by St. Jerome. It was on Jerome's work that he relied most consistently throughout the course of his own interpretation. Recognizing that it contained a veritable store of scholarship and information, he often paraphrased it, or picked up hints dropped by Jerome and developed them himself. The Latin authorities and sources utilized in the commentary (Augustine, Pelagius [Pseudo-Jerome], Gregory, the Ordinary Gloss, and the gloss of Lombard) occasion no surprise. It is when we turn to his Greek reading that some absolute novelties appear, namely, the homilies of St. John Chrysostom on Galatians and the Pauline catena attributed to Theophylact of Bulgaria.

Grosseteste read the homilies of Chrysostom directly in Greek. The extensive use he made of the work suggests that he was following not an anthology or catena merely but the unabridged text, for he evidently could refer to it for particular questions as they arose throughout the course of his work. To choose but one example: he rightly perceived that in the animated patristic discussion concerning the difference that opposed Peter and Paul (Gal. 2), Chrysostom was in fact in agreement with Jerome, who in his turn had followed Origen. Their combined point of view is reflected in the commentary, together with Augustine's opposing one. Grosseteste's feeling for the unity and fundamental agreement of the two apostles owed a good deal to the Greek homilist.

Theophylact's successful compilation attained a very wide diffusion in the Byzantine world. No trace of any Latin employment of it has yet been found prior to Grosseteste, who may not even have known the name of its author. He employed it liberally and even translated passages from it when commenting on chapter 2 of Galatians. Theophylact was a compiler who conveyed no personal message, but by the clarity of the résumé that he presented he gave strong reinforcement to the interpretation of St. Paul put forward by Chrysostom.

A large part of the distinction of the *Expositio* as a representative of the exegetical tradition must be located in its deliberate reliance upon the Greek expositors side by side with the Latin. A related distinction attaches to the use made of Greek for the elucidation of the text. Grosseteste was working from a copy of the Greek New Testament and the Septuagint, and consulting a Greek dictionary (the *Etymologicum Gudianum*). It can be argued without exaggeration that he produced the most philologically accomplished Latin commentary on Paul since St. Jerome.

The other noticeable distinction of the commentary is of the spiritual order. Grosseteste was not in search of originality but chose to concentrate all his intellectual effort upon the biblical text. Yet he was too individual an author to yield himself wholly to the constraints of the genre, with the result that on some occasions a more personal message resonated within the lines of his commentary. This is true, for example, of the vibrant pages that he devotes to the fruit of the Spirit (Gal. 5:22).[7] He emphasizes the unity of the single fruit by showing that "love, joy, peace, patience," and so on, are not a combination of disparate elements but are meant to be a series of perspectives upon a single reality; in other words, love *is* joy, peace, patience, and so forth. A further example is the wholly individual way in which he pursues the childbearing metaphor employed by St. Paul (Gal. 4:19) to dramatize the role of the evangelist and teacher.[8] In his analysis of the spiritual procreation that is the outcome of educative love Grosseteste shares his own experience as teacher and priest with his readers, in a moving and memorable way. His commentary may not sustain throughout its length the sublime level indicated by the foregoing remarks, for there is the more technical terrain of explanation to be got through, side by side with the high points of Pauline spirituality. But it can be said that the work he produced reveals him at the very height of his powers and at his best as a teacher of the Christian faith, for it is both erudite and wise, full at once of deeply pondered truths and of finely distilled experience.

On The Ten Commandments

Following the commentary on Galatians Grosseteste wrote on the commandments.[9] The absence of Greek learning in his treatise indicates that the work was aimed not precisely at a scholarly readership but at the growing number of learned priests whose ministry and general influence he was ever anxious to support: in his eyes there never were and never could be enough of them. He had considerable success, for his book was copied and read throughout the fourteenth and fifteenth centuries in England (all twenty-four manuscripts are of English provenance). One of the manuscripts entitles the work *de dileccione et x mandatis* ("On Love and the Ten Command-ments"); nothing more apt could be found to express the theme of the writ-ing. The commandments, after all, do remain in force within Christianity where, furthermore, they are surrounded by thickets of laws and regulations; how is this multiplicity to be understood and lived as a unity, in the light of the *mandatum novum* of love that is Christianity's unique precept? This is the perspective that governs the whole composition.

De decem mandatis can be placed broadly within the genre of *pastoralia*; it occupies, as it were, a place on the highest shelf of popular theology. It is at the same time a work of exegesis whose literary structure is given by Exo-dus 20:1–17. Grosseteste commented on each phrase and each word, even of the longer commandments. He was of course acquainted with the best Latin material on the commandments and related themes, and he made extensive use of (among others) Augustine, Jerome, Bernard, and Bede, as well as the Gloss, drawing upon his own *Tabula* for many of the topical ref-erences. *De decem mandatis* was written at a time when the teaching of the precepts was finding a secure place within what was an increasingly system-atic theology, yet it stands apart from this tendency and is in fact the first self-contained treatise on the subject since Philo (to whose writing, however, Grosseteste had no access).

The book is rich in brief *exempla* relating some aspect of the precepts to the society in which he lived. It is possible that they were not all his own inventions, but that is of comparatively little importance, considering how much they contribute to its savor. They would have been very easy for preachers to excerpt and retail. Grosseteste made much reference to the social structures of feudal society, both to reinforce all that he admired and to cas-tigate abuses, especially those of wealth and power. Side by side with this popular material he developed the Augustinian theology of ordered love, which pervaded his entire treatment of the commandments.[10]

On the Cessation of the Ritual Torah

Only a little can be said here about a work to which Grosseteste clearly de-voted much care and no little time, probably not long before or after his unexpected election to Lincoln, in 1235.[11] The theme of the work is the Old Law and its replacement by the New as regards all but its moral content (i.e., the commandments). This subject was much studied in the schools at the end of the twelfth and the beginning of the thirteenth centuries, by Peter

Lombard and William of Auvergne among others. It is in four parts, the first of which examines the error of the Judaizing tendency within the early Church. The second shows that Jesus is truly the Messiah announced by the prophets. The third exhibits the Church as the mystical body of Christ, whose Incarnation was predestined in independence of Adam's Fall. The fourth points out the harmful effects that the continued observance of the Mosaic Law would have produced within Christianity and underlines the central- ity of the action of the Holy Spirit in the Church. Within this broad frame- work a wide variety of topics is discussed, including the rules governing the spiritual interpretation of the Scriptures, the enjoyment of beatitude, the finality of nature, and the ages of the world. The Septuagint is used with frequency, but otherwise no Greek learning is exhibited. Two back refer- ences are made to the commentary on Galatians.

It used to be thought that *De cessatione* was a controversial anti-Jewish writing, but this is not in fact the case. It is a study of salvation history, and for the most part its author prefers to remain "in the footsteps of the Fathers," though Anselm of Canterbury is accorded recognition as an authority for the doctrine of the Incarnation. In its literary form, in the amplitude of its themes, and in its close reliance upon the Scriptures, the treatise belongs less to the genres of Grosseteste's own time than to the world of Augustine and Jerome. Despite that, he manifests great originality and boldness, in arguing without the support of any authority that the Incarnation would have constituted the central focus of salvation history even if the Fall had not occurred.[12]

The Hexaëmeron

Grosseteste's detailed exegesis of Genesis 1–2:16 was probably circulated during the final years of his theological teaching.[13] Adam Marsh devised chapter divisions and detailed titles that are still useful to the reader. For this work, which is the most important of its author's writings from a doc- trinal point of view, a manuscript exists that is corrected throughout three- quarters of its length in Grosseteste's own hand; it also contains *De cessatione legalium*, similarly corrected. Seven complete witnesses to the text are known, only one being conserved outside of England (Prague).

The desk at which he worked must have been huge, for he had the Vulgate, the Septuagint, and several patristic commentaries on Genesis con- stantly open before him. In no genre was the medieval author more conscious of following "in the footprints of the Fathers," for the very title of this commentary was embedded in tradition. His *Hexaëmeron* is a work of splendid erudition that uses no less than thirty-six authors and over a hundred titles. It incorporates generous quotations from Ambrose's *Hexaëmeron* and from the homonymous work of Basil the Great (on which the former was so largely modeled), from Augustine (especially *De Genesi ad litteram*), and from the *Hexaëmeron* of the Venerable Bede (referred to nineteen times). Among Grosseteste's favorite reading are pseudonymous works that his age was notoriously slow to unmask: *Hypomnesticon*, *De mirabilibus sacrae Scripturae*, *De spiritu et anima* (all attributed to Augustine), and *De corpore et sanguine Domini* (Paschasius Radbertus, wrongly attributed by Grosseteste to Rabanus Maurus). His use of Greek sources is extensive. Grosseteste employed existing translations where they were available: Gregory of Nyssa, *De hominis opificio* (Dionysius Exiguus); Pseudo-Dionysius (Scottus Eriugena); Damascene, *De fide orthodoxa* (Burgundio); Chrysostom, *Homilies on Genesis* (Anianus). Already in the lengthy *prooemium*, however, the author shows that he has access to hitherto untranslated Greek works.

The preamble to the *Hexaëmeron* includes his commentary on two letters of St. Jerome concerning the study of the Scriptures. Where mention is made by Jerome of Egypt (§12) and of Athena (§15), to mention only two examples, Grosseteste has resort to the *Etymologicum Gudianum* for etymologies. He reconstructs by conjecture Greek words that were garbled in the manuscripts of Jerome's letters. He is informed about the Byzantine pronunciation of Greek. From the *Suda Lexicon* he derives recondite lore about the brahmins. Above all, he has obtained access to homilies X and XI of the *Hexaëmeron* of Basil, of which no Latin translation existed. It was undoubtedly Grosseteste's deepening interest in biblical exegesis that motivated his study of Greek; in his commentaries on Galatians and Genesis we have the proudest results of his determination to study the New Testament and the Septuagint in the original texts, as well as to draw profit from Greek patristic exegesis.

Grosseteste's interpretation seeks to establish the literal sense of each verse, before exploring its value for the nourishment of faith and prayer (the spiritual sense, which can be allegorical, moral, or anagogical). A good deal of doctrine is covered under one or another sense, so that the book contains most of his characteristic emphases, sometimes developed more expansively in it than elsewhere in his writings. One example of this we have seen already: the creation of light and the Trinity of light.[14] Another is to be found

at the very beginning of the commentary, where its author, in an interpretation of John 17:20–21, proposes a Christocentric program for theology, one
that has deep affinities with the mind of St. Augustine. Theology should
study "the whole Christ, head and members," and every other reality, divine and created, strictly in relationship to Christ.[15]

When read with fuller understanding of its literal sense, Grosseteste
claims, the creation narrative does not omit the angels from its account, for
in the production of light on the first day we find an expression of their generation from the First Light.[16] Each angel is an image of the eternally active, absolute, and generative light that God is. Adopting ideas from Augustine, he suggests that the different phases of the single and simultaneous
divine act of creation are to be understood as moments occurring in the cognition of the angels. As moments they are distinct; as occurrences in a purely
spiritual intellect, however, they are simultaneous, since they lie outside of
time. By "the light of the first day" we understand the angelic nature as
turned toward the first light and made deiform in the image of its splendor—the daylight of existence succeeds to the darkness of nonbeing. The
angel's bright vision of eternal light includes the sight of its own creative
reason in the divine mind, by contrast to which the angel's reflexive knowledge of itself is a less clear awareness, similar to evening light. To evening
there succeeds again morning, when the spirit is borne back by contemplation of the Word's presence within itself, and is led to the praise of the light
that originated it. On the second "day" the angel contemplates the eternal
reason of the firmament, before perceiving in the dimmer evening light the
firmament as created, and returning praise of the Creator toward the morning of the third "day"; this pattern is repeated for the remaining "days" up
to the sixth. The principle governing this process within the angelic mind is
exemplaristic, the Neoplatonism of St. Augustine being at its source.

Expounding the words "In the beginning," the commentator makes a
forthright assault upon the Greek pre-Christian assumption that the universe is everlasting and without origin. He conveys a warning to "certain
moderns" who, he asserts, in attempting to palliate the relevant Aristotelian position, in particular, run the risk of attenuating Christian doctrine.[17]

Concluding his discussion of the physical heavens, Grosseteste reminds
his reader that God's disposition for the generation of the heavenly bodies
may in fact have been quite different from the hypotheses men have constructed to explain them.[18] Regarding a series of topics, all related (heavenly
motion, the number of the spheres, the conflict between the geometrical

astronomy of Ptolemy and the physical theory of Aristotle), Grosseteste expresses his own far-reaching skepticism vis-à-vis the historical attainments of science. His criticism expresses the frustration of a well-informed participant in the scientific movement, one who himself longed to have a system of the world that would satisfy all the criteria of truth, including both scientific and theological ones. A significant aspect of his criticism bears upon the limitations of recorded observations, all of which are lacunary, he complains: not a single planet has as yet been observed throughout its orbit, and in any case observations are only as good as the eyes that record them. Furthermore, nothing obliged God to make every feature of his creation evident to the human senses, with the result that there might well exist heavenly bodies that no one would ever see. His criticism should not be read as a disparagement of exploration, but as the expression of his awareness of the unreliability of much that passed for knowledge in his own day. He returns at the end with full sympathy to a point made by Aristotle: the study of the heavens is toilsome and involved, and its yield in terms of actual knowledge of the celestial substances is small, because of their remote nobility. There is a touching sincerity about this admission. Grosseteste had busied himself for years with the leading authorities on problems of celestial motion, but in the end he admitted candidly that he had reached no certain conclusions.

In the prologue to the *Hexaëmeron* the author warned that "when the attempt is made to predict future voluntary acts by astrology, it is indeed not science but a trap set by demons." He resumed his attack in part five, utilizing the arguments advanced by St. Augustine in *Confessions* and *De civitate Dei*.[19]

God speaks in the plural when he says, "Let us make man in our own image"—because God is three in one.[20] To know man, the image of God, Grosseteste remarks, one would have to know God, some reflection of whose infinity and mystery is to be found in his finite image. It is in "the highest face of the soul" (*suprema facies animae*) that the image of God is located. This supreme power is both one and three (the capacities of intelligence, memory, and love present in the human mind). It is the locus of the work of grace in the soul, and it orders the lower faculties by drawing them into its likeness. Its influence reaches even the body, so that it stamps the entire person with the seal of the divine life, much as the ether receives the light of the sun immediately and passes it on to each of the lower elements in turn, until it permeates at last to the thick earth, at which point the whole universe is illuminated by a single splendor.

It is a noteworthy fact that Grosseteste's exegesis, although influential in England already in his own lifetime, scarcely managed to cross the English Channel and exerted practically no influence at Paris, the leading center of theological studies. The *Hexaëmeron* was to be studied at Oxford by his immediate successors, Fishacre and Rufus, who quoted copiously from it. Roger Bacon had some firsthand knowledge of his hero's exegesis, in particular of Ecclesiasticus 43:1–5. *De decem mandatis* and *De cessatione* were copied fairly continuously up to the close of the Middle Ages, but in a general way we can say that a century or so after his death not very much of his influence remained, even within England. It was with John Wyclif and Thomas Gascoigne that Grosseteste's exegetical work was to find what the late Beryl Smalley once referred to as "late but warm recognition," once again, at Oxford.

De libero arbitrio

Grosseteste's work on the freedom of the will is not exegetical, but, on the other hand, it does not fit conveniently into any other category either.[21] It is the tribute of a distinguished logician to the Christian tradition, which counted notable probings by St. Augustine and Boethius, and then later by St. Anselm and St. Bernard, into the compatibility of human freedom with divine knowledge and action. All of these thinkers figure prominently among the sources of the treatise. Its author devoted considerable care to its composition and revision, and in fact three recensions of it can be distinguished. The work must have originated in disputations, but its final form was probably fixed about 1230. It is composed of two parts: arguments against free choice (including divine "foreknowledge"; statements about the future; prophecy; predestination; fate; grace; force used against freedom; and sin); and a defense of free will together with a positive account of its nature. Grosseteste was a master of the logic of his day. In this book he developed modal logic with reference to the different kinds of necessary propositions (absolute and simple necessity). Recent research has shown that the ideas expressed in *De libero arbitrio* exerted considerable influence on Oxford thinkers for a century or more after his death (Fishacre, Rufus, perhaps Duns Scotus, Thomas Bradwardine, Thomas Buckingham, Wyclif), but no trace of any influence on the continent has as yet been discovered.

How did Grosseteste's academic approach and outlook compare with that of his immediate contemporaries? R. W. Southern has mounted an assault upon what he regards as the misplaced desire of historians to domesticate Grosseteste and to draw his rugged individuality closer to the human (and, in particular, the academic) norm.[22] He has criticized the attempts of the Powicke School to fit him and his writings into the pattern of his times and to make a Scholastic out of a man who should, on the contrary, be regarded as quite unconventional in his career, thought, and writings. I do agree with part of this case: the intention attributed to Grosseteste (by D. A. Callus) of composing a summa is not supported by evidence; and the unusual degree of difficulty in relating what he wrote to what and how he taught is common ground. However, I believe that the classroom Grosseteste was much more scholastic than his published work allows us to discern. Even though he did not feel impelled to publish collections of *quaestiones* (he preferred the more discursive form of the treatise), some of his writings (in particular, *De libero arbitrio, De Dotibus,*[23] and his commentary on Galatians) contain clear internal references to disputations held in his school. We have besides that the firm and reliable testimony of Thomas of Eccleston to the effect that the friars were trained by him in disputation, as well as in exegesis. Furthermore, regarding the discussion of God as "the first form of all things" (*prima forma omnium*), which Southern regards as unscholastic by contrast to Albert the Great's handling of the same question, it is surely not without significance that the answer proposed by the Oxford master (God is not a "forma completiva ex qua et materia fit unum": God is not the sort of form that completes matter to make one thing) turns in fact upon the same distinction as that which Albert developed in his *Summa Theologiae*. If we take the academic situation as it is known to us, between 1200 and 1235, then Grosseteste was, I consider, clearly part of it: closer in style, admittedly, to some and further from others, but comparable in significant ways to, for example, William of Auvergne, his direct contemporary at Paris. Speaking in a general way, Grosseteste should be considered as belonging to the mainstream of the scholastic movement rather than the margins. After all, what we today are inclined to think of as the typically scholastic mold (the collection of questions into summas, commentary on authorities by means of questions, the dominant place accorded to the *Sentences*) all came into prominence after his teaching career was over.

So far as can be determined, the greater part of Grosseteste's theological writings was put into circulation during the last years of his regency at Oxford, that is, the five or ten years before 1235. On the hypothesis of Southern,[24] Grosseteste both learned and taught theology between 1225 and 1235, with the natural consequence that the resultant writings all came out late. I prefer to think that he taught theology at Oxford for something more like twenty years and that his published work reflects many years of detailed preparation, but that the earlier material that he assembled for purposes of teaching has, with only very limited exceptions, disappeared. Every academic career has an individual shape and depends on circumstances (such as access to libraries, the quality of pupils, and the availability of assistants and material resources—to say nothing of health and contentment), of which in Grosseteste's case we have little or no idea during the entire period preceding 1230.

There is, however, one ascertainable factor that certainly slowed Grosseteste down in his production, that is to say, his application to the Greek tongue (the same could not be said of his contemporaries, William of Auvergne and Philip the Chancellor, for example). He must have spent a great deal of time during the 1220s in learning the language and reading Greek manuscripts; it was slow work, but work that was to stamp much of his late production with his individual mark.

GREEK SCHOLARSHIP

It was as a translator from the Greek that Grosseteste was to achieve celebrity on a European scale. The most popular of his versions (the *Nicomachean Ethics*, the *Letters of St. Ignatius*, and the *Testaments of the Twelve Patriarchs*) far outweigh his original writings in numbers of extant copies, as well as outreaching them in geographical diffusion. Indeed the Ignatian letters and the *Testaments* were read well beyond the university and clerical setting that formed the intended readership of his other versions.

Learning Greek:
The Why and the How

The conventional date of 1232 for the beginnings of his Greek studies does not take account of either the breadth or the depth of scholarship that Grosseteste displayed in versions and commentaries within a very few years of then, and in reading and glossing even around that very time. There was no precedent at Oxford, or in England, for the learning of Greek and no ready-made collection of books to learn from, with the result that the question concerning his motivation for taking up the language must in the very last analysis receive an answer in terms of his own free initiative.

It was not Grosseteste's absorption in the logical and physical writings of Aristotle that impelled him to learn the Greek language: his motivation for

its study derived essentially from his devotion to the sacred books of his religion, and its earliest fruits are shown in philological and textual criticism
of the kind that had been the apparatus of biblicists in patristic and later
times. That he taught theology for some period of time in the way that he
himself had doubtless learned it, by glossing books of the Vulgate Bible for
class instruction while drawing essentially upon the Latin tradition of exegesis for information and interpretations, we have good reason to believe
on the basis of the surviving evidence pertaining to the Psalter (his commentary on Pss. 1–81) and the Pauline epistles. His decision to learn Greek must
be understood in the light of that conception of the theologian's task to which
he appears to have held steadfastly throughout his career: the theologian is
above all a teacher of the Scriptures after the manner of the Fathers of the
Church. He may and should employ all other forms of learning and of scholastic exercise in order to promote the one central aim, the knowledge and
appreciation of the Scriptures. This conviction became more and more ar-
ticulate and was expressed more insistently as he aged, but it does seem to
have guided his practice from the earliest stages of his teaching that are
known to us.

To read the New Testament in Greek, as St. Jerome had done, to go
behind the Vulgate (the text of which was widely acknowledged to suffer
from many corruptions), and to study likewise the Septuagint version of the
Old Testament: this was the ideal and the goal that moved Grosseteste to
take up, at an unusually advanced age, the serious study of Greek. To this
motivation we can subjoin circumstances that were propitious in the Western Europe, and even in the England, of his day.

The Latin invasion of Constantinople in 1204 and the ensuing coloniza-
tion of parts of the Byzantine territories had resulted in the establishment
of Latin centers of administration at Athens and Nicaea, as well as in the
capital itself. The violent way in which this new order had been brought
about embittered its victims, the Greeks, but the enforced contiguity of the
two peoples nevertheless intensified cultural exchange between them and
opened lines of communication that extended even as far as England, where
Grosseteste was to feel their impact. Shortly after his time William of
Moerbeke, the Flemish Dominican, was to become the Latin archbishop of
Corinth and, learning Greek on the spot, to attain to celebrity as the translator, on a large scale, of Greek philosophy. Already before 1235 Grosseteste
himself had a clerical friend, John of Basingstoke, who returned to England

with a knowledge of Greek and with some Greek books, after years of service in the duchy of Athens. John was appointed archdeacon of Leicester by
Grosseteste within a few months of his episcopal consecration. To trust him
so much Grosseteste must have known him before then. Perhaps it was from
John that he received help in learning Greek, hearing it spoken with the
Byzantine pronunciation, which Grosseteste describes with accuracy in the
prologue to his Pseudo-Dionysian versions. It was from John that he learned
of the *Testaments of the Twelve Patriarchs*. It is a testimony to the ease of com-
munications with the East that then prevailed that Grosseteste was able on
the basis of John's report to order the book in a copy that still survives—
perhaps the very one John had spoken of. Grosseteste translated it, and it
became one of his great successes. He had in his episcopal household a certain Nicholas Graecus, who was presumably one of the *adiutores* whom he
warmly thanked for their collaboration. We also know through Bacon's testimony that Grosseteste was accompanied in his Greek studies by his friend
Adam Marsh.

A teacher is important in the learning of a foreign language, but a grammar and a dictionary are even more so once one gets down to studying a text.
Our knowledge of Grosseteste's learning of Greek has been supplemented
by a recent study of one of the dictionaries he knew and that he employed
liberally in his published work, the *Etymologicum Gudianum*.[1] Side by side
with this work we can place the *Suda Lexicon*. The use made by Grosseteste
of both has long been known.[2] Let us begin with the second.

How his copy of the large Byzantine dictionary (compiled in the twelfth
century) reached Grosseteste is not known; one wonders whether it may have
been through the agency of the Franciscans, with their connections in Italy
and Constantinople and their incessant wanderings to representative chapters of the order, that he managed to secure some of the contents of his Greek
library. His copy was made in southern Italy, and it survives.[3] The *Suda* (or
Suidas) gives an encyclopedic coverage of classical, biblical, and Christian literature. It contains articles on personalities, writers and philosophers, places,
institutions, and events. Grosseteste exploited its rich linguistic and historical information when glossing and commenting on the works he translated,
as well as in his biblical exegesis. He even translated seventy or more entries
from it, many of which are extant but remain unedited. Among the surviving articles are, for instance, biblical entries (e.g., Abraham, Jesus, Mary);
philosophical biographies (e.g., Anaxagoras, Plato, Porphyry); exotic late

classical lore (e.g., brahmins, Serapis, Hermes Trismegistus); and conceptual studies (e.g., *pathos* [passion], *epithymia* [desire], *nomos* [law], *kosmos* [universe]). The two entries on Mary and Jesus were copied in isolation and achieved a wide circulation. The *Suda* was his reference work for Greek literature. When translating the Pseudo-Dionysius, for example, he drew his information on the Areopagus from it. When rendering the *Nicomachean Ethics* he employed it to elucidate hopelessly obscure references made in passing by Aristotle, such as the one to the dining clubs of Athens. The *Suda*, in short, was the main support of the strenuous efforts he made to elucidate for his Latin-only readership the linguistic, conceptual, and historical aspects of the texts he translated and glossed. Grosseteste often pursued the antiquarian side of his interest in Greek culture right down to the minutiae offered by the encyclopedia about the most varied subjects, such as the dates and places of events, the titles and authenticity of writings, and so forth, in a way that lends an individual character to his ambition, which was to enter the alien world of Greek literary culture by seeing it through the eyes of the Greeks themselves. In his old age he garnered more information about Greek life and literature than any Latin had had at his disposal since the close of antiquity.

The *Etymologicum* complemented the *Suda* through its copious linguistic information concerning a wide range of Greek vocabulary. Side by side with reliable grammatical and semantic data it offered etymologies of rather dubious quality; Grosseteste's extensive use of it shows that both these features appealed to him. Examples abound in his commentary on the Pseudo-Dionysius, where the semantics of words like *simbolum*, *ieron*, *agalma*, *agathon*, and *zelos*, together with many other terms, are determined by means of entries in the dictionary.

Grosseteste must have employed another sort of dictionary in addition to these two, for they are monolingual and he would have required a bilingual dictionary. It is known that John of Basingstoke compiled a dictionary (presumably a bilingual one) that he entitled *Donatus grecus*; Grosseteste may have known it. It is tempting to associate with him a Greek-Latin dictionary of around sixteen thousand words.[4] The surviving copy (dating from the end of the thirteenth century) was made in England, but the original was probably compiled in bilingual southern Italy, from the *Suda* and many other sources. It may well have been Grosseteste who acquired it. The case for its employment by him has been defended, but it will require more extensive exploration of his translation if the argument is to be clinched.[5]

The Translations from Greek

All medieval Latin translations were modeled to some extent on the Vulgate and imitated its literal word-for-word approach to the sacred text, in order to capture the meaning of writings each one of which was considered authoritative within the relevant context of study. Grosseteste valued uniformity of translation, and it appears that he mentally assigned to each Greek word a Latin equivalent, from which he rarely departed. This approach was to be roundly criticized by the later humanists, who seem to have considered it the product of a primitive form of Latin illiteracy. In his rendering of the *Testaments of the Twelve Patriarchs*, interestingly, Grosseteste departed from his own norm and produced a flowing, readable version. Why did he not adopt this easier and more pleasing style for the remainder of his translating activity? The answer is to be sought neither in a slavish conformity to St. Jerome as a model, nor in any lack of linguistic accomplishment on his own part (certainly not in his own Latin language!). His aim was to produce versions for serious study, not simply for reading through; he destined the *Testaments* for the widest Latin readership. Contrary to what the later humanists supposed, he did not translate Greek by the sheerly mechanical employment of one-to-one equivalences between elements of Greek and Latin vocabulary. The lack of flowing Latinity in his translations (a feature of which he was explicitly conscious) was the outcome of policy, not incapacity, on his part. In other words, he opted for a style of translating that mirrored the Greek text and allowed it to appear through the medium of Latin. The Latin he deploys is the faithful vehicle of the Greek meaning in all its irreducible difference and foreignness—a constant reminder to the monolingual reader that language is more than the clothing and unclothing of a naked thought that is the same for all minds; language is thought incarnate, and a foreign language, as he realized, is the sedimented meaning of an alien experience.

This brief survey of the Graeco-Latin versions produced by Grosseteste (all or practically all of them when he was already a bishop) may fittingly commence with a word about his translation of several writings by St. John of Damascus.[6] We do not know what occasioned this version, which was very likely his first. The reputation of St. John, and in particular of his masterpiece (generally known in Latin as *De fide orthodoxa*), may be sufficient to account for Grosseteste's decision, and it is clear from his use of it in personal writings that he himself placed a high value upon it as a guide to orthodoxy. This writing had attracted a good deal of attention during the latter half of the twelfth century. It can be considered as a systematic epitome (*Sententiae*, the Latins regularly called it—thus inviting comparison with Peter Lombard's work) of Greek theology, and in particular of Cappadocian thought. The Aristotelian logic and language to which Damascene subscribed as a theologian make another link between him and Grosseteste. The latter possessed one of the two existing Latin versions of the writing, that by the lawyer Burgundio of Pisa. This he reworked, altering words and phrases. This *re-translatio*, as we may call it, was to be printed three times in the course of the sixteenth century, out of a renewed interest in Damascene (Grosseteste's name did not appear). Unfortunately, no modern edition of the re-translation exists.

On the other hand, six minor works by Damascene were translated by Grossetese without reliance on any pre-existing version (there were none).[7] These included *Dialectics* (an explanation of logical terms designed for theological purposes), *The Hundred Heresies* (of the first six centuries), the *Discussion Between a Christian and a Saracen* (an appendix to the hundredth heresy), and *On the Hymn "Thrice Holy"* (*De trisagio*). The last named was a letter on the liturgical hymn which had come to be debated in the context of trinitarian theology. Grosseteste appended a personal note (*notula*) to his translation of it, putting forward his original viewpoint on the *Filioque* debate (see chap. 9). The authenticity of all these versions is not in doubt, for their translator himself took responsibility for two of them in his commentary on the *Celestial Hierarchy*, while the manuscripts interlink them all.

Grosseteste did not intend his most scholarly translations to be read on their own but accompanied them with glosses and commentaries as the necessary complement to their study. The paradigm of his success may be observed in his commentaries on the four writings of the Pseudo-Dionysius, a model achievement to which his other comments and glosses approximate in varying degree.[8] Each short section of translated Greek is followed by the scholia of "Maximus," rendered into Latin. An exposition ensues in which the text itself is taken up phrase by phrase, there to be woven into a more fluent discourse than the limitations of strict translation could admit of, a discourse that clarifies, orders, magnifies, and diversifies the wording of the version itself. Translation and exposition are joined in a unity that Grosseteste clearly wished to be indissoluble. In the sections of commentary immediately following he discussed the variants found in the three Greek manuscripts that he had had collated for his use, and examined the options of the earlier translators (Hilduin, Eriugena, and Sarrazen), making in effect a scholarly edition of the text. He explained the difficult words of the passage and suggested a small constellation of Latin terms, each one of which partly covered the meaning of the single Greek word. He tried to iron out ambiguities in the punctuation and in the construction of the text. He regularly related the progress of the discussion in hand to his author's discourse taken as a whole, reconciling apparent contradictions. He frequently ended by commending the thought of his author to the appreciation of his reader. These recurrent expository features focused relentlessly upon the meaning of the text and were aimed at recovering every nuance of meaning present in it. The reader is reminded at every turn of the specificity of Greek syntax and semantics; he is not allowed to relax as though he were in his native culture. The total recovery of the alien medium was the goal.

Grosseteste produced only one other translation, this time of Aristotle, which rivaled his Pseudo-Dionysian commentaries in the scope of its realization. Working from a preexisting translation of the *Nicomachean Ethics* (one that may have been complete but that has survived only fragmentarily), he made a full version, adding to it the translation of a voluminous body of commentary compiled anonymously in the twelfth century from various ancient and Byzantine sources.[9] In order to produce a corpus of peripatetic ethical writing he added the translation of a work on the passions (wrongly attributed to Aristotle), his own summary of the content of the *Ethics*, a personal commentary (preserved only in a very fragmentary form), and innumerable interlinear and marginal glosses of a philological nature.[10] The fruits of this imposing undertaking saw the light of day only in the middle 1240s, at about the time when Grosseteste took part in the First Council of Lyons (1245).

His skill as an interpreter of Aristotle's ethical thought is most evident in book 8. In the middle of the book the commentary of Aspasius, a second-century Aristotelian, ran out, but Grosseteste himself anonymously completed the commentary on the remainder of the book, which, as it happens, contains discussions of favorite themes of his, such as the love between spouses, their continuing duty to educate the children of the marriage, and the origin of kingship in natural law.[11] The majority of his notes and comments were designed purely to help his Latin reader to become (in hermeneutical terms) the hypothetical contemporary of the author of the *Ethics*. Grosseteste's tendency was to regard the latter as an edifying work, even though on occasion it was clearly pagan. Through his achievement

Grosseteste stands at the head of that academic tradition that still continues to read the *Nicomachean Ethics* as a classic of moral wisdom.

That Grosseteste should have tackled the translation of this corpus of ethical writing occasions little surprise, when we take into account his previous involvement with Aristotelian philosophy, his admiration for the method and contents of the *Ethics*, and in a general way the intellectual climate of his later lifetime, when Aristotle's thought was in the ascendant in the schools. If we leave aside his retranslation of works by Damascene, then we can regard a group of his versions as the expression of that passionate interest he took in the origins of Christianity and in its earliest history. His translations of St. Ignatius, Dionysius the Pseudo-Areopagite, and the *Testaments* run parallel to the theological explorations that he conducted in his commentary on Galatians and in *De Cessatione Legalium*. The *Testaments of the Twelve Patriarchs*, in particular, attracted Grosseteste (just as it had Origen long before him, and was to interest Roger Bacon and Vincent of Beauvais, not long after him) because the work seemed to be of Jewish origin yet to contain explicit prophecies of Christ. (In fact the work probably came into being at the end of the second century AD, as a Christian solicitation to Jews to accept the message of Jesus Christ.)[12]

Grosseteste regarded this group of Greek writings as illuminating the origins and beliefs of the primitive Church, and in consequence as helping to further that spiritual purification of the contemporary Church that was the goal of his own episcopal ministry. The great outlay of Church funds occasioned by the acquisition of Greek originals and the payment of collaborators was justified, at least in his own eyes, by the lively hopes he entertained of a spiritual vision recovered in all its pristine splendor.

The Superscriptio Lincolniensis and English Hebraism

Reliable evidence associates Grosseteste with a fresh Latin version of the Hebrew Psalter: Henry Cossey, O.F.M. (d. 1336), referred to it as a *superscriptio* because it was written above the Hebrew letters of the Psalms, and he stated that the bishop of Lincoln had it written in his Hebrew psalter.[13] Three manuscript copies of the *Superscriptio lincolniensis* survive. One of these (Oxford *MS Corpus Christi College 10*) has an anonymous prologue that Beryl Smalley attributed with plausibility to Grosseteste.[14] The author of the prologue takes responsibility for the publication but does not claim to be the translator. He deplores the existing variations between the Vulgate and the Hebrew text and expresses the wish that both tongues, and likewise both Scriptures, be known and allied with one another, for the sake of unity in Christ. The original of the *Superscriptio* is lost, but it was copied at least four times and was used by Nicholas Trevet, O.P., as a source for his commentary on the Psalms. Trevet's claim that Grosseteste "made many extracts from Hebrew glosses" lends support to the notion that he acquired some Hebrew learning, as also does the isolated statement carried by a manuscript to the effect that Grosseteste found a particular story in Hebrew and translated it into Latin.[15]

Grosseteste was fully alive to the scholarly requirement to go back to original languages. From the New Testament in Latin to the New Testament in Greek is a step that we know he actually made; the logical progression would have been to return from the Septuagint to the Hebrew text. It cannot be proven conclusively on the basis of the *Superscriptio* alone that Grosseteste learned Hebrew well enough to make use of the volume, but at any rate his patronage of the translation and his intention in its regard may be accepted on the basis of Cossey's testimony. Its interlinear form was in any case designed for the learning of the Psalms in the original language.

PERSONAL THEOLOGICAL STAMP

Did Grosseteste reach a rounded, strategic view of his subject? Several considerations are relevant when attempting to do justice to this question and to his achievements in theology themselves. In what follows the attempt will be made above all to discern the quality and individual bent of his mind.

Exegesis and Biblical Theology

Grosseteste taught essentially from the Bible, clarifying its books through questions that arose from the text, and expounding both literal and spiritual senses in ways conducive to devotion and preaching. In his stock of knowledge concerning the text and the meaning of the Scriptures, as well as in his acquaintance with the Christian exegetical tradition, he surpassed those of his Latin contemporaries who are known to us, in virtue of his access to the Greek text (of both Old and New Testaments), as well as to the Greek commentarial tradition. His reading included most of the stock-in-trade of the theologians at Paris (the *Sentences* of Peter Lombard; the *Historia scholastica* of Peter Comestor; the Ordinary Gloss). And like his direct contemporaries at Paris he was reading ancient and Arabic philosophy (Aristotle, Avicenna, Algazel, and some of Averroës's commentaries). The best-known Parisian figures who were roughly contemporaries of his, however, are each of them known for a large-scale work of theology with a structure sufficiently wide to embrace a variety of theological themes, handled either discursively (William of Auvergne, *De universo*) or by groupings of questions (the *Summa aurea* of William of Auxerre; the *Summa* of Philip the Chancellor). In Grosseteste's final years of teaching, his own former *socius*, or advanced student and helper, Alexander of Hales, was collecting theological glosses and questions in view of circulation; he was to become the named figurehead of a Franciscan Parisian summa (the *Summa Fratris Alexandri*), the first of a new genre that was to prove eminently successful and was to be imitated at Oxford (as we shall see) during Grosseteste's episcopate. Grosseteste himself remained aloof from such undertakings. He showed neither taste nor talent for the large-scale organization of ideas grouped thematically and developed sequentially. He was at his best when following a book (of the Bible; of Aristotle; of the Pseudo-Dionysius; perhaps of Boethius),[1] tracing the sequence of its ideas and developing those themes that had a particular appeal for him. To comment on a text, after all, does not require much initiative of a structural kind; on the other hand, the genre in no way inhibited him from making very personal and often quite unpredictable developments.

When he chose to depart from exegesis strictly speaking, Grosseteste still preferred to write what can be called a biblical treatise. *De decem mandatis* takes the only structure it exhibits from the order of the biblical precepts. In the case of *De cessatione legalium* the structure is his own; however, the logic that governs its detailed articulation is not always transparent, save in a rather general way.

It would be wrong to bewail the lack of any systematic overview of theology on Grosseteste's part, for to wish the case otherwise than it is would be to undervalue all that makes up the richness and uniqueness of his particular intellectual contribution. Very few attempts have been made to survey his theology, mostly because anyone who ventures upon the task finds himself called upon to intervene continuously, by selecting the sequence in which the most characteristic thoughts of the Oxford regent may be ordered.[2]

Grosseteste's theology can be summarily and selectively presented on two levels: first, in its leading characteristics and in a very general way, then thematically. In what follows, his original and most personal positions will be sketched according to the order that he prescribes in the one text in which he discusses how the various themes making up Christian theology should find their due internal coherence.

General Features

It can be said in a general way that Grosseteste's theology is trinitarian, Christocentric, and biblical in character, its biblicism being of that mystical-allegorical and spiritual variety that goes right back to Origen (whom Grosseteste read, in part at least through the sometimes lengthy extracts quoted or reported by Jerome), and that Ambrose and Augustine developed with particular conviction within the Latin Church. He adopted with approval Augustine's rationale for the application of the allegorical method.[3] He remained within the patristic trinitarian outlook, which found the tripersonality of God revealed and manifested in creation and in both Testaments, as distinct from the Aristotelian-inspired theological approach that was just beginning to show itself at Paris during his old age. This new theology regarded the existence of God as provable by arguments taken from creation, but considered that the mystery of the Trinity was revealed in the New Testament exclusively. The Christocentric character of his theology will receive particular attention in what follows. His ecclesiology was centered upon the Augustinian vision of the Head and body of the Church as being one, but a new emphasis on ecclesiastical hierarchy showed itself from the time when his interest in the Pseudo-Dionysius became apparent (from ca. 1230 onward). It is possible that his attraction to the latter and his efforts to harmonize Augustinian and Dionysian thought (especially in mystical theology) point to an affinity between Grosseteste and the "school" of the Abbey of St. Victor at Paris.[4]

Personal Theological Positions

The Subject Matter of Theology

At the opening of the first part of his *Hexaëmeron* Grosseteste devotes a discussion, unique in his writings, to the subject matter of theology.[5] Here he is at pains to avoid placing theology, that is, the revealed word of God and its appreciative study, under the generic concept of science. *Sapientia* (wisdom) is his preferred designation of sacred science; the very name privileges it and underlines its transcendence with regard to all purely human knowledge. In the duality of *sapientia-scientia* with which he works there is a clear indication of his conscious adherence to the theology of St. Augustine.

Wisdom, just like the sciences, has a subject matter. Some locate it in the whole Christ, that is to say, in the Incarnate Word together with his body, the Church. Perhaps, Grosseteste suggests, the unity referred to by St. John (17:20–21) might more fittingly be taken as the object of theology: "I pray not only for these, but for those also who through their words will believe in me. May they all be one, Father, may they be one in us, as you are in me and I am in you, so that the world may believe that it was you who sent me." The unity in question comprises four unions: the hypostatic union; the union of Christ with his Church together with the eucharistic expression of this bond; the union of Christ with the Father and with the Spirit; and, finally, the union we enjoy with the Trinity through the mediation of Christ. The all-embracing unity of John 17:20–21 includes the tri-unity of God, and also the Incarnate Word, the Church, and grace that unites the redeemed with the Trinity. Each department of wisdom, taking one of these unions as its object, will stand in a definite relationship to the whole of wisdom. Creatures belong to theology by their flowing out from the divine unity and returning to it, but in other respects they lie outside of it and fall as subjects of study under the sciences. Evidently theology was in Grosseteste's eyes identical with the interpretation of the divinely revealed message of salvation.

The distinction between Christian wisdom and human science is developed with consistency in the course of the discussion. The subject matter of theology sets it apart from the particular sciences that human reason constructs. Wisdom elaborates on the basis of revelation an understanding of the totality of being. Each branch of wisdom abstracts one dimension of unity from the whole, but the parts remain intimately related to the whole through the centrality that Christ holds both in each division and in the entirety of being. The unity of theology is thus guaranteed by the mediating presence of Christ in each part, so that the structure of wisdom will reflect the order of the real, where the universal ontological mediation of the Incarnate Word assures the cohesion of the entire circle of being. Wisdom, the study of the totality, stands apart from the sciences, which can flourish only by methodological abstraction, that is to say, by breaking down into a series of manageable regions the unity of the whole of what is. Normally a science takes its origin from self-evident truths and proceeds by way of demonstration to its conclusions. Not so wisdom: its entire object is assumed from faith alone, because in wisdom belief is the presupposition of understanding. The reason for this is that its object does not fall within any division of being as human philosophy differentiates it; it is not finite *or* infinite being but the unrestricted totality which wisdom takes as its subject matter. The totality is not susceptible of reduction into categories, any more than it is definable in terms of limited extension, since it itself is not a specific nature (such as the object of Aristotelian science must be), but rather the locus of that wisdom that the wise of this world are not able to discover; Grosseteste at this point invokes Job 28:12–14, 18, 21.

Propositions to which believing assent can be given are of two kinds. They may be such as to contain an intrinsic probability that justifies their acceptance, or they may be accepted on authority. It is only by accident that statements of the first kind occur in wisdom; the second constitute its proper domain, because in the Scriptures we are offered truth upon God's own guarantee. Whether the statements of the Bible proceeded through the mouth of God's prophets or through his Son, their authority is undifferentiated, belonging as it does to God. Insofar as the statements contained in the Scriptures are all of them equally accepted on the authority of God, it is otiose to attempt to establish among them an order of priority, whether in the temporal or in the logical sense of the word. Moreover, as they are all accepted on faith, no one truth is better known than any other. The only difference that may exist among them is that they are imaginable with greater or lesser facility, which is why the Scriptures, proposed as they are to the belief of mankind universally, commenced in the Book of Genesis with the sensible things of this world, to the extent that these fall under faith, that is to say, as regards their origin and the order of their creation.

Grosseteste's position regarding the general shape of theology is indebted to St. Augustine, who constantly emphasized the centrality within Christian reflection of "the whole Christ, Head and members." Grosseteste himself had a twelfth-century precursor in Robert of Melun, who proposed a similarly Christocentric organization of theology. His own contemporary at Paris, the Dominican Hugh of St. Cher, appears to have shared his views. But is it is above all the Aristotelian methodology of science that forms the immediate backdrop to his discussion and lends it its clarity of outline. Grosseteste insists upon the essential difference between, on the one hand, science, which pursues demonstrable knowledge by deduction from self-evident principles, and, on the other, Christian wisdom, which is established only within submission to the authority of God's word. He remains firmly Aristotelian in recognizing the autonomy (as well as the limits) of the particular sciences, which theology will not invade. It emerges from his discussion of the subject matter of theology that wisdom is to be elaborated on the basis of the biblical revelation. In its pursuit, faith is in search of understanding; faith is likewise the precondition of any understanding that results. Grosseteste identifies a very definite structure for theology; however, it is highly unlikely that he himself would have aimed at realizing it in the form of a summa. No doubt the theory was intended to elucidate his own mature practice as a theologian, with the result that his biblical treatises, in particular, and the various developments of Christian doctrine that he injected into his exegetical writings, can be thought of as exemplifying in a general way the Christocentric theology that he advocated in the opening lines of the *Hexaëmeron*.

It is significant, above all, for his outlook that his search for a general structure for theology led him not in the direction of the *Sentences* of the Lombard, but to a word of Jesus Christ in the Gospel according to John.

The Absolute Predestination of Christ

In the third part of *De cessatione legalium* Grosseteste raises the question as to whether the Word would have become incarnate even if Adam had not sinned.[6] He refers his reader to Augustine, Gregory, and Anselm ("whose arguments are clearer than light"), for proof that the one who came to liberate mankind from sin and to lead it back to its lost glory must be both God and man. The reader will find (he informs us) that all the commentators of the Sacred Page have offered at least some reasons why the restoration of fallen man had to be effected through the passion of the Son of God. However, unless his memory fails him (Grosseteste continues), none of the commentators (*expositores*) has ever determined whether God would have become man even if man had not fallen. On the contrary, they seem to imply that if man had remained in the original state of justice the Incarnation would not have taken place—in other words, that the redemption of humanity from sin is the sole reason for the Incarnation. Yet there do, Grosseteste claims, seem to be conclusive arguments to show that God would have become man in any case; and so, excluding from his treatment all questions concerning the redemption and the reasons for it, he will inquire whether the Incarnation would have taken place even in the absence of sin. Grosseteste's arguments are numerous (nineteen in all) and often interconnected. They can be grouped into five considerations, as follows.

1. God withholds from the universe no goodness that it is capable of receiving, for he intends the perfection and beauty of the whole created order to be a varied participation in his infinite power, wisdom, and goodness. The Incarnation is an undeniable enrichment of each thing and of the whole, and we know that the universe is capable of receiving it.

2. The capacity of human nature for union with the Word cannot either have resulted from sin or been enhanced by its arrival. It cannot be the evil of sin (a privation, not a positive reality) that grounds the possibility of the Incarnation.

3. Redemption and justification are independent needs of mankind. However, to reduce the humanity of Christ to the function of a purely material prerequisite for redemptive suffering is to attribute to it an incongruously small role in the divine plan. It seems that we would have been adopted as sons of God even if sin had not entered the world. As it is, however, we are made sons of the Father through becoming brothers of Christ, and it is by his assumption of our humanity that we become sharers in his divinity. We could be none of these things apart from the Incarnation.

4. The Church and its sacraments derive from the Incarnation. Are we to suppose that the dignity of marriage and the mystery of the Eucharist were not an original part of the divine plan for mankind?

5. The last consideration was the most decisive in Grosseteste's eyes; it both merits and requires a somewhat fuller résumé.

Grosseteste identifies in the Incarnate Word the causal principle of the created universe. How could it be that this unique focal point of the unity of all being, both uncreated and created, was merely the agency of redemption from sin? He develops a theology of the Incarnation that reposes upon the double principle of the divine generosity and the universally representative status of the human nature adopted by the Word. He makes the philosophical doctrine of man as the unique microcosm of creation into the vehicle of an outlook that has in fact much more in common with Cappadocian thinking (Maximus Confessor, Gregory of Nyssa), than with Latin theology.

The angel and the human soul are linked to one another by their common spirituality, while soul and body meet in the unity of human personhood. The soul recapitulates in itself the life activities of all vital things. In the body the whole diversified richness of the physical universe can be discovered, from the spheres of heaven to the four elements making up the earth. Man thus shares in the nature of every creature, visible and invisible.

Through the Word's assumption of humanity all natures are turned back into a circular fulfillment (*in complementum circulare*). Even if we bracket the Fall we can see that the Incarnation was still supremely fitting. It was within God's power, as we know, and it is in no way unbecoming; on the contrary, without it the universe would lack true unity. Granted the Incarnation, the universe attains to its full and fitting unity. When God becomes man, the chain of being is turned back into a perfect circle to include the whole of reality, both divine and created. Now since it is a greater good for the universe to be united in such a complete, circular unity than to be deprived of it, and since it is possible both for God to confer it and for the universe to receive it, Grosseteste is enabled to conclude that the very perfection of unity actually implies its providential realization.

After setting forth his arguments Grosseteste reverts to his introductory remark, in which he indicated that the basis of his thesis on the Incarnation was not authority, but reason. Reasons of the kind he has given certainly appear to support the assertion that the Incarnation does not depend upon sin, but whether this can be definitely affirmed he confesses that he does not know, and he admits that his ignorance perturbs him. In the lack of any explicit authority in favor of his proposal he neither wishes nor dares to commit himself, granted the poverty of his own wit and the modest extent of his knowledge. It would seem, in short, as though Grosseteste was aware that the Fathers of the Church never discussed the Incarnation in hypothetical terms, that is, by opposing the actual situation of sinful man to a possible state of continued innocence. There is much patristic support, on the other hand, for the belief (expressed already in the hymns of Ephesians and Colossians) that Christ was predestined from eternity to be the unity in which all things hold together. The hypothetical formulation of the question went back only to the twelfth century, to Rupert of Deutz and Honorius of Autun, both of whom answered it in the affirmative. Grosseteste shows no sign of dependence on either, but the question they had raised still hung in the theological air; he seems to have been the first to explore the whole issue in depth.

A theologian of Grosseteste's bent, one who preferred the positive study of the sources of theology to the more systematic application of dialectical method, could not be completely content with giving an unreservedly positive answer to a question that was not raised in the Scriptures or discussed by authoritative commentators. In other writings Grosseteste in fact reemployed some of the arguments he had used in *De cessatione legalium*, in order to support the absolute primacy of Christ within the *present* order of salvation history, no reference being made to the hypothetical question. In the Pauline doctrine of the headship of Christ (Col. 1:16) he found support for his belief that the Word, in and by whom all things were created, is the Word Incarnate. He understood the Apostle as maintaining that the Word made flesh had primacy over all creatures and was the primordial element in God's plan. In his developed treatment of the universal primacy of Christ his entire life's work as philosopher and exegete was placed at the disposal of a Christology that made the Incarnate Word the focus of the created universe and the true and ultimate unity of all being.

His teaching was not forgotten at Oxford, where, forty years after his death, Duns Scotus defended the absolute predestination of Christ.

The Friendship of Christ for Mankind

Grosseteste's study of Aristotle triggered an original idea in his mind as to how the redemption might be elucidated by reference to the model of friendship, which shows us how one friend can act in the place of another, being in truth the "other self" of his friend. Shortly after his translation of the *Ethics* (or perhaps concurrently with it) Grosseteste composed an essay on the redemption.[7] In the context from which the following extract is made, he has been developing the argument that Christ made satisfaction for the sins of all men by virtue of his unity with mankind. But how are we to understand the unity in question? Here Grosseteste makes an original use of the model of friendship, as Aristotle proposed it: in order to make satisfaction for sin Christ became the "other self" of mankind, in such a way that his action is inseparably his own and that of his friends, on behalf of whom it was undertaken out of sheer love. The idea is, then, that Christ is the *alter ipse* of each of the redeemed, the one who out of pure friendship took all the faithful into solidarity with his own person and substituted himself for them (much as Orestes and Pylades, in classical lore, each wished to die in order that the other might be spared), with the result that they act in him and he acts (both in his passion and ever afterwards) on behalf of them and in them.

I do not know of any other place in his writings where Grosseteste expressed this idea. I translate the passage as follows:

> Now no one should think that an objection to the views we are developing might be made on the grounds that the one who is in person God and man is someone quite apart from any given sinful man. In reality, someone who cleaves to him with true faith, firm hope, and persevering

charity is no longer a separate being but is united to his personality and is one Christ with him. To such an extent is this true that it is no longer the individual in question who performs the works of faith, hope, and charity, but it is Christ who effects these in him. Moreover, the things that Christ performs on his behalf, the one united to him actually does through Christ and in Christ. According to the law of friendship, each of two friends is his friend's "other self," in virtue both of the bond of love and of the unity it forges between them, and also through "unity of will regarding moral right and wrong."[8] Equally, the son is the "other self" of his father. Keeping this in mind, can we not say that all [believers] are one in him, far more than is the case even regarding friends, when we consider that they are by creation the sons of God-made-man; that their rebirth reinforces their sonship; and that they are sons by sharing in his nature, as well as by receiving his illumination, and being as it were all glued together by an indissoluble love?

The Infinite, Voluntary Suffering
of the Redeemer

Robert Grosseteste appears to have been alone among medieval theologians in arguing that the wounds inflicted on Jesus during the relatively short hours of his passion and crucifixion were not of themselves sufficient to bring about his death. Rather, his sacrifice of his own life consisted in the voluntary sundering of his soul from his body, a separation that entailed infinite suffering, because so long as the body is not vanquished by its own inherent tendency to material dissolution, no finite power is sufficient to cancel the natural care of the soul for the body that it vivifies.[9]

On at least six occasions Grosseteste returned to his personal view of the passion, refining and developing the central notion of the voluntary nature of the self-immolation of Christ. The emphasis changed subtly from one context to another but the idea received consistent development. In *De cessatione legalium* the accent fell upon the sign of divinity that can be read in the crucifixion.[10] It lies wholly beyond the power of any creature to divide the soul from the body for as long as body and heart remain sound. It was by his divine power, Grosseteste argued, that Jesus on the cross freely and of his own will breathed forth his spirit. His members were still sound, for the perforation of his hands and feet without the infliction of any further wound would not have caused sufficient loss of blood to claim his life in only three hours of suffering. He should have retained the blood of the heart and of the interior organs, together with vital heat, for longer, as the young, strong and healthy man that he was. There was, after all, plenty of blood left to flow from his opened side after he expired. Besides, if his blood supply and vital warmth had already given out, he could not have cried aloud as he did, articulately and meaningfully, in prayer to God the Father (Lk. 23:46). It cannot have been from the violence of his wounds alone that he died, but in virtue of that power that alone can join soul to body, and alone can sunder the soul from a body still functioning and retaining its vital heat. The centurion, seeing that he died while crying aloud, acknowledged that this man was truly the son of God (Mt. 27:54).

In a later sermon, *Ex rerum initiatarum*, the emphasis has shifted within the context of redemption: the God-man redeemed the whole of mankind by an immolation that transcended all the suffering of history and everything that could be inflicted by a mere creature.[11] The redemption thus won reaches every member of the fallen race. In another sermon the argument is generalized by means of an appeal to infinite power: no finite power could withdraw even the most insignificant form of life from its carrier; Christ's soul loved its union with his body with an infinite love; if the power that separated the soul of Christ from his body was infinite, then his suffering was likewise infinite.[12]

St. Anselm is to be sought in the background of this infinity argument. In both John Chrysostom and Avicenna Grosseteste found the Stoic motif of the soul's care for the body. Taken as a whole, however, the idea to which he was so resolutely attached was entirely his own creation; it was born with him and it died with him. It went almost unnoticed in the schools, although it did in fact draw a suitably respectful criticism from Roger Marston, O.F.M. The reason for its lack of impact no doubt was that there is something implausible about it. Grosseteste made no allowance for the weakened state of Jesus, as he approached his crucifixion debilitated by an entire night of agony and torture, and he gave no sign of realizing that the death of the crucified resulted not so much from the loss of blood as from asphyxiation, as the sufferer became less and less capable of supporting the weight of his tortured body.

Grosseteste's deeply pondered meditation on the passion and death was meant to stir his readers to pity, gratitude, and wonder. In his lively devotion to the crucified he may well have owed something to St. Francis of Assisi.

The Creation of the World in Time

An outburst in the *Hexaëmeron* registers Grosseteste's violent disagreement with efforts just then being made at Paris by someone whom he knew well to palliate Aristotle's teaching on the eternity of the cosmos:

> Our opposition is directed against some of our contemporaries, who are attempting to make the heretic Aristotle into a Catholic, against the sense of Aristotle himself and his commentators, as well as that of the patristic commentators [on the Scriptures]. With astonishing blindness and presumption these men think they can arrive at a more limpid understanding and a truer interpretation of Aristotle on the basis of a corrupt Latin text, than philosophers, both pagan and Catholic, who had the most complete knowledge of him in Greek texts, uncorrupted and unabridged. Let them not delude themselves nor sweat in vain to make Aristotle a Catholic, lest they consume their time and waste their mental powers, and while turning Aristotle into a Catholic, make heretics of themselves![13]

In the *Physics* Aristotle postulated the everlastingness of movement and the coeternity of the Prime Mover with the cosmos. A century before Grosseteste, Thierry of Chartres and William of Conches proposed a harmonization of Aristotle with both the *Timaeus* of Plato and the creation narrative of Genesis: Aristotle meant that the origin of the universe and the beginning of time were coeval; he did not think that the universe had no beginning, but simply maintained that there was no time before its creation. This conciliating view was winning increasing support in Grosseteste's own day. Alexander of Hales refined it by arguing that the creation was a miraculous event, revealed in the Bible but of course not falling within the purview of the natural philosopher, who as such is interested only in the continuity of change. Aristotle, he argued, maintained that the existence of the universe covered the totality of time; not touching at all upon creation, he did not teach in an absolute sense the eternity of the world.

Grosseteste's anger was aroused by what he considered to be a false and even a dangerous view. Very likely he was particularly dismayed to find that it was being propounded by someone whom he personally knew, a former collaborator of his. Even when striking a polemical note, however, Grosseteste had the decisive advantage in terms of knowledge, which came from his having worked carefully through the text of the *Physics* and having come personally to the firm conclusion that its doctrine on everlastingness quite simply contradicted the faith; any attempt at the harmonization of the pagan teaching with the biblical doctrine could only lead, he was convinced, to confusion on the part of Catholics. The new interpretation he considered a piece of pseudo-sophistication, flying in the face not only of the ancient interpretation of Aristotle (Themistius and Simplicius) but of the Arabian one (Al-Ghazzali, probably); worse still, it bypassed entirely the ancient Christian rebuttal of pagan pantheism (Ambrose, Augustine, and Boethius). In the wake of his own glosses on the *Physics* Grosseteste composed a treatise devoted to the finitude of movement and time, many of whose arguments reappeared in the *Hexaëmeron*.[14] The crux lay for him in the inability of the pagans to raise the heart (*affectus mentis*) in love to the all-powerful God, and consequently in their incapacity mentally to grasp (*aspectus mentis*) the absolute difference there is between simple eternity and temporal mutability:

> Know that what deceived the ancients into positing no beginning to the universe was that false imagination especially which drove them to fancy before all time yet more time, as the imagination pictures outside all place yet more place and outside all space yet more space, and so to infinity. This error can only be purged by way of the cleansing of the mind from worldly affections, in order that the mind's eye, freed from phantasies, may transcend time and may understand simple eternity, which has no extension in time and whence all time proceeds.[15]

In a word, the ancient mind was clouded by the imagination.

The discussion was to continue through renewed confrontations long after this early polemical thrust.[16] Grosseteste's contribution lay in his decisive statement of the abyss that separated the pagan and Christian positions from one another. In doing so he set the agenda for his immediate successors at Oxford, Fishacre, Rufus, and Thomas of York.

Latin-Greek Understanding

By the time he became bishop Grosseteste's growing appreciation of the Greek fathers offered him daily confirmed evidence of the harmony in orthodox faith that had prevailed over the countless heresies that had plagued the early Christian centuries. Like Latin Christian Hellenophiles before and after him (Scottus Eriugena; Nicholas of Cusa), he was anguished by the quarrels that divided East and West. A note that he appended to his own translation of the *Trisagion* ("Holy, Holy, Holy . . .") of St. John Damascene deserves to be quoted in full (as Duns Scotus did in his two major writings), for the ecumenical and eirenic quality of the confidence it professes, that the major stumbling block in the way of unity in faith, namely the *filioque* controversy, could and should be removed.

> The Greeks maintain that the Holy Spirit is the Spirit of the Son, but that he does not come forth from the Son but only from the Father, through the Son however. Now this conclusion seems contrary to ours, which holds that the Holy Spirit proceeds from the Father and the Son. It may well be, however, that were this apparent contradiction to be discussed by two doctors, a Greek and a Latin, each of them a true lover of the truth and not of his own expression of it for its own sake, it would eventually be clear to both of them that the difference which opposes them is not so much real as verbal. The only alternative is that either the Greeks or we, the Latins, are nothing less than heretics. But who is so foolhardy as to accuse the author of this work, John Damascene, together with the Blessed Basil, Gregory the Theologian, Gregory of Nyssa, Cyril and other such Greek Fathers, of heresy? And who on the other hand dares to make a heretic of Blessed Jerome, Augustine, Hilary and other such Latin Doctors? It is probable, consequently, that the opposing statements quoted do not correspond to any real conflict between the saints, for this reason, that what is said is said in a variety of ways. For example in this context: "of this person," and similarly "from this or that person," or again "by him." Now it may well be that if this wide range of expression were more subtly understood and analysed, it would emerge clearly that the doctrine which finds opposing expressions is in fact the same.[17]

It goes without saying that it did not occur to Grosseteste to doubt that the *filioque* was an authentic expression of trinitarian theology. He was convinced, on the other hand, that the different Latin and Greek formulations of doctrine agree in substance, beneath the surface verbal variations. The difficulties posed by the differences between natural languages and between distinct theological traditions were present to his mind, just as markedly as partisan loyalty was absent. Here is a concrete case wherein his preference for scholarship over dialectic allowed him to bring the full warmth of his humanity to bear upon a difficulty that to the great majority of his contemporaries appeared irresolubly great.

The Order of Love

The scholastic debate concerning the relative priority of the intellect and the will arrived on the Parisian scene a generation after Grosseteste wrote. He had, however, his own individual way of expressing the manner in which love shapes and extends the intellectual horizon. We have already seen how he appealed to the couplet *affectus/aspectus mentis* to explain the failure of the pagans to comprehend the simplicity of eternity. His insight can be paraphrased thus: "[T]he mind's range of vision cannot extend further than its range of love."[18] Grosseteste appeals to the priority of love within the intellectual life in a multiplicity of contexts, using his own *aspectus/affectus* distinction in ways that reveal the pervasive influence upon him of St. Augustine's ideal of *amor ordinatus*. In some ways his reflections on love developed in quite individual ways; these can be only briefly exemplified here.

Stated rather baldly, the theology of love elaborated by the *Doctor amoris* required that the ordering of reality, as that is appreciated within faith, should be accepted as the measure of the love apportioned to each thing or experience. If we measure our love according to being then we will love God without measure, since God is without measure; we will love the neighbor as ourselves, since we are measured alongside each other in virtue of our common creation; and we will love the body and bodily creatures less than spiritual ones. The finality of lower things is to serve human liberty, while the finality of liberty itself is the liberating service of the neighbor and God, or rather of the neighbor (and the self) in God; or, better still, of God in all realities. Love "fulfills the law" (Gal. 5:14; 6:2), because love is truly love only before and within the totality.

The invincibility of love (*caritas*) is a recurrent motif of Grosseteste's thinking.[19] Charity cannot be conquered by any pleasure, desire or fear; it cannot be lost against our will but only through our own volition; in other words, its invincibility is the measure of its freedom. The love that is the highest activity of a spiritual creature unites the latter with the God who is the source of all love and places it above the material creation, which no longer has power to subject it in servitude. If the soul clings to God by God's own power, then nothing created can intervene, save a perverse act on the part of the soul itself, of falling away from God's love.[20]

God, the unmeasured measure, should be loved immeasurably by his spiritual creature. Working from hints supplied by St. Bernard and St. Anselm, Grosseteste expounded the First Commandment in a wholly original way, as the requirement to place no strange love before or above our supreme love:

He who loves God above all clings lovingly to him as the supreme good and believes that he alone is the supreme good. For if he believed something other to be a good equal to or greater than that which he loves supremely, then that which he loves supremely would not be God, since God is that greater than which cannot be thought, and is indeed greater than can be thought. Therefore, since faith is nothing other than thinking with assent (as Augustine says), if he believed in, and thus thought, a good equal to or greater than that which he loves supremely, then that which he loves supremely would not be God, and so he would not love God.[21]

Grosseteste's purpose is to show that the contradiction identified by St. Anselm (*Proslogion* 2–3) applies not only to the intellect but to the will as well. It is, according to Anselm's argument, contradictory to pretend to conceive of a greater being than "that than which no greater can be thought." For Grosseteste, however, it would be equally contradictory to assent to the thought of a good that would be better than "that than which no better can be thought." His concentration upon the transcendence of God focuses upon the requirement to *love* God, to love God *alone*, God incomparably *above all* creaturely objects of love, God, furthermore, above all *conceivable* objects of affection.

There can be no doubt that St. Anselm would have recognized in this page a legitimate and genial extension of his own argument to the order of the will, as well as to the exegesis of the First Commandment.

Love has, Grosseteste was convinced, the foundational role in education. Taking his cue from Galatians 4:19 ("My little children, whom I am in labor to bring forth again"), he pursued the metaphor of conceiving and childbearing in order to find expression for his personal view of spiritual procreation.[22] (He was helped, of course, by the Latin language, which referred to the idea or thought as *conceptus*, on the analogy of the fetus.) Think of the teacher first as the father, then as the mother of the disciple. As a father, he reaches union with the mind of the hearer and procreates the seed of the word within it. The word is conceived within the womb of consciousness and follows the development of embryonic life, growing, moving, kicking—until it is ready to be born and to enter the world in the form of action. The teacher's love is more maternal than paternal in quality, however, for it accompanies intimately the entire process of education from conception throughout the stages of birth and childhood. Like a mother, the teacher fears the possible miscarriage and stillbirth of the understanding and love he has generated in the pupil's mind; he bears it and finds deep joy in its birth; he gives it nurture from himself and rears it with care, preparing it for maturity by correction and encouragement; he delights like a mother to see his offspring develop. "This kind of begetting," Grosseteste avers, "is greater than physical generation, and the readiness of the teacher to beget should be proportionately greater." It is clearly out of his own experience of educative love that he is writing.

Finally, Grosseteste found in the *Ethics* of Aristotle the idea that spouses could be truly friends.[23] Struck by the relative novelty of Aristotle's notion, he commented upon the place of virtue within married love. All three kinds of Aristotelian friendship, he pointed out, can be present in marriage. Mutual help and enjoyment have their part, but they can be crowned by the elevated, moral friendship that is joined by two people who love each other because each of them is good, and whose aim it is to bring about moral virtue and the good in each other. Grosseteste was moved to translate the *Ethics*, and no doubt was sustained in that exacting task, precisely by the delight he experienced in recovering insights like this one, which had largely been occluded during the centuries preceding him.

Theological Influence

Some of Grosseteste's translations from the Greek were very widely copied and read, as we have seen. The same is true of his commentary on the *Posterior Analytics*, and in some measure of a collection of his philosophical and scientific writings, which was available here and there on the continent of Europe. When we turn to his exegetical and theological works, however, the evidence concerning their copying and diffusion suggests that few of them ever reached a readership outside of England. Through the Franciscans it is likely that St. Bonaventure had some insight into the metaphysics of light (which features in his own theology), but apart from him it is difficult to find at Paris any echo of Grosseteste's theological style, or indeed of the distinctive positions that he espoused. Grosseteste certainly set part of the agenda for the generation that succeeded him at Oxford (Marsh, Rufus, and York among the Franciscans; Fishacre among the Dominicans). In particular, his views concerning the nature of theology and the eternity of the world were widely known. However, no school formed around his major impulses. In particular, his Greek scholarship, though widely admired, was not imitated by thinkers in the age of more dialectical, speculative theology, with the result that Grosseteste was to remain the only prominent figure of the medieval schools (after Eriugena) to become a translator—and vice versa: he was the only translator from Greek who had a distinct theological gift. Duns Scotus could still locate Grosseteste's books at the friary library at Oxford, where he lived, and he cited some of the most characteristic of his theological stances. Yet long before his time Grosseteste's exegetical style was regarded as unfashionable and attracted but few admirers. It was left to Wyclif and, later still, to Gascoigne to revive his biblical and pastoral works, which they did, but in writings that were little read and that ignored the Greek language.

PASTORAL WRITINGS

The impact of the Fourth Council of the Lateran upon the life of Grosseteste has not up to the present been given its full weight. The year 1215 marked the culmination of the activity and influence of the most imposing and innovative pope since Gregory VII. The council Innocent III convened carried his message of pastoral renewal, of ecclesiastical liberty of action and of administrative centralization to every corner of the Latin Patriarchate. Grosseteste's pastoral writings and his activity as bishop (including the influential set of statutes he promulgated for the diocese of Lincoln) all bore the stamp of the great reforming council and shared its conviction that the guidance of souls (*regimen animarum*) was the art of arts. The postconciliar period witnessed the proliferation of a pastoral literature expounding the sacraments, the articles of faith, the commandments, and the virtues and vices. This new literature was aimed at the academic and practical formation of priests—for parish priests were to be given a new consciousness of their vital local role, and supplied with the means of instructing the faithful in simple and memorable terms. Thanks to a number of recent editions, principally of writings on confession, Grosseteste's part in this general movement can at last be appreciated.

Pastoral Writings

There is a sense in which almost all that Grosseteste wrote, whether as regent master or as bishop, was pastorally motivated. He was committed to the traditional view of the purpose and function of theology, as offering to future priests and pastors a deepened knowledge of the Scriptures and an understanding of the faith (*intellectus fidei*) based upon the Church's tradition. To take an example: his book on the Decalogue has been discussed in the chapter on his exegetical writings; however, it could with equal justification have been included here. If, on the other hand, we are guided by a rather more precise notion of what constituted pastoral literature in his time, then we can delimit a number of his writings that come undisputably under that heading. Three broad categories of pastoralia have been identified and studied in recent scholarship: preaching, confession, and ecclesiastical discipline. Grosseteste made contributions to all three, and we may take them separately.

Preaching

Bishop Grosseteste's renown as a preacher was great, not only in the mouths of contemporaries of his such as Matthew Paris, but throughout the fourteenth and fifteenth centuries, when collections of his sermons were still circulating in England. Unfortunately, the sermons as a whole have not yet found an editor; only about ten items have been edited in recent decades.[1] It is to be hoped that the rich and varied remains of this large homiletic corpus, the work of one of the greatest of medieval pastors, will find an editor worthy of it, and soon. It was once thought (by S. H. Thomson) that 129 sermons could be identified, almost all of them in collections, but recent research suggests that there are in fact only about forty extensive and independent items (as distinct from his *Dicta*), another nineteen in abbreviated or summarized form, and about thirty-three fragments, or sets of sermon notes.[2] It was their author's practice to preach in Latin to the clergy and in the vernacular to the laity, but all the surviving material is in Latin; presumably he employed Latin notes even when preaching in French. Some of the sermons to clergy may have been rewritten by the bishop for wider circulation, for they are learned and very lengthy, more like conference pieces. The simpler sermons are full of biblically based metaphors and employ the spiri-

tual sense of Scripture in order to invite practical, personal application of
the sacred words to the lives of the hearers.

Confession

Several authentic writings by Grosseteste are connected with confession.
They reveal Grosseteste as a man of the tradition, willing to adapt the ways
of the Fathers in the interests of good pastoral practice, and satisfied that
the substance of the ancient penitential tradition could be conserved and
updated for his own times, divested of its onerous code of tariffs.

We begin with a book, *Templum Dei* ("The Temple of God"), the popularity of which is attested by the hundred or so surviving copies, by the
numerous excerpts made between the thirteenth and the fifteenth centuries, and by a medieval English verse translation.[3] Its aim is to prepare the
priest for the examination of the penitent, but the material it comprises
extends to the virtues and vices, the Lord's Prayer, the Beatitudes, the sacraments, and some elements of canon law. Nearly three quarters of the text
consists of charts, lists, and diagrams that serve to highlight the principal
contents and to facilitate reference to the text. The information it contains
is of the most practical order and is presented in mnemonic form as a direct aid to the confessor and pastor. The structure of *Templum Dei* is an
allegorical extension of I Corinthians 3:17: "For God's temple is holy, and
that temple you are." The design of the temple is twofold: corporeal, to
receive the human nature of Christ, and spiritual, to receive the divine
nature. The physical temple is the human body, distinguished by its several members. The spiritual temple, the dwelling place of God in man, is
that space in the soul where faith, hope, and love reside. Faith lays the
twelve foundation stones (the twelve articles of faith), hope forms its walls,
and love makes its roof. The whole of life consists in building up and
maintaining the structure; in that task the confession of sin is of paramount
importance. It is not unlikely that the popularity of the allegorized temple,
which lasted in England well into the seventeenth century (with the poet
George Herbert), is due in some measure to the impact made by this im-
mensely successful writing.

Several other works on penance to help confessors flowed from the pro-
lific pen of Grosseteste. The longest and richest of these, *Deus est*, is a hand-
book intended for learned priests.[4] It is structured chiefly by means of the

offenses against faith, hope, and charity, and in a subsidiary way by the seven deadly sins and the four cardinal virtues. The lengthy preamble is a masterpiece. It sketches the plan of creation, placing a notable emphasis on its grades, beauty, and hierarchy, and examines the fall of Lucifer, the creation of man as the splendor of God's handiwork, the Fall of Adam and Eve, and the divine plan to redeem and restore mankind to godlikeness. It is striking both in its scope and in its notable employment of terms and ideas derived from the Pseudo-Dionysius, a consideration that inclines one to place its composition within the episcopal career of its author.

Grosseteste also composed a confessional formulary, addressed to the penitent, instructing him on how to examine his conscience and confess his sins.[5] It probably reflects the penitential discipline that prevailed in his own episcopal household. It studies the seven principal vices, adding a list of sins regarding the sacraments and the commandments. The tone of the formulary is familiar and personal. For instance, a number of examples of sins against the fifth commandment are drawn from the life of the student: in the schools he has defaced books, stolen wax from candles, and purloined the belongings of his colleagues. The conclusion is most interesting from a linguistic point of view: confession should be made in French (*gallice*) or in the native tongue (*idiomate*) better known to the penitent (i.e., any English dialect), and should be completed with a formula of contrition, which the author offers in French as well as in Latin. This emphasis on confession in the vernacular is somewhat unusual in the penitential literature of the period; perhaps Grosseteste was thinking in the first place of members of his own household, where Anglo-Norman French was the daily language (along with Latin). The work attractively combines informality with disorder. It is known in a single copy.

Another writing on confession ascribed to Grosseteste is *Perambulavit Iudas* (cf. I Macc. 3:8), but its authenticity is less certain than that of the others.[6] It is composed in the form of a letter to a friend, evidently a monk in orders, and the self-examination is correspondingly subtle and searching, in every way worthy of a man of Grosseteste's spirituality. A short group of meditations conserved in two manuscripts is also probably authentic. It is at once pastoral and spiritual.[7]

A brief Anglo-Norman work, *Confessioun*, is ascribed to Grosseteste, although it would be difficult to establish that he actually wrote it in Anglo-Norman rather than in Latin.

Ecclesiastical Discipline

Bishop Grosseteste composed a set of constitutions that occupy about ten pages in modern print. These were intended for the parochial clergy of his diocese and were widely read in England for two centuries after him. They were the best-known set of English episcopal statutes (twenty-three manuscript copies survive) and formed the basis for synodal statutes in four other English dioceses. The bishop eschewed length and comprehensiveness in the framing of his statutes, in favor of legislating solely for the parochial clergy and in relation to practical and immediate realities. The penalties that appear at the end of the statutes are identical with the excommunication clauses of the Oxford Council of 1222, which, along with the decrees of the Fourth Council of the Lateran, are the sources upon which Grosseteste chiefly drew. The statutes may be dated to 1238–1239, although some additions may have been made as late as the middle of 1240, when they were circulated to the archdeacons of the diocese.

The pastoral content of the statutes concentrates on the priest's functions of administering the sacraments, preaching, and teaching. The opening passage sets the tone for the rest: every single pastor of souls must know the Decalogue and should frequently explain it to the people:

> Since the observance of the Decalogue is necessary for the salvation of souls, we exhort you in the Lord, firmly enjoining that every pastor of souls and every parish priest shall know the Decalogue, that is the Ten Commandments of the Law of Moses, and shall frequently preach on them and expound them to the people in his charge.

He should know the seven deadly sins and be able to preach on them. Likewise he should know the seven sacraments of the Church, and in particular all that belongs to the devout practice of the sacraments of baptism and penance. It is recommended that he recite the Office in the church and surround it with prayer and Scripture reading. He should teach the laypeople frequently in their common tongue. Each pastor should possess at least a simple understanding of the faith as it is contained in the creeds. The statutes also regulate the reverent celebration of Mass and devotion to the Blessed Eucharist. The sacramental care of the sick and dying is spelled out in detail. The children of the parish are to be taught the Lord's Prayer, the Creed, the Hail Mary, and the sign of the cross. Adults who come to confession should be examined as to their knowledge of these and be instructed as far as may be. The statutes were, in short, the work of a conscientious bishop, one who drew upon wide experience—his own and others'—and who was possessed of a practical and realistic sense of the pastoral conditions of priests and people.

Grosseteste's pastoral purposes were pursued in more than one literary genre, and indeed in more than one language; it is to his writings in the Anglo-Norman dialect of French that we shall turn in the following chapter.

ANGLO-NORMAN WORKS

Robert Grosseteste was intensely conscious of the burgeoning of lay life in his own times. One way in which he sought directly to influence the mental and spiritual life of the laity was through his poems and other writings in Anglo-Norman, his native dialect of the French language. We should assume that the few surviving writings represent a larger output.

Up to thirty years ago it was widely accepted that England was a bilingual country until around the middle of the thirteenth century. French was regarded as a vernacular in the true sense, that is, a native, spoken language. It has been argued in recent decades, however, that Anglo-Norman, far from being a vernacular in almost universal use in the England of about 1200, was a language that the great majority of the inhabitants of the island were incapable of speaking, in particular the mass of the peasants.[1] The ethnic English, if they aimed at becoming administrators, were obliged to learn Anglo-Norman French as a foreign language. Thus in the England of the early thirteenth century there was only one true vernacular, namely English, and there were two nonvernacular languages of culture, and increasingly of administration, namely, Latin and French. French was being used as an administrative language even before 1200, because it was more generally understood and spoken than Latin. In the first half of the thirteenth century Anglo-Norman was beginning to be used to reach a reading public wider than the narrow range of those literate in Latin. A limited number of

146

works on religion, medicine, and science were either turned into Anglo-Norman or written in it. In particular, the Fourth Council of the Lateran (1215) precipitated the composition of works of religious instruction, such as the *Evangile des Domees* and the anonymous *Corset*, a treatise on the sacraments. The writers of these instruction books were obliged to create a vocabulary by transfer from Latin to Anglo-Norman. Grosseteste fits into the company of known writers who worked their way from Latin into the French dialect with a religious purpose, and who were conscious that their writings (or translations) in Anglo-Norman would appeal to the laity (i.e., persons who could not read Latin). His purpose was to instruct in matters of religion as widely as possible and to evangelize; one means that he determined to employ among others was the use of his native language. It is thought that most French speakers belonged to the ruling class; if that was so, then Grosseteste was an exception, perhaps even a rare one: a writer who came from peasant stock and who had French as his mother tongue.

Let us make a little tour of inspection of the writings in Anglo-Norman that are currently attributed to Grosseteste.

A brief work called *Confessioun* is attributed to "Saint Robert the Bishop of Lincoln" in the two copies that survive. Its structure follows the seven deadly sins, concluding on each occasion with a formula containing a prayer for mercy. It is not certain that Grosseteste actually wrote this piece in Anglo-Norman; it could possibly be a translation of a Latin writing by him.

Another writing attributed to Grosseteste is called *Les Reulles de Seint Robert*. When he was bishop, he wrote an ordinance for the conduct of his own household and the domains attaching to the see; it is known as *statuta Familiae*. The editor of both works, D. Oschinsky,[2] presents the *Reulles* as an amplified version of the *statuta*. (The French text was later translated into Latin, and the Latin in turn extracted in English.) Grosseteste is claimed as the author of all of them. The *statuta* are genuine. The French *Reulles* was sent to the countess of Lincoln when she was widowed and faced with the management of her large estates. There is a case for regarding Grosseteste as the principal author of the *Reulles*, and of course the immediate author of such of them as are taken more or less directly from the *statuta*. The dating of the *Reulles* is unproblematic: the countess was widowed in 1240, so that her request for assistance must have been made, and met, before she took the easy way out of estate management, by remarrying, in 1242.

Two prayers of Grosseteste's in his native language have been preserved in a manuscript (*Lambeth Palace 499*)[3] that throws an intimate light on his episcopal household. The shorter is introduced by the phrase (in Latin), "He used to say this after a meal." The prayer begins, "Deu seit od nus par sa pite. . . ." I translate it as follows:

> God be with us through his mercy, and defend us from evil and sin, and grant us to do his will, and keep us in health, and lead us to be agreeable to the living and merciful to the dead. And may God grant us to live well and to die well, and to come to the great joy. And may God be with us and grant us his grace and a good end and *vitam eternam*. And first *Benedicite*, and the response [given in Latin], May the Lord keep us and defend us against all evil and lead us to eternal life.

A prayer to St. Margaret is authenticated by the words, "Oracio *eiusdem* ad sanctam Margaretam, quam eciam dicere solebat magister Salomon socius eius" ("A prayer *of the same* [bishop] to St. Margaret, which Master Solomon, his assistant, used to say also"). Solomon of Dover was a trusted member of Grosseteste's *familia*, who served for a time as the bishop's personal chaplain before succeeding John of Basingstoke as archdeacon of Leicester in 1252. Regarding Grosseteste's devotion to St. Margaret we may recall that he held the living of St. Margaret's, Leicester, during the years when he was archdeacon of Leicester (1229–1232). (If his mother was called Margaret, that would account for his predilection for the name; but we shall never know.) In the prayer, Robert of Lincoln comes before his "Dame Seinte Margarete" like a knight pledged to uphold her honor before the whole world, while at the same time suing for her intercession with the king on his behalf:

> Glorious lady, Saint Margaret, I come to implore you, and thank you again, that you have pity on me, in the same way that I have chosen you next to God and His gentle Mother, Our Lady Mary, and before all others. And to you will I turn above all other ladies now or to be, and I will love and honor you above all other ladies to the best of my ability and the grace that God will grant me as a result of your request. As truly I have never, by the grace of God, had it in my thoughts to pollute my body with the stain of the flesh, or any other stain, and also truly because I have honored to the best of my feeble ability all women, for the love of you whom I love above all others, and especially those who are named after you, [I pray you] be my help in front of God the all-powerful, my Creator. May He have mercy on me in His holy pity and through your holy prayer, and may He pardon my sins and give me grace so that I may be able *sic transire per tempora* ["to go through this world"] *ut non amittam*

eterna ["in such a way as not to lose eternal life"]. And please heed my prayer for your assistance in front of my Creator, so that through His mercy and your prayer I may, if it please Him, feel His grace abundant in me. And I promise faithfully to you that if God grant that I may be a worthy man on this earth, I shall give all the honor I can to you, and shall attract others to honor you, and shall honor you in such a way that others will be edified by the good example shown in me by our Lord, through His grace which is our help.[4]

The prayer finishes with a Latin concluding formula: "Quod mihi prestare dignetur et cetera" ("Which may He deign to grant me, etc."). It makes a notable claim to the preservation of its author's chastity. As a prayer it may be a bit long-winded for modern tastes, but it is warmly devotional, in the style of the prayers to saints by St. Anselm of Canterbury, who was a model for later prayer writers and was indeed the inventor of the genre. Phrases of Latin are incorporated into it, for its author's tongue was ready in both languages when it came to praying. To have this glimpse into his private devotional life adds a welcome touch of intimacy to our knowledge of the man he was.

An anonymous treatise, the *Peines de Purgatoire*, has been ascribed to Grosseteste, but its authenticity is open to serious question and it will be left aside here.

A poem entitled "Le mariage des neuf filles du diable" ("The Marriage of the Nine Daughters of the Devil") is attributed to Robert Grosseteste in both surviving manuscripts containing it.[5] The theme is given in the rubric of the *MS Rawlinson Poet. 241*, in French: "Here begins a treatise on how the devil marries off his nine daughters to people of the world, and on Holy Church, according to Robert Grosseteste." In the allegory each daughter is married to a class of society: Simony to clergy, Hypocrisy to the religious, Rapine to soldiers, Sacrilege to farmers, Simulation to servants, Theft to merchants, Usury to city-dwellers, Worldly Pomp to matrons, and Luxury to the greedy.

"Le Chasteau d'Amour" is (despite its appearance) a modern title, given by S. H. Thomson to Grosseteste's longest writing in Anglo-Norman. It consists of 884 octosyllabic couplets, the first twenty-one of which constitute a prologue. A medieval title is found in one of the nineteen manuscripts (Oxford, *Corpus Christi College 232*): "Carmen de creatione mundi" ("A Song about the Creation of the World"). That is fair enough as far as it goes, for the poem admittedly begins with the creation, but it goes on to recount the

history of salvation in allegorical form. It has been hailed as one of the few
really successful medieval allegories.[6] The theme of the "Castle of Love"
turns up also in his *Dictum 43*, as the "house of the body" idea; in the poem
the castle for man's protection is the Virgin Mary. Some of the manuscripts
have a prose preface in Latin that outlines the contents and explains why
the work is written in the *lingua romana*; two manuscripts have an adapta-
tion of this in French. Here is an extract from it (l. 15ff.):

> But not all can know well the language
> Of Hebrew, Greek and Latin
> To praise their Creator.
> May the mouth of the singer
> Never fail to open in praise of God
> Or to announce His holy name,
> And may each one in his own language
> Know in himself without fail
> His God and his redemption.
> I begin my statement in Romance
> For those who do not know well
> The letters of the clergy

He begins, that is to say, in Latin. The poem reflects Grosseteste's concern to deepen the knowledge and living of the Christian faith. In it he
conveys a rich theological content in an easily memorizable versified form.
Beginning with the Creation and the Fall, he relates the Old Testament
prophecies of the Messiah to the Incarnation, the redemptive death and
the resurrection of Jesus Christ. He includes a remarkable reflection on
the infinite suffering of the redeemer and his mother's anguish by the cross
(l. 1173–1185):

> Hail! most glorious Queen
> Mary, Mother and Virgin,
> For piety I cannot enumerate
> Your dolors or call them to mind.
> But now there is accomplished
> Perfectly the prophecy of Simeon,
> For more than in your body,
> You were wounded by a sword in your soul.
> But your joy will be doubled a hundred times over

When he rises from the dead.
The passion would have had no value
If it were not for the Resurrection.[7]

The same passage expounds Grosseteste's ideas on the soul's relationship to the body and the infinite suffering of the redeemer caused by the sundering his soul from his body.[8] Comparison with the other contexts in which these notions turn up suggests that the poem was written after *De cessatione legalium*, that is to say, no earlier than circa 1235.

The history of salvation is continued by the Church, whose foundation is recalled, and by its sacraments. The poem looks forward through history to the eschaton: the final destruction of the natural world through fire; the last judgment; the joys of heaven; and the pains of hell. Grosseteste weaves into his writing allegorical, anagogical, and tropological motifs; in other words, he tries to convey the spiritual sense of the Scriptures to his audience, or readership.

The chief literary interest of the work is attached to the two extended allegories, of the Four Daughters of God (l. 205–456) and the Castle of Love (l. 567–878). The four daughters of a mighty and just king, with whose help he ruled, were called Mercy, Truth, Justice, and Peace (cf. Ps. 84). A servant of the king transgressed and was handed over to his enemies and imprisoned. Mercy pleaded that the prisoner be ransomed, since the enemies of the king had deceived him by a false promise. Truth advised that transgressions be punished so that majesty might be feared. Justice asked for the punishment of death, since the prisoner had deserted Mercy, Truth, Justice, and Peace and had chosen punishment and sorrow, which are described (l. 337–370). Peace spoke up: she has deserted the country and will not return until her quarreling sisters are united in judgment. The king's son, moved to pity for the prisoner by the pleas of Mercy, determined to take the servant's clothing and suffer punishment in his place, so that peace and justice might embrace and the whole country be saved.

The Son is the Good Shepherd, and also the Wonderful Counselor prophesied by Isaiah: wonderful, because he takes on human nature and becomes like all men, while he unites that nature to his divine nature. To become man he must be born of woman; here the second allegory is introduced.

God's habitation on earth is a castle of love, built upon a rock, with a keep, deep ditches, four towers, three baileys, and seven barbicans, each with a gate. It is painted in green, blue, and red but inside it is pure white. In the keep there is a well from which four streams run and a throne of white ivory mounted by seven steps. Above that is a rainbow shining with all the colors (l. 567–658). In the interpretation the castle is revealed as the body of the Virgin Mary, our defender against the enemy. The colors represent faith, hope, and charity; the turrets are the four cardinal virtues; the baileys are the maidenhood, chastity, and marriage of Mary; the seven barbicans represent humility, love, abstinence, chastity, generosity, patience and gladness, by which the seven deadly sins are overcome; the well stands for grace and the ditches for the voluntary poverty of the virgin. Through this castle, when God descends, the devil loses his power. (The author pauses to ask for admittance to the castle of love, because he is attacked by foes.) When the child is born, Mercy is heard, Peace covers the earth, and the beauties of nature are enhanced.

Regarding the redemption, the work is notable for its combination of two theories of the devil's rights. According to the ransom theory, God gave his son to the devil as a ransom for imprisoned man (cf. Gregory of Nyssa and the Greek tradition). In the theory of the abuse of power, the devil broke the contract, which stipulated the limits of the divine and the diabolic spheres of power, by an abuse of power directed against the Son, who alone of all men was outside his influence (Augustine). The author of the poem may accord more attention to the ransom theory, but he incorporates and combines the two in the dialogue of Christ and the devil in the desert (l. 1057ff): God must pay a ransom, for the relationship between God and the devil has been stipulated by covenant.

In the poem Grosseteste used existing writings but elaborated their themes, in particular by developing feudal and juridical notions. He took the allegory of the *Quatre filles* from the *Rex et Famulus*, a Latin prose treatise, and probably also drew on St. Bernard's sermon on the feast of the Annunciation (*P.L.* 183: 383–390). The allegory, which is also found in Hugh of St. Victor, goes back to midrashic interpretations of Psalm 84:11–12 (sixth century and earlier). While the castle was popular as a basis for allegorization after circa 1100, no direct source has been found for the allegory of the Castle of Love; on our present knowledge it would seem to be original to Grosseteste. It contains "perhaps the richest and most varied version of the castle-of-the-body idea adapted to the Blessed Virgin."[9]

There were half a dozen or so longer poems in the Anglo-Norman dialect, and Grosseteste's proved to be among the most popular of them, to judge by the number of manuscripts. It belongs to the literary history of England just as much as to that of France, for it was translated four times into Middle English, in versions of varying length. No modern version or even a thorough study of the language and theology of the poem exists, nor has it been satisfactorily edited.[10] It was probably meant to be sung at live entertainments. It shows an otherwise unsuspected side of Grosseteste's sentiment, revealing his willingness to use every medium at the disposal of his talents to inculcate faith and encourage piety. He recognized the vital importance of Anglo-Norman, his native dialect, for pastoral communication, and he manifested in verse form his ability to express in it his beliefs and views as they are known from his Latin writings, with undiminished originality.

THE EARLIEST FRANCISCAN
MASTERS AT OXFORD

We are fortunate in being able to follow quite closely the development of one of the early Oxford schools of theology, that belonging to the Franciscan Order, and to record something of the debt it owed to its first master. Although the chronicler Thomas of Eccleston, O.F.M., was not himself a scholar, he devoted particular attention to the place held by studies within the life of the English Province, from the arrival of the first friars up to the time (ca. 1258) when his narrative ends.[1] Nine Franciscans landed at Dover on 10 September 1224, at a time when St. Francis himself was still alive. The founder of the order had appointed as the minister for England Fr. Agnellus of Pisa, formerly guardian of the Paris house. Before the end of October two of the nine, Richard of Ingworth and Richard of Devon, were staying with the Dominicans at Oxford. They rented a house, which rapidly became too small as students and bachelors joined the movement. A larger house was bought for them, and near it Agnellus of Pisa had a school built. Agnellus made the decision to invite Grosseteste to lecture rather than any of the friar theologians he might have requested. Under him, Eccleston proudly records, "within a short time they made incalculable progress both in scholastic discussions [*in questionibus*] and in subtle moralities suitable for preaching."

Grosseteste very likely gave up his own school entirely and transferred his daily lectures on the Bible, when he foresaw that he could have the deepest impact upon these future preachers. He taught there from 1229 or 1230 until he was elected bishop of Lincoln, in 1235. Three more secular masters followed him during a period of seventeen years: Peter, who went to a bishopric in Scotland; Roger de Weseham, afterward dean of Lincoln (ca. 1240) and bishop of Coventry (1245)[2]; and Thomas of Wales, who acceded to the see of St. David in 1247. Only at that point did the succession of Franciscan masters begin, with Adam Marsh (1247 to at least 1250); Ralph of Colebridge (ca. 1249–1252); Eustace of Normanville (erstwhile chancellor of Oxford, date unknown; *regens* at Cambridge); and Thomas of York (incepted 14 March 1253, remained *regens* until 1256). Under the friars' provincial, William of Nottingham (1240–1254), Grosseteste's close friend and confidant, the house at Oxford and to some extent that at Cambridge became the training grounds for lectors and masters in theology throughout the province. When William left office, Eccleston was able to count thirty lecturers "who solemnly disputed," and three or four in addition who simply lectured. The pattern was set of each house in England's having a lecturer, and in addition a student's being prepared at Oxford or Cambridge. The reputation of the province for learning spread to France and Italy: Elias of Cortona, the third minister general, sent for two brothers, Philip of Wales and Adam of York, to lecture at Lyons; Sanson the Englishman, lector at Parma in 1238, and Stephen the Englishman, who taught at Genoa and Rome in obedience to the second minister general, John of Parma, were likewise products of the Oxford school.

Through the eyes of Thomas of Eccleston, then, we can follow the rise of a school from its very origins to its flourishing state twenty years later; we can retrace the continuous succession of its teachers and observe the transition from its secular masters to its own Franciscan regents. By the prestigious agency of Grosseteste the first provincial of England managed to associate the life of the house intimately with that of the university, thus establishing a link that was to endure for two centuries and more. The effect of the development initiated by Agnellus and given substance and body by Grosseteste was to make the friars insiders to the university and to place their best-trained theologians on an institutional par with their secular colleagues. The impact of university life and activity, at Paris as well as at Oxford and Cambridge, upon the ideals and practices of the order has been the object of sharply divergent evaluations; however, that controversy cannot occupy us here.[3] As A. G. Little remarked,

One of the characteristics of the English Province which stands out most clearly in the pages of Brother Thomas is that the early friars combined

zeal for poverty with love of knowledge. . . . [F]or some years the friars
of the English province reconciled ideals which St Francis regarded as
incompatible.[4]

This feature, introduced by the alliance of Agnellus and Grosseteste, ensured
in turn that for a hundred years after the foundation of the Franciscan school
a large proportion of the leading lights in theology at Oxford were to be friars and that for most of that period their school was simply the best place to
study theology at the university.

Adam Marsh, O.F.M.

The name of Adam Marsh, O.F.M., will forever be associated with that of
Robert Grosseteste, for the two men were linked by the deepest philosophical and religious affinities. Their names are joined in the unique manuscript
of Grosseteste's *Tabula* by the words, "with an addition by Friar Adam
Marsh." Tables to Grosseteste's *Hexaëmeron* were drawn up by Marsh.[5] A
summary of the metaphysics of light associated principally with Grosseteste
has recently been attributed to him; it seems to have been meant for St.
Bonaventure.[6] More than fifty letters from the friar to Robert Grosseteste
have survived, as against only two going in the other direction. It may well
have been Marsh who opened Grosseteste's eyes to the importance of the
Pseudo-Dionysius, for Marsh is said to have passed several years (ca. 1230–
1235) in study at Vercelli, where Thomas Gallus (who made influential summaries and commentaries on the Dionysian works) implanted the traditions
of the school of St. Victor (Paris). Grosseteste relied on Marsh for confiden-
tial advice about possible nominations of clergy within the diocese of Lincoln and important political and administrative matters—for Marsh knew
simply everybody, and was beloved of all.

Marsh may not have been all that much younger that Grosseteste, but he
was certainly the latter's pupil. He was described as being already old at the
time of his entry into the friars, circa 1227. After his death he was sometimes
referred to as *Doctor illustris*. Thomas of Eccleston claims that Master Adam
Marsh was "famous over the whole world," and Salimbene, the Italian
Franciscan chronicler, tells us that he was a "great scholar" and that "famous
in England, he wrote many books." Marsh was a Doctor of Theology, and
in fact, at an advanced age, in 1248, he became regent at Oxford, the first

Franciscan to do so. His regency was relatively brief: Thomas of York, O.F.M., succeeded him in the chair in 1253.

Roger Bacon testifies that Marsh and Grosseteste spent forty years together in the study of the sciences and mathematics. We can be certain that the two men shared a great deal of their reading, not only in ancient and Arabic philosophy and science, but in theology also. Both were erudite patristic scholars and both could read Greek, so that in these regards Marsh doubtless prolonged Grosseteste's influence at Oxford, when it finally came his time to teach there. But what did he add of his own? The corpus of 247 letters, which is all that survives of what must have been an imposing intellectual output, is not very informative theologically, although it is a precious source for the English and Franciscan history of the period. As we might expect, Marsh certainly was very attentive to the spiritual sense of the Scriptures. He was of a mystical, contemplative tendency. He assimilated the theology of the Pseudo-Areopagite, showing a particular interest in the nature and functions of the celestial and ecclesiastical hierarchies. Finally, a straw in a wind blowing from the south: Marsh wrote to Grosseteste (Ep. 43) sending him "some particulars from various expositions of the Abbot Joachim [of Fiore], brought to me some days ago by a friar coming from abroad." In fact, Marsh was a friend of Hugh de Digne, O.F.M., and it may even have been Hugh who sent the Joachite material that reached Marsh in England and was shortly to be conveyed in summary form to Grosseteste.[7] Marsh believed that, as he said to Grosseteste, Joachim's writings were "the interpretations of a holy man who is justly credited with having a divine spirit of understanding the prophetic mysteries." It was to Joachim as a spiritual interpreter of the Apocalypse that Marsh was drawn; indeed, he himself wrote a partial (and lost) commentary on that book. However, the mixture of sanctity, allegory, and prophecy that was typically Joachite was very heady stuff; it was to seduce Franciscans even more markedly than it had done some of Joachim's own Cistercian reformed monks, in ways that were promising division already in Marsh's own lifetime and that were to reach cataclysmic proportions soon after his death, tearing the order apart and actually threatening its continued existence. What Grosseteste said by way of reply to Marsh we do not know. Nor can we tell to what extent Marsh's Oxonian lectures reflected his own reception of the abbot of Fiore's writings. However, it may be suspected that Robert Grosseteste was too well anchored in more sober scriptural exegesis to feel much sympathy with the nascent cult of Joachite illuminism. In theology, Grosseteste was a disciple of Augustine, in all matters relating to time, providential history, the ages of the world, and the last things. Nowhere does he give any sign of thinking that a utopia of the Spirit would or ever could come about within history, to replace the institutional Church of Peter with the eschatological community of John, the rock of earth with the eagle of the spiritual air.

Thomas of York, O.F.M.

One of Marsh's letters (no. 192) carries an extensive report of the inception of his confrère, Thomas of York (14 March 1253), and describes the conflict between the Franciscans and the university that came about because Thomas was not a Master of Arts. Marsh clearly thought very highly of the latter's intellectual and human qualities. Thomas lectured at Oxford for at most three years. In 1256 he succeeded William of Melitona as regent at the Cambridge studium. Several minor writings of his have been preserved, but it is his extensive (though incomplete) *Sapientiale* (1253–56)[8] that must earn him a place in even the most cursory survey of early Oxford thought. It is a wide-flung discussion of metaphysical and theological problems that draws on an extensive knowledge of ancient philosophy, the Arabic commentators on Aristotle, and Jewish writers (in particular Maimonides), as well as of course the Latin Fathers. Thomas habitually presented all the attempted solutions to a problem, quoting generously from his authorities, with the result that it is often quite difficult to discern amid the abundance of his anthological tendencies where exactly his own preferred solution lies.[9]

Thomas devoted a learned and comprehensive chapter intended, according to its title, "To establish Aristotle's meaning concerning the proofs that he brought forth for the eternity of the world, and to distinguish the opinions about the question, and to respond to the arguments adduced for the eternity of the world."[10] He opened it with a review of the position of Aristotle, using Maimonides and Averroës as authorities, and of Plato, drawing on Themistius via Averroës.[11] Maimonides's view was extensively quoted: Aristotle offered only probable arguments; philosophical reasoning by itself leads to his position. The traditional conciliation of the *Timaeus* with Christian belief was echoed by Thomas, with the proviso that the disordered state that preexisted the creation had itself no beginning. Thomas drew from an anonymous contemporary (who was himself indebted to Grosseteste) a series of arguments to show the impossibility of the Aristotelian position:

1. Nothing can confer being on itself; everything must be preceded in time by its own efficient cause.
2. The non-being of the world before creation is really located in the divine eternity.
3. The whole of past time has the present moment as an extreme point, but whatever has an extreme point must be finite.
4. The infinite cannot be traversed.
5. Whatever has a future had a beginning; therefore every past thing had a beginning in time.

Thomas had wide learning but not great speculative powers. His mid-century state of the question concerning the eternity of the world indicates the growing importance of Averroës and Maimonides in the debate, and reveals that the viewpoints of Alexander of Hales, O.F.M., and Grosseteste (who was presumably Thomas's teacher) had become part of the tradition at Oxford.

THE ARRIVAL OF THE *SENTENCES*

On becoming bishop of Lincoln, in 1235, Grosseteste left Oxford. The fifteen years that followed his departure witnessed a growing influence of Paris upon Oxford, through the importation of the practice of commenting on the *Sentences* of Peter Lombard. By about 1250 both Richard Fishacre, O.P., and Richard Rufus, O.F.M., had completed commentaries on the *Sentences*. Grosseteste's resistance to the new style had some effect, as we shall see, but he was not able to counteract the novelty. On the other hand, the influence of some of his ideas was felt by both writers, in a way that lent a measure of material continuity to the changing structure of theology. I shall study these developments in some detail, on the basis of the latest research.

Grosseteste more or less identified theology with the study of the Bible and filled the morning hours of classes (*lectiones ordinariae*) with exposition of the text. Indeed he deliberately underlined his adherence in this regard to the practice of the Paris regents of the time of his own youth. In doing so he was no doubt reflecting a broad consensus among the regents who were his contemporaries at Oxford. Robert Bacon, O.P., for instance, has left a lengthy book of moralities on the Psalter, in which several short *quaestiones* are included.[1] After him, Simon of Hinton, O.P., teaching between 1248 and 1250, wrote on the Gospel according to Matthew in the traditional style of lengthy, diffuse commentary containing long questions that represented a classroom exercise. An anonymous postil on Exodus fits neatly into the same tradition of continuous commentary on the text, interlaced with questions that arise in some way from it. Later still Thomas Docking, O.F.M., composed (between 1260 and 1265) an exceptionally voluminous commentary on the Pauline Epistles, stocked full of traditional authorities, with frequent questions and digressions. These are all witnesses, Franciscan, Dominican, and secular, to the practice at Oxford of attaching theological teaching to the Scriptures, holding disputations during the lecture course, and writing up commentary and *quaestiones* together without any regard to brevity or summary. It would appear that Oxford held conservatively to the older Parisian practice of circa 1200, during the very years when Paris itself was moving in a new direction.

The novelties of Paris are made evident by a formal analysis of works from the first thirty years of the century. Hugh of St. Cher headed a Dominican team at St. Jacques that compiled, from 1230 onward, a complete postil on the Bible, one that was to prove influential during later medieval and even early modern times. "Hugh intended his postils as a supplement to the *Gloss*. They were to introduce the student to the achievements of biblical scholarship in both literal interpretation and moralities, between the compilation of the *Gloss* and his own professorship."[2] The Parisian style of commentary leaned toward concision, and theological *quaestiones* were circulated separately from it. The questions tended increasingly to become a literary device (as they were in summas of theology), for although they derived from the text, they were no longer made the object of classroom discussions. Paris, in other words, was moving toward theological specialization, while Oxford persisted for some time in the earlier practice of Paris itself. Fifty years ago, B. Smalley uttered the suspicion that two currents of opinion, and even a disagreement, were felt at Oxford from circa 1240, when the Dominican Richard Fishacre introduced the distinction between moral instruction, to be given on the basis of Scripture, and theological questions, which he himself developed by commenting on the *Sentences*. Recent research has confirmed Smalley's suspicion and clarified the nature and extent of the disagreement, which merited the intervention of the local ordinary, the bishop of Lincoln.

Fishacre's Inaugural Sermon on Wisdom

Alexander of Hales it was who, already during the years 1223–1227, made the *Sentences* and not the Bible the ordinary text for his lectures at Paris, "antequam esset frater" (i.e., before he took the Franciscan habit, ca. 1236). It is now widely acknowledged that by circa 1240–1245 this practice had become common. When Richard Fishacre adopted the *Sentences* as a text at Oxford, he could claim, with good reason, to be simply following the newer but already well-established practice of Paris. This is the claim he advanced in his *sermo principialis*, or inaugural sermon, which served as the prologue to his commentary:

> This science, therefore, which makes a double approach to a single reality, has two parts. The first concerns the union of the will (*affectus*) with the highest good, the other the union of the mind (*aspectus*) with the highest truth. The former, which is about the union of the will in this life with the highest good, consists of moral instruction, while the latter, which is about the union of the mind [in this life] with the highest truth, consists of the discussion of difficult questions about the articles of faith. I maintain that each of them is contained in the sacred canon of the Scriptures, in a global and undifferentiated way. The first part only [moral instruction] is taught by the modern masters when expounding the holy books, whereas the second is reserved for disputation, as being the more difficult. At present this more difficult part is removed from the commentary on the Holy Scriptures and located in the book known as *Sentences*. And so, in this instance there is no difference between expounding and disputing.[3]

Fishacre's informative words justify the drawing of two conclusions. In the first place, the Parisian practice to which he was referring divided theology (or the science of Scripture) into two parts. All moral instruction was based upon the Bible and was given at the ordinary morning lectures, whereas the disputations on matters of faith were held at a later time of day. Second, Fishacre himself proposed to follow the innovation introduced by Alexander more than fifteen years beforehand, and to make the *Sentences* the ordinary morning text in the faculty, because he regarded doctrinal questions (the object of disputations) as belonging to the understanding and interpretation of the Scriptures. His innovative practice had the effect of abolishing the distinction between, on the one hand, the exegesis (*lectio*) of the one truly and supremely authoritative text in the faculty, and, on the other, the more speculative disputations that only very recent academic practice had introduced. The proposal could not but create disquiet among the older masters at Oxford. The dismay with which Bishop Grosseteste reacted to it was no doubt rather widely shared at his old university.

Bishop Grosseteste's Letter
to the Regents of Oxford

The letter that the ordinary addressed to the regent masters at Oxford is well known, but it has to be read in the context of the innovations at Paris and their recent introduction to Oxford, in order to yield its full meaning.

The location of Grosseteste's undated Letter to the Regents within the collection of his official correspondence indicates that it was written in 1245 or 1246. It is couched in his familiar and personal style and is larded with biblical references. It opens upon an allegorical motif, the house of God, which it sustains and embellishes throughout. This Pauline motif (Eph. 2:20–22) serves a double function in the letter. In the first place it highlights the responsibililty of the theologian as an architect and builder of the house, one who constructs the edifice of truth upon the only sure foundation, namely, the prophets, the apostles, and Christ the cornerstone. Second, in accommodating the motif of building up the house of God to his purpose, which is to have exegesis restored to its rightful place, he is enabled to draw upon the Bible in its own defense, with the result that form and content coalesce in the letter itself. The regents are exhorted not to weaken the foundations by using stones that are not chosen for the weight they must support; no architect wants to place at risk the solidity of a construction.

> But the time most appropriate for placing and fitting in at the foundation the stones we have mentioned (for there is a time for laying foundations, as there is a time for building [Eccl. 3:3]) is the morning hour of your ordinary lectures. All of your lectures, especially these early ones, should be drawn from books of the New Testament and of the Old. If this is not done the foundational stones will be interspersed with or even replaced by others. Besides, the time fitted for such business will not be alotted to it (which is against the teaching of Scripture and the natural order of things), and a departure will be made from the footsteps of the Fathers and of our predecessors, and from conformity with the regent theologians at Paris. Therefore, because we wish that you do all things uprightly and in order, as the Apostle commands [I Cor. 14:40], we ask, warn, and exhort you in the Lord Jesus Christ, with all the affection and devotion of which we are capable, to draw all your ordinary lectures at the morning hour from the New or the Old Testament. We want you to be like fathers of families, indeed to be such, bringing out of your treasures new things and old [Mt. 13:52]—not, however, things other than the New or the Old; no intermediary, not even the edifices built by the

Fathers upon the teaching of Scripture, can be substituted for the study of the foundations; some other time can be more fittingly set aside for such reading.

Grosseteste weighed his words and chose a formula (*rogamus, monemus, et exhortamur in Domino Jesu Christo*) that he intended to be binding on all masters teaching at Oxford, that is, within his jurisdiction. His own wish would have outrun his formal ruling: *all* ordinary lectures should consist of "reading" the Sacred Page. This he recommended as a practice, without however imposing it as a command. The letter is insistent and admits of no ambiguity.

Grosseteste's letter in its turn drew a reaction, and did so from the highest quarter of all: an *epistola secreta*, emanating from the papal curia at some time between 1245 and 1247, commanded the bishop of Lincoln not to prevent "Br. R. of the Order of Preachers then teaching at the Faculty of Theology at Oxford from lecturing *ordinarie* on the *Sentences*," but to encourage him.[4] Evidently the Dominicans had been able to interest someone at the curia in Fishacre's affair. Very likely the curia found it unacceptable to discourage at Oxford what was being practiced at the metropolitan center, Paris. Looking back from the 1260s, Roger Bacon continued to deplore the innovation that had so elevated the *Sentences* within faculties of theology, and he made a retrospective defense of the position of revered earlier figures, naming Grosseteste and Marsh.

Another voice joined the discussions, a Franciscan one, which attempted to accommodate new practice to revered tradition, and thus to steer a middle course. Richard Rufus, O.F.M. (or *Cornubiensis*—of Cornwall), in the introduction to his commentary on the *Sentences*, reveals the existence of a conflict of opinion within the faculty. Rufus was the first Franciscan to comment on the *Sentences* at Oxford, and his is only the second commentary known from there. It was compiled circa 1248–1250, not long after the death of Fishacre, which took place in 1248. Brown has argued persuasively that the introduction to the work was a direct response to the Dominican's position.[5] Here is Rufus's statement:

> Some like to use this prologue to debate general points concerning theology itself, and do so on the occasion of this *Summa* of the Master. Such a thing does not appear to me to be necessary, since this *Summa* is not theology itself nor any part of it. Sacred Scripture is whole in itself, perfect without this *Summa* or any other. Works like the Lombard's are a

sort of clarification, useful for our benefit, of things which are said obscurely in Scripture. However, since it is customary, we also will say some things.

Grosseteste would have been pleased with this assertion of the sufficiency of Scripture, and with the conjoint exclusion of the *Sentences* from theology in the strictest sense—the only sense then current—of Scripture itself and the study of Scripture. Yet it would have been plain to him that he had lost the argument with the faculty, for Rufus, just like his Dominican predecessor, was delivering his ordinary lectures on the Lombard's work because it was rapidly becoming a recognized task of the theologian to do so. By presenting the *Sentences* in the pedagogical light of an elucidation of things expressed with deliberate obscurity in the Bible, Rufus was clearly distancing himself from Fishacre's claim that there are two parts to the study of theology, and that both belong in some way to the canon of Scripture. It did not enter Rufus's head, by the way, to suggest that Fishacre wished to extend divine inspiration to the *Sentences*; his protest was made against the separation of *lectio* from *disputatio*, which Rufus himself proposed to reunite within the curriculum.

Theology at Oxford in the Mid-Century

Richard Fishacre, O.P.

The Order of Preachers came to England in 1221. Richard Fishacre, who hailed from Exeter, joined it at an unknown date. He was a Bachelor of Theology by 1240, for he commented on the *Sentences* between circa 1241 and 1245. In his commentary he avowed that he suffered from a weak constitution. He died, probably still fairly young, in 1248, the same year as Robert Bacon, O.P., his own master and Grosseteste's friend and former colleague. According to the chronicler Matthew Paris, Fishacre was a notable popular preacher. The wide readership his commentary found is attested by the existence of fifteen complete and partial witnesses to the text. Other surviving works of his include questions about heresies and a question on the Ascension;[6] a number of sermons, and perhaps a work on the theological virtues, whose authenticity has not been satisfactorily established.

The dominant motif of Fishacre's thought was the relationship between theology and the liberal arts or philosophy. In this regard he employs the traditional allegory: Abraham's child by Hagar the servant (*ancilla*) was born before Sara could conceive. Fishacre uses ideas and information deriving from physics, astronomy, meteorology, and botany, in order to illuminate and illustrate the truths of faith. The desire to know all things is innate in mankind (Aristotle); both philosophy and theology attest it. Using the three-book topos, Fishacre argues that the book of life (the divine ideas) having been closed to us by the Fall of Adam, the book of creatures has become indecipherable; recourse must be had to the book of Scripture in order to interpret creation, which is seen, by means of the word, which is heard. An armillary sphere, he reminds us, would serve little purpose of instruction concerning the heavenly bodies, if we did not have Ptolemy's words to accompany the visual model. Divine wisdom is found in the Scriptures as word, and in the creation before our eyes; the conjoint learning by means of eye and ear can alone return the human spirit to the hidden wisdom of God. Fishacre's theological program, as one can see, is Augustinian in character: the liberal arts and philosophy (if consulted with discernment) hold messages of truth and moral precept (Augustine, *De doctrina Christiana* 2.4; 2.40), and are the handmaidens of wisdom. This traditional model of knowledge is the key to Fishacre's attitude even to the *Book of Sentences*, which he regarded as a faithful companion to the exegesis of Scripture, not a work of knowledge or wisdom in its own right. It is in the light of a thoroughly traditional outlook that Fishacre's innovation, in making the *Sentences* part of the study of Scripture, must be assessed. In the same vein, his insistence on a broad philosophical preparation for theology highlights once again his Augustinian conviction about the finality of all knowledge, which is to serve the opening of the *liber scripturae*, in which all truth, both practical and speculative, is contained, at least in an indistinct way.

In Fishacre's comment on *I Sent.*, dist. 3, we can observe the extent to which the content as well as the form of his theology was indebted to the Paris faculty, for his arguments for the existence of God might just as well have been written there as at Oxford; they bear, on the other hand, no relationship to any known page of Oxford theology up to his time.[7] Can the existence of God be shown by rational argument? Does the existence of God indeed require to be proven—is it not an evidence of the rational mind? In addressing these issues Fishacre had before him a dossier of texts assembled by William of Auxerre and included in the *Summa aurea* (1215–1231), a work that evidently made a considerable impression upon the English Dominican. For Paris theologians down to Aquinas, the collage of texts drawn from

St. Augustine, St. John Damascene, and St. Anselm, which William had mounted, was a widely received *status quaestionis*. It put into circulation a causal argument for the existence of God but overshadowed that by promoting a distorted formulation of St. Anselm's argument in the *Proslogion*, making the claim that God's existence is self-evident to every mind. Fishacre endorsed this ontological argument, in pages that closely parallel the *Summa fratris Alexandri*, which was being compiled contemporaneously by Franciscans at Paris. In language that owes much to Aristotle's affirmation of the senses' role in the foundation of knowledge, the Dominican unfolded the classical Augustinian theory of knowledge: the senses are the occasion for the soul's immaterial acts of cognition; all truth is inscribed in the mind from the beginning, and the Light of God is even more present to the mind than the mind is to itself. We may conclude that much of Fishacre's program and materials was directly related to the contemporary theological developments being pursued at Paris, whereas Grosseteste's finesse in meeting Aristotle's epistemology from a Catholic perspective largely passed him by.

Fishacre proposed formally to separate biblical and moral teaching from speculative questions, so that his program was innovative. It became controversial in the Oxford context. When we turn from theory to practice, however, it is something of a surprise to discover the extent to which moralities figure in his commentary. Indeed, Grosseteste himself would have been very approving of these moral instructions, in respect of both their quantity and their content. A contemporary compiler was so struck by the numerous *exempla* and life lessons that he excerpted them extensively, apparently for the edification of the Cistercians of Fountains Abbey in Yorkshire, and for possible application in meditation and use in sermons.[8] Fishacre's proposal for the formal separation of theology into two branches sounded more radical than it in fact was; it was in great part attenuated by his own practice. To put it another way, the pastoral purpose of sacred studies asserted itself quite naturally in his commentary, which reads in part like a source book for sermon writing.

Grosseteste's presence at Oxford had resulted in the availability there of an impressive array of Greek patristic sources; Fishacre and Rufus could scarcely fail to be exposed to this side of his legacy. Fishacre remained within the ambit of Oxford theology in another way, for he made liberal use of the *Hexaëmeron* of Grosseteste, which he evidently admired.[9] He paraphrased its lengthy attack on the Aristotelian teaching concerning the eternity of the world, omitting most of the patristic quotations, save for Ambrose. In a similar way he took over much of Grosseteste's rebuttal of the "false, heretical, and unscientific" claims of astrology, repeating selectively the main points, paraphrasing much more, and quoting the conclusion of the discussion.[10] Moreover, the very personal treatment afforded by Grosseteste to the image of God in man was taken over in abridged form in Fishacre's commentary, including many of the authorities drawn from the Greek Fathers. Finally, the *affectus/aspectus* distinction became a commonplace in his commentary, and the metaphysics of light made a limited impact on his thought: in a scholastic question concerning light, he took up an issue that Grosseteste had raised in the *Hexaëmeron* but passed over without much ado, as to whether light is an accident or a substance. Fishacre argued that light is not a spiritual thing nor an accident but is the most subtle of bodily substances. The term "light" can also signify the accident caused by light, that is, lighting up or illumination. Fishacre proposed an original view regarding the ontological status of light (the metaphyscial question): the "matter" of substantial light, he argued (not without originality), does not emanate from the sun or come from the element of air but is unceasingly being created by God. Fishacre's views were contested by Rufus in his commentary on the *Sentences*. In this discussion the metaphysics of light launched by Grosseteste at Oxford knew a limited afterlife.

Fishacre's discussion of free will (the longest chapter in his commentary) merited the praise of Lottin, as a very personal and original essay.[11] Regarding the existence and the source of free choice he relied extensively on Grosseteste's treatise on the same subject, but he inverted Grosseteste's firm position regarding the priority of the will over the reason, in a way that foreshadowed the later Dominican position.[12]

Only when the edition of Fishacre's commentary has appeared will the full extent of his debts to his contemporaries (William of Auxerre, Hugh of St. Cher, and Robert Grosseteste) be revealed, and an informed and balanced estimate of his originality be made possible.

Richard Rufus, O.F.M.

Richard Rufus may well have been saved from complete oblivion by the forthright denunciation made of him by his fellow friar Roger Bacon.

> The one I knew best was the worst and most stupid of them all. He was the inventor of these errors. His name is Richard of Cornwall, very famous among the stupid masses, but the wise thought he was absurd. And

he was rejected in Paris for the errors he had invented and promulgated, while lecturing there on the *Sentences* solemnly from the year 1250 onwards, after he had lectured on the *Sentences* at Oxford. From that time, 1250, on, therefore, most people persistently followed this master in his errors, and it has mainly weakened Oxford, where all this nonsense started.[13]

The precise nature of the errors referred to by Bacon has not yet been satisfactorily clarified. Rufus had in him nothing of the innovator; his theological views, when they can be discerned, do not stand out in relief over against those of his contemporaries.

The reliable Eccleston recorded Rufus's entry into the order (at Paris, probably in 1238) and underlined his repute at Oxford, and later at Paris, "where he read the *Sentences cursorie*." He was given permission by the general to return to Paris in order to continue in theology there (1248), but his weak health (he was subject to depression, according to Marsh) kept him at Oxford where he lectured on the *Sentences*, circa 1250. (His commentary remains unedited.)[14] Rather unexpectedly, he left Oxford for Paris in 1253, where he again lectured on the *Sentences*. In 1256 he became the fifth lecturer at the Oxford convent. He died at an unknown date (after 1259). His life does not appear to have been an easy one; his writings were quickly bypassed and forgotten.

What did he write? The Oxford commentary on the *Sentences*, extant in a single complete manuscript copy, is the best authenticated of his works. Internal evidence places it between 1245 and 1250. An abbreviation of Bonaventure's commentary on the same writing, containing independent notes and additions, has been attributed to him; it certainly originated in Oxford, but its ascription to Rufus is open to serious doubt.[15] A *Scriptum super Metaphysicam*, written probably at Oxford and in the Franciscan milieu, somewhere between 1235 and 1250, is attributed to Rufus in one early copy, but its authenticity has not been established beyond doubt.[16] No trace of his Paris commentary has been found. Seven of the unedited disputed questions attributed to him can be considered authentic.[17] His interest in Aristotle gave rise to a commentary on the *Meteorologica* that was known to Bartholomaeus Anglicus.

It was with an air of embarrassment that Rufus introduced his commentary to the Oxford public, claiming that the enterprise was imposed upon him by his university role, but that it was not itself theology or a part thereof (as Fishacre had approached it): *theologia* is found in the Scriptures, and is done in the attempt to unfold their meaning and message. There can be no doubt that as he wrote in these terms he was conscious above all of the bishop of Lincoln's express command to the masters, of the exceptional place the bishop had occupied within the faculty, and of the universally recognized debt that Rufus's own confrères, the Franciscans, continued to owe him. Commentaries on the *Sentences* are but footnotes to theology properly speaking, he claims, a sort of appendix in which some biblical notions are clarified and parabiblical issues are discussed, by human and fallible minds. Rufus's own practice, however, diverged from this fully Grossetestian theory of the relationship between theology and *quaestiones*, for the mode of discourse he found congenial issued directly from his own dialectical formation at Paris and bore little resemblance to what Grosseteste prized and practiced, that is, the careful scrutiny of each word of the text, philological elucidation, and moral and spiritual elaboration of the biblical message, intended for the nourishment of meditation and the formation of preachers. Not surprisingly, Rufus felt himself squeezed between a venerable practice that he himself could neither abjure nor follow and an emergent one for which he could offer no satisfactory theoretical justification. One supposes that he was not alone in this uncomfortable situation.

Rufus's discussion of the vexed question concerning the eternity of the world has been edited and studied.[18] He had Grosseteste's *Hexaëmeron* open before him and followed it closely, citing the same authorities and seeing in the pre-Christian position the denial of the created character of the universe. Like Grosseteste and Augustine, he located the source of pagan error in the imagination that falsely represented eternity in terms of indefinitely extended time. On occasion Rufus diverged from the former Oxford master. For example, when arguing against the idea that the divine creativity may be subject to any form of necessity, he placed a greater accent upon the eternal, free causality. The resulting contingency of creatures and their dependence on God's will must be balanced, he felt, to avoid all suggestion of arbitrariness on God's part. Is the universe temporally posterior to eternity? How is eternity prior to time? Was the world creatable from eternity? Rufus was noticeably more intrigued by the intellectual puzzles involved in the relationship between time and eternity than Grosseteste had been, and his arguments gained in sophistication over those propounded by his source. Besides the *Hexaëmeron*, he turned up Grosseteste's treatise on the finitude of motion and time in the library of the house where he lived, and evidently gained from its perusal. Prominent among the sources of his discussion was

Maimonides, whom Grosseteste had only mentioned. Rufus did not think highly of his book: it should be read either with caution or not at all, he declared, since there are many false and frivolous things in it.

Curiously, Rufus often appears to quote the *Hexaëmeron* of Grosseteste through Fishacre (on the harmfulness of astrology, for instance), even though he himself had direct access to it. He took over the triple distinction of the natural, reformed, and deformed image of God in man. He passed over the metaphysics of light in silence, and opposed Grosseteste's theology of the absolute predestination of Christ, advancing a soberly soteriological perspective on the reasons for the Incarnation.

In a word, Rufus borrowed extensively from Grosseteste, but in certain questions he succeeded in developing his own positions while grappling with the thought of the former regent—positions that incline more to the newer Aristotelian framework of reference than to the spiritual commentary on the Bible, or to Neoplatonism, both of which Grosseteste had favored. Much of the intrinsic interest of his thought must lie in the relative confidence with which he expounded Aristotle's ideas and applied them within theology, as well as in his apparent struggle to come to grips with the challenges presented by a new intellectual framework, one with which the older generation at Oxford had not been confronted in the same way.

Roger Bacon's vituperative outburst directed at Rufus remains largely unexplained. Why should Bacon call him "very stupid," and even "mad"? Raedts identifies three characteristics that he attributes to the best-authenticated writings of this author: a florid, exclamatory, and irritating manner of writing; an intellectual diffidence that amounts to indecisiveness; and a pervasive lack of organization. Bacon, of course, was intemperate in his judgments; yet he was rarely altogether wide of the mark. Rufus's idiosyncratic, not to say displeasing, form of expression, together with his too-frequent passivity before selected authorities and his recurrent "nescios," may well be what drew upon him the merciless strictures of his intolerant fellow Franciscan.

CONCLUSION

Much still remains to be done before the picture of Oxford University during its formative and early years can be filled with all the detail the sources can be made to yield. Some of its features, such as faculty regulations, are likely to remain for the most part a matter of guesswork. A great deal of what was written by masters has disappeared. As good as nothing is known with any certainty of the teaching of the arts there between the time of John Blund, in the earliest years of the century, and that of Adam of Buckfield, who was active around 1250. To add to the present obscurity of our knowledge, a number of extant writings by early masters of theology remain still to be edited, as we have had several occasions to note. These comprise for the most part biblical commentaries and sermons, and include several substantial writings by Robert Grosseteste. The history of early Oxford theology will one day be written with much greater precision and richness of detail than are to be found in this study, but it is unlikely that the general outline of the story told here will be very significantly altered by further research.

In the 1260s Roger Bacon looked back on the evolution of theology at Paris and Oxford. From his own (admittedly rather singular) point of view he drew a picture of decline verging upon the betrayal of truth. He bewailed the "replacement" of the source of Christian faith, the Bible, by novelties. The newer Parisian practice of making the *Sentences* the object of the ordinary lectures was the principal novelty he denounced.

The introduction of the *Sentences* at Oxford was accompanied by controversy and provoked opposition. However, the ecclesiastical authority responsible for the university, in the person of Bishop Grosseteste, found itself unable to enforce the traditional approach to the teaching of theology and failed in the attempt to keep the exposition of the Bible in its unchallengeably central place. A statute of the university, dating from the year of the bishop's death (1253), in effect recognized the existing lack of consensus among the masters and attempted to enshrine a compromise by allowing a choice to the theologian preparing to incept: he must hold lectures on a canonical book of the Bible, or on the *Sentences*, or on the *Historia Scholastica* (of Peter Comestor); and he must of course preach.[1] This formal proposal took account of the apprehensions felt by some concerning the increasing dominance of the *Sentences* in the formation of theologians at Paris and the clearly discernible trend in the same direction at Oxford. Whether the compromise had any real effect on teaching practices is not clear; at any rate it was formally abandoned in 1267, when the faculty of theology at Oxford capitulated to the ways of Paris and imposed the *Sentences* as the ordinary faculty text. It was precisely the central place accorded to the *Sentences* that Bacon was to deplore as a pernicious novelty.

The same commentator drew attention to the dominant role played by Grosseteste during the early years of the faculty of theology, associating Adam Marsh closely with him in outlook, intellectual convictions, and achievements. In the same breath as he lauded their attainments he regretted the failure at Oxford of their program. Bacon himself was a product not of Oxford but of Paris (which is the reason that he does not figure in this volume); but looking across the channel from Paris he continued to regard Grosseteste's regency at the younger university as a moment of great significance, but one from which the insular institution had proved lamentably unable to draw any lasting profit. In this judgment Bacon was surely close to the truth. Grosseteste was indeed the dominant intellectual personality of the early years, and yet his teaching evidently failed to create a school. Indeed it was Roger Bacon himself rather than any immediate pupil of Grosseteste's or Marsh's who perpetuated important elements of their theological practice, at least in the role of a publicist (admittedly a very isolated and ineffective one) of their outlook. Bacon may have been a Parisian by formation, but his spiritual attachment to Grosseteste and Marsh made him an Oxonian in mentality—if we understand by that term the Oxford of the 1230s.

Grosseteste's explicit preference was to follow in the footsteps of the fathers of the Church, but he also went by untrodden ways. In neither respect was his legacy claimed by his successors. The theological practice of Paris in the years on either side of 1200 gave way to the growing specialization and systematization of theology there, which the decade of the 1220s began to witness. After a time lag, Oxford found itself drawn by the example of the metropolis of ecclesiastical learning. The more personal of the impulses Grosseteste imparted—the mathematical interpretation of some portions of the Old Testament and the application of Greek philology to exegesis—had no effect at all outside of England, and at Oxford itself probably did not outlive the regency of Adam Marsh.

Grosseteste's approach to theological teaching had by the last decade of his teaching career acquired distinctive features. Why did his program fail so completely to leave progeny? One important reason must be that the academic structures of the times simply made no space for the study of Greek by young theologians. The very limited number of men who learned Greek for scholarly purposes did so in their spare time, as it were, and out of a personal conviction regarding its value. They did not teach it or require it of their students, and they were regarded as exceptions, to be admired but not imitated. The idea of a trilingual college for budding theologians was indeed to be launched early in the following century, but it took little real hold upon minds until the Renaissance.

The truth is that it was Paris that set the pace in theology and influenced the curriculum of studies at all other centers in Latin Christendom, during the twelfth and thirteenth centuries; Oxford was no exception to this rule. Grosseteste's mathematics, philology, and translating activity did indeed open up a line of distinctiveness at Oxford, and for a short period of years raised the bare possibility of a theological approach differing from the Parisian norm. However, the likelihood of Oxford at this period developing a particular theological identity was never very great. Even in Grosseteste's own eyes, Paris in its older tradition retained a normative status, in terms of the program of studies; he was not inclined to think of his own innovations as amounting to or requiring a change in the theological curriculum. As Paris changed, the younger scholars at Oxford changed with it, evidently feeling no temptation to develop their own distinctive approach or to link up with any native tradition. The adoption of the *Sentences* spelled the end of Grosseteste's style, both in its firmly traditional and in its innovative aspects—as Bacon rightly observed, when reviewing twenty years of developments of which he himself was a witness. Oxford, it is true, was never quite submerged by Parisian scholasticism (as Duns Scotus and Ockham were to prove), but the opportunity for a real distinctiveness, the chance that Grosseteste created toward the close of his regency, was lost with his removal to Lincoln.

There is some truth to the suggestion that Paris and Oxford "received" philosophy and science into their theology, in ways that began to diverge toward mid-century.[2] To the Paris condemnations of teaching from the natural and metaphysical works of Aristotle (1210; 1215) there is nothing that corresponds at Oxford. Parisian theologians, on the other hand, did not write studies of Aristotelian works in the way that Grosseteste did of the *Posterior Analytics* and the *Physics*, during his regency. It remains true that the incorporation of philosophical content into theology, together with the idea that theology itself must look more like a rational science and even *be* more like one, was a feature of Paris before it can be said truly to have affected the Oxford climate. Between Grosseteste and Robert Kilwardby Oxford masters without exception regarded philosophy as the *ancilla* (or handmaid) of Christian wisdom and cultivated it deliberately in those terms. Some of them studied Aristotle very seriously, particularly concerning the eternity of the world, yet it was from the biblical and Christian standpoint that their arguments and refutations were conducted: not even methodological reasons could induce them to move completely inside the philosophical perspective; the divinely created character of the universe was not to be bracketed by John Peckham any more than it had been by Grosseteste or Thomas of York. Theology at Paris tended to become more philosophical in its articulation, foreshadowing and preparing the great period of speculative scholasticism, but at Oxford theology was queen and philosophy remained at her service.

A SAMPLE OF
GROSSETESTE'S PREACHING

A Sermon of Robert Grosseteste on Galatians 5:24

Introduction

In a sermon on the words of St. Paul, "And they that are Christ's, have crucified their flesh, with the vices and concupiscences" (Gal. 5:24; Douai Version), Grosseteste expressed that interior spirituality of the cross, a spirituality that he shared, notably, with the Franciscans. The sermon is included in his sermon collection. It has recently been edited and studied.[1] Brief though it is, it repays attention, for it instantiates its author's biblical and practical approach both to theology and to the interior life of the believer. It is carefully constructed. Its substance could in fact be conveyed by means of a series of diagrams of cruciform outline. The variations on the cross theme were designed in order to facilitate their memorization by alert listeners. John Wyclif admired this sermon and summarized it in *On Civil Lordship*. A long extract from it has turned up in Middle English, in a Lollard collection of sermons. No date of composition can be assigned to the sermon. I have edited the Latin text from four manuscripts, three of them conserved in the Bodleian Library, Oxford, and the other in the British Library.

Translation

"And they that are Christ's, have crucified their flesh, with the vices and concupiscences."

177

1. We may take "flesh" in this verse to mean the very substance of our human flesh and body, together with the acts that are natural to the members of the body. The vices are evil wills, along with their acts. The concupiscences are desires of feeling, which set themselves in motion even against the rule of reason. According to the Apostle, "they that are Christ's" are required to crucify all three of these. But [we may ask], since "crucifying" means "nailing to the cross," to which cross are the above to be nailed? I maintain that they are to be nailed to more than one.

Now, "they that are Christ's" begin by preparing a cross for themselves in their mind. For from the center of the mind, which is love or the will, they aim their love upward to God, to love Him above all things. From that very same center they aim love at their friends, to love them in God "as themselves." Furthermore, they aim love at their enemies, to love them "as themselves," for God's sake. Now these two extensions of conscious love, that is, to friends and enemies, are like the two arms of a cross extended to the right and to the left. In the fourth place they aim their love at their flesh, since [it is written that] "no man ever hated his own flesh" [Eph. 5:29]; and they aim it also at other bodily creatures, in order to love them to the extent that they are matter for the knowledge, love, and praise of God. Since these creatures are of lower dignity than man, the love that is extended to them is like that cross-line that is directed from the center downward.

2. And so, just as in the physical cross the four lines forming the cross are drawn from a unique central point (one reaching upward, two going out to the right and left, and the fourth extending downward), in the same way it comes about spiritually in the cross of love, that the love of God is a line working its way upward; the love of friends a line stretching out to the right; the love of enemies a line going left; and the love of one's own flesh and of other corporeal creatures a line reaching downward. Thus in this cross the flesh is crucified, since all the works that are done through the members of the body are directed in accordance with one of these four loves.

3. In Christ the man this cross of love was present, for he directed his human love upward toward the Father, and to the right, as it were, toward his friends, to his enemies to the left, and to corporeal creatures, as it were, downward. Now that cross of love it was which made him mount the cross of wood. For out of love for the Father he, who was "obedient unto death" [Phil. 2:8], willed to be nailed to the wood of the cross, in order to redeem both friend and foe and to restore the other creatures to their ancient dignity. Thus we are required to join the cross of our love to that cross of love

which was in Christ the man, and through the mediation of that cross to the wood of his cross, in order that, finally, we may crucify "our flesh with the vices and concupiscences" on the wood of the cross of Christ.

4. But the cross of love is unavoidably accompanied in our case by the cross of penance. For he who loves God, and loves his friend and his enemy, and also the creatures of the world, grieves and does penance for the sins he has committed against God and against his friend, his enemy, and the creatures of the world. And this penance, once it is divided into four parts, is spread out like a cross. Since *contrition* also, which inseparably accompanies the aforesaid love, stretches as it were upward in hatred of sin, and downward, *letting go* of the object of sin, and to the left and right, as it were, toward *confession* and *satisfaction*; in the cross of love there is therefore a twofold cross of penance, in each one of which the flesh is crucified, when the flesh is punished in accordance with the requirements of the four parts of penance enumerated above. There can be no doubt that on these crosses the vices of the flesh meet their final extinction, when the concupiscences are mortified.

5. According to Rhabanus, however, the four cardinal virtues make up a cross, since they go out from the single root of charity in the following manner: *prudence* stretches upward from charity to take the upper place in the cross-form; *justice*, which "gives to each one what is due to him," has the downward place; *fortitude*, in turn, reaches out to the right; and *temperance* to the left. Doubtless, this cross of quadripartite virtue is present in that cross of fourfold love that we have already delineated: the flesh is crucified, "with its vices and concupiscences," on the cross of the virtues in the same way as it is on the cross of love.

6. According to Rhabanus, furthermore, in his book *On the Cross*, the fourfold Gospel, and in addition the seven gifts of the Holy Spirit enumerated by Isaiah [Is. 11:2–3], and also the eight Beatitudes that Truth itself lists in Matthew [Mt. 5:3–12], are laid out in the form of a cross. In each of these the flesh is crucified, the vices are put to death, and the concupiscences are mortified, in the way that we have outlined above. For in the cross of love there are to be found the cross of the keeping of the Gospel teaching, the cross of the Seven Gifts, and likewise even the cross of the Eight Beatitudes.

7. From another point of view: granted that heaven is as high up as could be and hell equivalently far down, the way between them is like a line mounting from the lowest to the highest place. On the other hand, the extension from the beginning of the world to its end is like a latitudinal line, which, on being joined to the former line, makes a cross shape. On this cross also

we can crucify the "flesh and its vices and concupiscences." We do this when we think of the punishments of hell, and then mount up from these to meditate on the joys of heaven, after which we concentrate upon the state of paradise, man's dignity in it, and his fall from it; and from that extend our consideration to the final end of the world and the fearful judgment. Who, concentrating his attention upon this, will not take charge of the works of the flesh, and kill the vices and reduce the concupiscences, when [he finds that] fear, coming from one direction, inhibits him from evil, even as the sweetness of good things, coming from the other, exerts its powerful attraction over him?

ON CHRISTIAN LIBERTY

*Extracts from Grosseteste's Commentary
on Galatians, Chapters 4–6*

Introduction

In his Letter to the Galatians, St. Paul argued vehemently against "false teachers" who would reimpose circumcision upon all believers in Christ, whether of Jewish or of gentile origin. Grosseteste's deep interest in the beginnings of Christianity expressed itself in a commentary on the Letter (see chap. 7). This writing reflects the character and quality of his teaching during the last part of his regency. It is an ambitious work, for the commentator's preparatory reading was thorough. He was using a Greek copy of the New Testament, as is shown by his knowledge of the vocabulary and semantics of the Pauline discourse. References to the lengthy commentary of St. Jerome on the same letter are frequent, as are quotations from it. Grosseteste had a rounded knowledge of the exegetical tradition, both Greek and Latin, of the Letter to the Galatians, something that enabled him to write with erudition and depth. Yet his purpose was the advanced instruction of preachers and teachers of the faith. The commentary has been critically edited (McEvoy, 1995). No translation of it exists.[1]

Chap. 4, v. 31 to 5, v. 1

He continues: *And so, brothers*, and so on, as though to say: from the Scripture quoted predicting the future, it follows now that *we are not sons of the maidservant*, that is, of the Old Testament or the Synagogue, or the spirit of fear, or of Scripture understood according to the letter, *but* we are *sons of the free woman*, that is, of grace, of the New Testament and the Church, of the spirit of adoption, and of Scripture understood according to the Spirit. Therefore, where it is said that we ought not to return to slavery (and in case we should ascribe to ourselves that liberty), he shows that we are free not merely by the freedom of our free will but *by the freedom with which Christ has freed us*, giving himself on the cross as the price for us, and so liberating us from the combined debts of evil desire, of the death of Gehenna, and of satisfaction for the first man, and also from servitude under the yoke of sin and of the ceremonial law; and also granting the grace by which our free will could avoid evil and do good. The philosopher Seneca says: "To serve philosophy is true freedom"; and again, the same: "Contempt for the body is true freedom"; and again, the same: "If you seek to be freed, then be the slave of no thing, no necessity, no chance happenings." Christ himself is the Wisdom of the Father and the one and only philosophy; to be conformed to him with obedient will, and so to serve him, is the only true liberty. He himself through grace brings about in us this conformity and full power of operating, and grants to us for love of him to despise the pleasures of the body and to be a slave to no passing reality, no necessity, no chance happenings.

> Chap. 5, v. 1: "For freedom Christ has set
> us free. Stand firm, therefore, and do not
> submit again to a yoke of slavery."

But he calls the burden of the law a yoke, as the Apostle Peter did in Acts, when he asked, *Why do you try to impose a yoke which neither we nor our fathers were able to bear?* [Acts 15:10] The Law he calls a yoke, meaning, according to Jerome, that it is "hard and difficult, an imposition that consumes its keepers day and night with heavy labor." Now a yoke weighs on two and joins them forcibly to each other despite their resistance, lest they be free to walk in different directions. So the Law was given in order to compel, by means of fear of punishment, the spirit and the flesh, which are struggling against each other, to walk the way of the commandments, not in different directions. Now the New Law was given in order that under it spirit and flesh should walk agreeably, quickened and attracted by the sweetness of love; whence this is the law of liberty. For what is done freely in virtue of love is done liberally.

Chap. 5, v. 13: "For you, brothers, have been called to liberty."

Because they could say, "But we are freed: we can do freely what we like, and so return to the carnal understanding of the law and provide for the care of the flesh in our desires," the Apostle counters by saying, *Only do not give your liberty as an occasion to the flesh*, as much as to say: *this liberty*, with which you can do what you will: *do not give* it *as an occasion to the flesh*, or of the flesh, that is, of the carnal observance of the law of carnal concupiscence and will. For he is truly free who does what he wills, not with an erring will nor with a will subject to the slavery of the concupiscence of the flesh: in that case he would be the slave of his slave.

Again, because they could say, "If we are free and have been withdrawn from the yoke of slavery to the law, then we ought to serve no one, nor should we be subjected to any yoke," the Apostle once again rejoins wisely, saying that they must *serve one another by the charity* of the spirit and be subjected to *the sweet yoke* of God and *the light burden* [cf. Matt. 11:30], which is charity. This, therefore, is liberty: to do what you will, with a will that is upright and in command of the flesh. Such a will wishes to do to the other what it wishes to be done by the other to itself [cf. Matt. 7:12]; therefore it serves freely and liberally the utility of each "other." This liberty, then, does not exclude but includes the servitude that is of one another, and it places on the neck the sweet yoke of the love of God and neighbor. For this liberty wishes—as is only proper—to be loved by all, whence also it loves all in the way that it ought; that is to say, God more than itself, the neighbor as itself, but the body and bodily irrational creatures less than itself. Therefore this liberty does not serve the law of the flesh, it does not serve the elements of the world, it does not serve the will of the flesh; for it cannot serve these, unless by diminishing liberty and subjecting its dignity to something lower and worse that pushes and draws it down. On the other hand, it serves (without being diminished or suffering loss, rather indeed with elevation and increase of itself) the majesty of God, the special utility of the neighbor and the finality of lower things. And so, by serving thus, through charity it fulfills the whole law.

*Chap. 5, v. 18: "But if you
are led by the Spirit, you are not
subject to the law."*

He continues: *But if you are led by the Spirit, you are not under the law*. That is, if you follow the guidance of the higher reason that is conformed to the Holy Spirit, *you are not under the law*, that is, you do not follow the law through fear of punishment, but being with the law you follow it through love of justice. Or thus: *you are not under the law*, that is to say, you do not require the written law as the giver of instructions. For he who by virtue of true loving choice [*dilectio*] follows the guidance of the Spirit wishes to each his best good and no evil; indeed he even hates evil occurring to anyone else. Hence true love, spontaneously and without the Scriptures commanding, avoids killing, adultery, and theft; indeed it does, effects, or thinks simply nothing evil; on the contrary, it honors parents and gives back to each what is his own. In this way it is not under the law, since it does not require the law. For whatever the law lays down concerning good behavior or forbids regarding evil behavior, that is just what love would do by itself and without the precept or prohibition of the law. That is why the Apostle says elsewhere, "The law is not imposed on the just man" [I Tim. 1:19]: for in what way is it imposed upon one who would fulfill it even if it were not there? Upon the just man, therefore, only the ceremonial law is imposed, not the law of the moral commandments.

Now this, once again, is read in accordance with the consequence of the Apostle's doctrine concerning the ending of the Torah, and the sense is: *If you are led by the Spirit*, that is, by the spiritual intelligence of the written law, *you are not under the law*, that is, under the carnal and historical understanding of the law, and you are no longer *debtors of the law* to be kept carnally. Jerome raises the question here, whether Moses and the Prophets at once "were impelled by the Spirit *and* lived under the law; [but he concludes that] the Apostle denies this here." Either they were impelled by the Spirit and were not under the law, or else "living under the law they did not have the Spirit—something that it would be utterly wrong to believe of such great men." He gives his own view: they were not themselves under the law, but on account of the weak they were under the law, in order to profit these; to the weak they were made in a way under the law, keeping the law by a dispensation.

Chap. 5, v. 19: "Now the works of the flesh
are obvious."

They are, however, called *works of the flesh*, not because they all pertain to the desire of sense, which in a strict sense is called the concupiscence of the flesh, but because they all pertain to the soul that is not conformed to the Spirit, but subjected to the flesh by the perversion of reason. Now some of the list [of vices] pertain properly to the will of the flesh, like fornication, uncleanness, self-indulgence, drunkenness, and riotousness. However, others enumerated here do not pertain properly to the will of the flesh but are among the vices that do not occur necessarily through the body: for the devil has vices of this kind even though he does not have flesh. Alternatively (according to Augustine), he here calls "flesh," man determined to live according to himself. . . .

He continues: *But the fruit of the Spirit is love, joy, peace*, and so on. The works of the flesh are done by us alone, and are called "works" of the flesh because they are, as it were, laborious and heavy, not smoothed out by the help of the Holy Spirit. On the other hand, those works that are good are done not by us alone but by the cooperation of the Spirit from above, wherefore they are called the fruit of the Spirit; for they are not burdensome, but through the aid of the Spirit they are light and by his sweetness they remake the soul. Now, the freedom of the will, that will which bears fruit in the Holy Spirit, is given to our soul like a seed. Therefore, whether the fruit is of the Holy Spirit and our spirit conformed to the Holy Spirit, that is, the fruit of the uncreated Spirit in our created spirit, or whether the fruit is our created spirit [reformed] by the uncreated Spirit, it brings about those virtues that are enumerated in what follows, of which the first is *charity*, that is to say, the root and cause and power of the other virtues, as upon it *the whole law and the prophets depend* [Matt. 22:40]. And it is only right that since the Holy Spirit is of his essence love [*dilectio*], the first thing that he forms in our Spirit is a quality of loving choice that, so long as we love the incorporeal [is invincible] by any sensual pleasure, and likewise by any desire or fear. For if it could be overcome, it would not have the greatness that merits the name of charity. If therefore charity is true, although we are able while in this life to cast it away of our own volition, yet we cannot lose it against our will.

And so out of charity as out of a root there come forth like branches the remaining virtues. Now, charity bursts forth at once in *joy*, for by loving choice of God and neighbor, in God it has God in itself and the neighbor in God, and in addition it has itself by loving choice of itself. But these are the closest goods: God and the neighbor in God, and the loving choice itself by which each of the others is chosen and loved. Therefore, charity holds the greatest goods, which it greatly desires.

Now, joy is the expansion of the soul coming from the possession of the good desired. But as Jerome says, the Stoics distinguish between joy and delight, saying that joy is "elation of mind about things worthy of the one experiencing elation, whereas delight is unrestrained elation of mind that knows no measure, even in things that are vices."

Again, from charity *peace, patience, and long-suffering* shoot forth. For, as it was said, charity is invincible; therefore it may not be disturbed by any passions. But, as Jerome remarks, *peace* is with you "if a tranquil mind is not disturbed by any of the passions"; and this peace will be completely perfect when the flesh will in no respect revolt against the Spirit, but with the flesh subjected to the Spirit, the heart and the flesh of the whole man *will exult in the living God* [Ps. 83:3]. Here, however, this peace will be possessed proportionately to charity, and just as charity is invincible with regard to lapse, so also peace itself is imperturbable in respect of fall. And since charity is invincible (*for many waters have not been able to extinguish charity nor streams to drown it* [Cant. 8:7] and, as the Apostle says, *no creature will be able to separate us from the love of God, which is Christ our Lord* [Rom. 8:38–39])— because, as I say, it is so invincible, it stands unmoved before every impulse of fear and tribulation; for which reason charity is patient. For *patience* is not to be crushed or stricken by any degree of fear or tribulation.

Furthermore, because charity is invincible, just as it is not moved or stricken by the magnitude of things to be feared, so also it is not tired when they go on and on; whence charity is *long-suffering*. Not to be worn down by the continuance of fearful things [patience] is furthermore not to be terrified by their extent. Moreover, he who truly loves consents to the justice of God, whence (since no one suffers tribulation unjustly) even in his tribulation he joins in the rejoicing at the justice of God, and looks upon that tribulation, because it is just and fitting, as a benefit, and upon the giver of the tribulation as the conferer of a benefit. That is why, with soul unmoved by the magnitude of the tribulation and its continuance, he not only bears it with patience and long-suffering, but even pays out benefit through *goodness* and kindness. We have it on the testimony of Jerome that, as the followers of Zeno define it, goodness is virtue that is of benefit, or virtue from which benefits derive; or affection that is typically a spring of benefits. And *kindness*, on the other hand, similarly is in the Stoic definition a virtue that is ready freely to do good. And although goodness and kindness agree in this, they differ inasmuch as goodness can be the sadder, and wrinkled of brow with strict conduct—sufficient indeed to act well and to deliver what is required, but not able to be attractive in relationship and to invite all with its sweetness. However, kindness, as Jerome says, "is a mild, welcoming, tranquil virtue, adapted to the company of all the good, inviting to friendship with itself, in address appealing and in conduct balanced." Goodness, therefore, acts for the advantage of all in so far as it can; but kindness is agreeable and pleasant to all. . . .

According to Jerome and the Greek text, after faith in this list there is placed *gentleness*, a virtue that (as Jerome reminds us) is opposed to wrath, quarrels, and disagreements, and that is never provoked to things contrary to its nature.

So gentleness cannot be provoked to wrath, quarrelling, and disagreement. In a similar strain, Augustine and Gregory describe gentleness as the virtue by which we restrain our soul from anger and dispute, while Chrysostom considers gentleness to be the virtue by which we easily and quickly put behind us all things that bring harm. And so this virtue follows well from charity, since loving choice, as we have already remarked, counts injury a benefit and the one doing the injury a benefactor.

Furthermore, from charity there follows *moderation*, since true loving choice does not exceed the measure; moderation is the bringing back of deeds and words to limit and measure. Again, from charity follows *continence*, for he who loves restrains himself from all things: even if they are permitted they are not required [I Cor. 6:12ff.]. For this is the proper nature of continence: abstinence even from what is permitted, just as chastity is restraint from what is forbidden, together with the right use of what is permitted.

Chap. 6, v. 3

He continues: *If someone thinks he is something, though he is really nothing, he deceives himself*, as though to say: "Let each one bear the burden of the other, and let him seek not only those things that are his own but those that are the other's. For if someone who is seeking only what are his own interests, not pouring out the true worth of his mercy upon others, thinks himself to be in himself and through himself something, whereas a man of that kind is nothing, he deceives himself." For believing himself to be self-sufficient, being content with himself he attempts to show that he will receive a reward with his goods. But in this he is deluded and deceived, just as if the eye in the body wished to see for itself alone and not for the work of the hand or the stride of the foot, thinking that it would nevertheless receive the reward due to members serving well, it would in fact not receive it, but would induce corruption by seeing for itself alone and not for the other members [cf. I Cor. 12:14–26]. But he who looks solely to his own advantage, not considering the common utility, will lose not only the common utility but his own as well.

Or understand thus: Bear your burdens for one another, and let no one, however great, believe that he does not need to be supported by someone else, as though he alone were able to carry himself. For just as a member in the body cannot be content with itself alone unless it receives aid from the other members (as, for instance, the foot is incapable of walking or the hand of working without the eyes looking before, nor is the eye of any use in seeing unless the foot walks according to it or the hand works according to it), so in the body that is the Church: he who, without being aided and supported by the other members of the Church, thinks that he is something, whereas without their support he is nothing, deceives himself; for he loses both the common good of all the members and his own, despite having convinced himself that he would obtain both. Therefore burdens are to be borne reciprocally, because no one is anything unless he at one and the same time carries the rest and is carried by them, just as a member is worth nothing in the body unless it both receives help from the other members and in its own turn repays the help given it.

APPENDIX 3

ON EDUCATIVE LOVE

Introduction

In his comment on Galatians 4:19 ("My little children, whom I labor to bring forth again . . .") Grosseteste allowed himself to reflect in a personal way on the role of the master in teaching. He stated his belief that teaching is an expression of love that, as it were, procreates the word and idea in the mind of the student and brings it to birth in the world of action. The teacher is like a father, but he is even more like a mother, giving birth to spiritual children. Grosseteste explores the metaphors of procreation, parenthood, and childbirth as expressions of the unitive power of love. The love of the *magister* for his disciple aims at unity, and if union comes about, something is procreated in the mind of the learner—a word is formed in his consciousness. In the conviction that all love seeks to bring together the lovers and to make them as one we can recognize at once the Augustinian influence at work here.

The inspiration for this passage is to be sought not in any of the patristic commentaries or in the Gloss, but in the prayer composed by St. Anselm of Canterbury to St. Paul. Thinking of the same verse of Galatians, Anselm wrote,

> O St. Paul, where is he that was called the nurse of the faithful, caressing his children? Who is that affectionate mother who declares everywhere that she is in labor for her sons? Sweet nurse, sweet mother, who are the

sons with whom you are in labor, and whom you nurse, but those whom by teaching the faith of Christ you bear and instruct?

There is a striking similarity between Platonic love and Grossetestian educative love. Among other things, neither writer was embarrassed about the essential inequality in the friendship between teacher and pupil. The love of the good is the crystallizer of friendship. In this passage the author shares with his readers his own experience as a teacher and preacher, shaped as that was by the influence of the Church and the schools upon his life.[1]

Galatians, chap. 4, v. 19:
"My little children, whom I am in labor
to bring forth again, until Christ
be formed in you."

When he says *little children*, he shows a parental affection for them. Elsewhere he presents himself as a father, saying "if you have ten thousand teachers, still you have not many fathers" [cf. I Cor. 4:15]. Here he speaks out of maternal affection, which is the more severe. The words he speaks recall those of Moses: *Have I not conceived* in my womb *this whole people?* [Num. 11:12]. These words teach us how much love we owe to disciples and what great pangs we are to endure, in order to bear them to Christ. Furthermore, by using the diminutive he conveys two things, namely, at once how young they are in Christ and how tender his own love for them is. For we develop the habit of calling by pet names those small children whom we love tenderly.

Now the preacher stands [as a father] to those he teaches, for he casts the seed of the Word out of which they may be given life in Christ. And he is at the same time their mother, for he devotes the affection of his love to the minds of those he teaches, and it is really he who conceives the seed deposited in the understanding of his hearers. He conceives by the unheard-of love for them with which he is aflame that they may understand the Word, to love it and do it. It is he who conceives, rather than those who listen to him. Therefore, when at the price of the teacher's love, that love which becomes one with the mind of the disciple, the disciple's mind receives the Word in loving intelligence, that very love coming from the teacher it is which in the union receives the seed of the Word and conceives. The seed conceived is there in that union coagulated with the words in the memory; it is strengthened by deliberation as to how the word conceived may be brought forth into deed. Like a fetus in the womb, it is formed through reflection and effort and struggle; it is being brought to birth, as it were, and when the word is delivered in the deed, behold! the fetus is born.

Now since it is the painstaking and watchful love of the teacher that brings about this entire process in the learner, it is not without reason that educative love is compared to the maternal role. And when, by long-continued care taken in reprehending and rewarding, the teacher succeeds in getting the action once brought forth to be repeated constantly and from that frequent repetition to be strengthened, he is bringing the child, like one rearing it, through the stages of growth until it reaches full maturity.

In the measure that this kind of begetting transcends carnal generation the teacher should be the more ready to procreate. As father, his desire to beget is the stronger, but as mother, he is rather solicitous to bear the child, is more devoted in feeding it, more fearful of a miscarriage, and more grief-stricken should it occur, more tearful over a stillbirth, more joyful should he witness the development of the child. In saying *again* ["whom I am in labor to bring forth *again*"], he implies that the Galatians were born but have died; he longs like a mother, with all the anxiety of grief, to bear them again into life.

NOTES

PREFACE

1. *The Philosophy of Robert Grosseteste*, Oxford 1982 (corrected reprint and paperback, 1986).

I. FROM SCHOOLS TO UNIVERSITY

1. This chapter, devoted to learning at Oxford during the later twelfth century and to the founding of the university, in 1214, is heavily indebted for the shape and for most of the detail of its narrative to the following study by the leading authority on the subject: R. W. Southern, "From Schools to University" (1986).

2. Ibid., pp. 15–20.

3. J. Goering, *William de Montibus (c.1140–1213)* (1992). This outstanding study of William's life and writings offers first-time editions of many of his works. William was known as "Lincolniensis," until by the middle of the thirteenth century the appellation passed definitively (although not without some ensuing confusion) to Robert Grosseteste.

4. The leading authority on Alexander Nequam was the late R. W. Hunt, whose study of his life and writings was published posthumously: *The Schools and the Cloister* (1984). Alexander's unedited sermons, and also his poetry, pose problems of authenticity that are explored critically in this learned work.

5. "If you are good you may come; if evil, strictly not." The reply may be translated, "If you wish, I will come; if not, there's no more to be said." The words "Tu autem" open a formula for bringing a liturgical prayer to a close (e.g., "Tu autem, Domine, miserere nobis").

6. Transl. Southern, "From Schools to University" (1986), p. 22.

7. Hunt, *The Schools and the Cloister* (1984), pp. 125–149, draws up a catalogue of the manuscripts and editions of Alexander's varied output.

8. Alexander Nequam, *Speculum Speculationum*, ed. R. Thompson (1990).

9. Iohannes Blund, *Tractatus de anima*, ed. D. A. Callus and R. W. Hunt (1970).

10. C. H. Lawrence, *St. Edmund of Abingdon* (1960). One of the writings referred to is by Matthew Paris; it has recently been translated and annotated by Lawrence: *The Life of St. Edmund by Matthew Paris*. Translated, edited, and with a biography by C. H. Lawrence (1996).

11. In the deposition he made in view of the canonization process: "specialissimus scolaris, auditor et socius."

12. Helen P. Forshaw, *Edmund of Abingdon. Speculum Religiosorum and Speculum Ecclesiae* (1973).

13. Lawrence, *St. Edmund of Abingdon* (1960), p. 118. One of the seven, Stephen of Lexington, was to be elected Abbot of Clairvaux, in 1243.

14. Lawrence, *St. Edmund of Abingdon* (1960), p. 182.

15. Southern, "From Schools to University" (1986), p. 25.

2. A LIFE POORLY KNOWN

1. J. Goering and F. A. C. Mantello, "*Notus in Iudea Deus*: Robert Grosseteste's Confessional Formulary in Lambeth Palace MS 499" (1987), p. 272.

2. These and other stories related by Eccleston are printed in McEvoy, *The Philosophy of Robert Grosseteste* (1982), pp. 43–46.

3. Transl. by R. W. Southern, *Robert Grosseteste: The Growth of an English Mind in Medieval Europe,* 2nd ed. (1992), p. 65. On de Vere, see J. Barrow, "A Twelfth-Century Bishop and Literary Patron: William de Vere," in *Viator* 18 (1987) 175–189.

4. D. A. Callus, "Robert Grosseteste as Scholar," in *Robert Grosseteste, Scholar and Bishop*, ed. Callus, Oxford, 1955, pp. 1–69.

5. R. W. Southern, *Robert Grosseteste* (1992).

6. This briefest of summaries cannot hope to do justice to Sir Richard Southern's hypothesis in all its novelty, intricacy, and learning. The interested reader should become acquainted, at first hand and at leisure, with (preferably) the second edition of this richly documented book.

7. M. Haren, *Medieval Thought: The Western Intellectual Tradition from Antiquity to the Thirteenth Century*, 2nd ed. (1992); see pp. 227–235. I have taken the translation of Sutton's statement from pp. 234–235.

8. It is once again Haren who deserves the credit for this hypothesis.

9. Southern, *Robert Grosseteste* (1992), p. lxii.

10. Southern, *Robert Grosseteste* (1992), pp. l–lv.

3. THE COUNCIL OF LYONS AND ITS AFTERMATH, THROUGH GROSSETESTE'S EYES

1. The most detailed and well-rounded account of the council (including a selection of the official acts in translation) that I have come across is H. Wolter, S. J., and H. Holstein, S. J., *Lyon I et Lyon II*, Paris, 1965.

2. A. Melloni, *Innocenzo IV*, Genoa, 1990. On Grosseteste and the pope, see pp. 221–228.

3. On the canonization of Edmund, see C. H. Lawrence, *The Life of St. Edmund by Matthew Paris,* Oxford, 1997, pp. 90–99.

4. Grosseteste's continuing contact with the family of Edmund is witnessed to by his appointment of Margery of Abingdon as prioress of Catesby, performed in 1245, when as bishop of Lincoln he intervened and quashed a previous election.

5. J. Goering, *Viator* 18 (1987), p. 262.

6. *Epistolae* 71–72, 90–95, and the treatise, 127.

7. See Wolter and Holstein, pp. 122–123, for a nuanced judgment on Innocent's achievements and failures.

8. J. le Goff, *Saint Louis*, Paris, 1996, pp. 783–785.

9. Salimbene, *Chronica* 4, Monumenta Germaniae Historica, Scriptores xxxii, pp. 226–232.

10. S. Gieben, "Robert Grosseteste at the Papal Curia, Lyons 1250. Edition of the Documents," in *Collectanea Franciscana* 41 (1971): 340–393. The recent study, which I summarize in what follows in this chapter, is by J. Goering, "Robert Grosseteste at the Papal Curia" (1997).

11. This deep conviction found expression through the terms "hierarch" and "hierarchy," which Grosseteste took over from the Pseudo-Dionysius and made a central part of his own thought; see the detailed and convincing argument to this effect in C. Taylor Hogan, "Pseudo-Dionysius and the Ecclesiology of Robert Grosseteste," in McEvoy, *Robert Grosseteste: New Perspectives* (1995), pp. 189–213.

12. L. E. Boyle, "Robert Grosseteste and the Pastoral Care" (1979), in *A Distinct Voice: Medieval Studies in Honor of L. E. Boyle, O.P.*, ed. J. Brown and W. P. Stoneman, Notre Dame, 1997, p. 22.

13. See chap. 5 for the later medieval and early modern interpretations.

14. The letter has been critically edited by Frank Mantello, who has also translated it into English. See Mantello, *"Optima Epistola*: A Critical Edition and Translation of Letter 128 of Bishop Robert Grosseteste" (1997). The passages given in translation are adapted from his version.

4. RELATIONSHIP WITH THE MENDICANTS

1. This chapter is heavily indebted to a recent study by Servus Gieben, O.F.M., Cap., "Robert Grosseteste and the Evolution of the Franciscan Order," published in McEvoy, *Robert Grosseteste: New Perspectives* (1995), pp. 215–232.

2. The word translated here as "house" (*locus*) was the authentic name used by Francis's followers for the "place" they temporarily lived in, for in their parlance they, like their founder, deliberately eschewed the overtones of stability conveyed by words such as "house," "monastery," or (religious) "order."

3. Goering and Mantello, "The *Meditaciones* of Robert Grosseteste" (1985), p. 127.

4. See Gieben, "Robert Grossesteste and the Evolution of the Franciscan Order" (1995), p. 219.

5. Ibid., p. 230.

6. Ibid., p. 231.

7. *Memorandum*, transl. R. W. Southern, *Robert Grosseteste* (1992), p. 259.

8. For the influence of Grosseteste on Adam Marsh and Thomas of York, see chap. 12; for his influence on the Franciscan Richard Rufus and the Dominican Richard Fishacre, see chap. 13.

9. The Temple functioned as an international exchange and delivery service, but its officers were careful to avoid usurious practices.

10. They could, of course, actually minister to the Anglo-Norman speakers.

11. Lambert le Bègue (= "the stutterer"), a contemporary of St. Francis, founded a poverty movement known as the Béghards/Béguines.

12. *Chronicle of Lanercost, 1272–1346*, transl. H. Maxwell, Glasgow, 1913, pp. 159–160.

5. THE MYTH OF THE PROTO-REFORMER

1. Goering, "Robert Grosseteste at the Papal Curia" (1997).

2. *John Wyclif and His English Precursors*, transl. from the German with additional notes, by Peter Lorimer, 2 vols. (1878; 2nd ed., 1881; rev. ed., 1884).

3. *The Life and Times of Robert Grosseteste, Bishop of Lincoln*, London (Christian Knowledge Society), 1871. Perry was chiefly responsible, it is said, for the commissioning of the window in the Chapter House of Lincoln Cathedral,

which depicts Grosseteste rebuking Pope Innocent IV in the company of the curia. We may add here that a stained-glass window (1922) dedicated to Grosseteste is found in the St. Andrews Chapel of Great St. Mary's Church, Cambridge, and that the College of Education at Lincoln commemorates Bishop Grosseteste in its title ("The Bishop Grosseteste College of Education").

4. J. Felten, *Robert Grosseteste, Bischof von Lincoln. Ein Beitrag zur Kirchen-und Culturgeschichte des dreizehnten Jahrhunderts,* Freiburg im Breisgau, 1887.

5. *Church and State in the Middle Ages*, Oxford, 1913, p. 170.

6. *Matthew Paris,* Cambridge, 1958; the standard work.

7. Southern, *Robert Grosseteste* (1992), pp. 6–13.

8. My attention was drawn to this passage of the *Dialogus* by Prof. John Kilcullen of Macquarrie University, N.S.W., Australia, who is preparing a critical edition of the work. I have adapted the translation that he kindly sent me.

9. The most recent discussion of the relationship between Wyclif and his source has been given by Southern, *Robert Grosseteste* (1992), pp. 289–307. For the Lollards and Grosseteste, see pp. 307–309.

10. Ibid., pp. 309–313.

11. *The Acts and Monuments of John Foxe*, fourth edition, revised and corrected by the Rev. Josiah Pratt, vol. 2 , London (The Religous Tract Society), 1900; see pp. 523–534: "The Story of Robert Grosthead, Bishop of Lincoln."

12. Gratius Ortwinus, *Fasciculus rerum expetendarum ac fugiendarum, prout ab O.G. editus est Coloniae, A.D. 1535*, London (Edward Brown), 1690 (in-fol., 2 vols). Samuel Pegge preserved some details concerning Brown. A native of Rochester, he was an M.A. and a Fellow of Clare Hall. He was collated to Sundridge by Archbishop William Sancroft and was inducted on 12 February 1689, where he died about Michaelmas in 1698 or 1699. Pegge describes him as "an excellent scholar, a spirited writer, and singularly well versed in the controversy between the Protestants and Romanists." S. Pegge, *The Life of Bishop Grosseteste, the Celebrated Bishop of Lincoln, with an account of the Bishop's Works and an Appendix*, London, 1793, pp. 3–4.

13. Samuel Pegge, *The Life of Robert Grosseteste*.

6. CONTRIBUTION TO PHILOSOPHY

1. Edited for the most part by F. C. Baur in *Die philosophischen Werke des Robert Grosseteste* (1912).

2. Only those works whose authentic character is generally admitted will be discussed here.

3. J. Moreton, "Robert Grosseteste and the Calendar," in McEvoy, *Robert Grosseteste: New Perspectives* (1995), pp. 77–88.

4. Fully translated by Crombie, in Callus, *Robert Grosseteste, Scholar and Bishop* (1955), pp 116–119.

5. Ed. J. McEvoy (1974).

6. Ed. P. Rossi (1981). See Rossi, "Robert Grosseteste on the Object of Scientific Knowledge," in McEvoy, *Robert Grosseteste: New Perspectives* (1995), pp. 53–75.

7. Quoted in McEvoy, *The Philosophy of Robert Grosseteste* (1982), pp. 329–330.

8. A. C. Crombie, *Robert Grosseteste and the Origins of Experimental Science* (1953).

9. A Koyré, "The Origins of Medieval Science: A New Interpretation," in *Diogène* 17 (1957): 1–22. French and German versions exist of this important study: "Les origines de la science moderne: une interprétation nouvelle," in *Diogène* 16 (1956): 24–42; "Die Ursprünge der modernen Wissenschaft: ein neuer Deutungsversuch," in *Diogenes* 4 (1957): 421–448.

10. In his treatise *De lineis, angulis et figuris* ("On Lines, Angles and Figures") Grosseteste proclaimed: "There is an immense usefulness in the consideration of lines, angles and figures, because without them natural philosophy cannot be understood. They are applicable in the universe as a whole and in its parts, without restriction, and their validity extends to related properties, such as circular and rectilinear motion, nor does it stop at action and passion, whether as applied to matter or to sense . . . For all causes of natural effects can be discovered by lines, angles and figures, and in no other way can the reason for their action possibly be known."

11. McEvoy, *The Philosophy of Robert Grosseteste* (1982), pp. 206–222.

12. Ed. R. C. Dales (1963).

13. Edited by Baur (1912). The critical edition is being prepared by N. T. Lewis, who has already published the text of the First Recension: *Mediaeval Studies* (1991), pp. 1–88.

14. K. Hedwig, *Sphaera Lucis* (1980).

15. Ed. F. C. Baur (1912). Several English translations exist, the most accessible of which is *Philosophy in the Middle Ages*, ed. A. Hyman and J. J. Walsh, Indianapolis, 1973, pp. 434–440.

16. *Hexaëmeron* I.8.2, ed. R. C. Dales and S. Gieben (1982), p. 78.

17. Ibid., pp. 223–224.

18. Ibid., p. 222.

19. Dictum 55, MS Cambridge, *Gonville and Caius 380*, fol. 51ᵛ. Cf. Eph. 5:13–14: "But everything exposed by the light becomes visible, for everything that becomes visible is light."

20. S. Gieben, "Robert Grosseteste and Adam Marsh on Light in a Summary Attributed to St. Bonaventure" (1993).

7. EXEGETICAL WRITINGS

1. This work has been noticed along with Grosseteste's philosophical writings (see chap. 6).

2. Edited by J. McEvoy, *Roberti Grosseteste Expositio* (1995), pp. 27–30.

3. By P. W. Rosemann (1995). Rosemann has discussed the *Tabula* in McEvoy, *Robert Grosseteste: New Perspectives* (1995), pp. 321–355.

4. In a Toronto Ph.D. thesis by James R. Ginter. Dr. Ginther has kindly allowed me to see a copy of his work. I am indebted to him for much of the information and many of the views expressed above.

5. Southern, *Robert Grosseteste* (1992), p. 118.

6. J. McEvoy, *Roberti Grosseteste Expositio* (1995).

7. See appendix 2.

8. See appendix 3.

9. Edited by Dales and King (1987). See the study of *De decem mandatis* by J. McEvoy, "Robert Grosseteste on the Ten Commandments" (1991).

10. See chap. 9.

11. Edited by Dales and King (1986).

12. See chap. 9.

13. Edited by Dales and Gieben (1981). A full translation exists: *Robert Grosseteste: On the Six Days of Creation. A Translation of the* Hexaëmeron, by C. F. J. Martin, Oxford (Auctores Britannici Medii Aevi 6 [2]), 1996.

14. See chap. 6.

15. See chap. 9.

16. *Hex.* II.7.1 (pp. 94–95).

17. See chap. 9.

18. *Hex.* III.6.1–8.3 (pp. 106–109).

19. *Hex.* V.9.1–10.8 (pp. 165–170).

20. *Hex.* VIII.2.1. (p. 218).

21. Edited by Baur (1912). The critical edition is being prepared by N. T. Lewis, who has already published the text of the First Recension: *Mediaeval Studies* 53 (1991), pp. 1–88.

22. Southern, *Robert Grosseteste* (1992), chap. 2: "Grosseteste and the Pattern of Scholastic Thought."

23. Edited by J. Goering in *Mediaeval Studies* 44 (1982): 83–109.

24. Southern, *Robert Grosseteste* (1992) , pp. 70–75.

8. GREEK SCHOLARSHIP

1. C. Dionisotti, "On the Greek Studies of Robert Grosseteste" (1988). Her invaluable study goes a long way toward reconstructing Grosseteste's Greek library. I draw upon some of her conclusions in what follows.

2. For a detailed study of Grosseteste's debt to the *Suda*, see C. Dionisotti, "Robert Grosseteste and the Greek Encyclopaedia" (1990). J. B. Lightfoot (1885) and E. Franceschini (1933) were both aware of a connection between the two Byzantine compilations and Grosseteste's translating work. However, Dionisotti was the first to explore it and reveal its extent.

3. MS Leiden, *Bibliotheek der Rijksuniversiteit, Voss. gr. F.2.*

4. London, MS *College of Arms, Arundel 9.*

5. M. Holland, in McEvoy, *Robert Grosseteste: New Perspectives* (1995), pp. 121–147.

6. For Grosseteste's view on language and translation, see J. McEvoy (1981), reprinted in McEvoy (1994).

7. These have all been edited by Meridel Holland in a Harvard Ph.D. thesis (1980), but not as yet published, "An Edition of Three Unpublished Translations by Robert Grosseteste of Three Short Works of John of Damascus." See her article "Robert Grosseteste's Translations of John of Damascus," in *Bodleian Library Record* 11 (1983): 138–154.

8. J. McEvoy, *The Philosophy of Robert Grosseteste* (2nd ed., 1986), pp. 74–90.

9. Edited by H. P. F. Mercken (1973; 1991).

10. He also produced a version of something he called *De laudabilibus boni*s; it seems to be a fragment of the *Eudemian Ethics* of Aristotle.

11. J. McEvoy, "Grosseteste's Reflections on Aristotelian Friendship: A New Commentary on *Nicomachean Ethics* VIII. 8–14," in McEvoy, *Robert Grosseteste: New Perspectives* (1995), pp. 149–168.

12. M. De Jonge, "Robert Grosseteste and the *Testaments of the Twelve Patriarchs*" (1991).

13. The translation was critically edited by Raphael Loewe more than fifty years ago but has not yet been published. For further information, see R. Loewe, "The Medieval Christian Hebraists of England: The *Superscriptio Lincolniensis*" (1957). A publisher is being actively sought.

14. Smalley, *The Study of the Bible in the Middle Ages* (2nd ed., 1951), p. 343.

15. The story in question is printed by D. Wasserstein in McEvoy, *Robert Grosseteste: New Perspectives* (1995), p. 371 (together with a skeptical discussion).

9. PERSONAL THEOLOGICAL STAMP

1. A usually reliable bibliographical tradition attributes to him a commentary on the *De consolatione philosophiae*, but it has never been identified.

2. The most recent attempt is also the most enlightening: Southern, *Robert Grosseteste* (2nd ed., 1992): "Grosseteste's Theological Vision," pp. 205–232, expounds successively the theology of creation; the centrality of man; the unity of

God and nature; the necessity of God's entry into nature, the pastoral theology (*Château d'amour*); and theology of reconciliation.

3. *De cessatione legalium* I.9.4–7 (pp. 49–51).

4. Grosseteste admired Hugh of St. Victor, the founding figure of this Augustinian abbey, and studied his commentary on the *Celestial Hierarchy*. He likewise knew John Sarracen's versions of the four writings of the Pseudo-Dionysius, and he was friendly with Thomas Gallus, abbot of Vercelli, whose reception of the *Mystical Theology*, in particular, runs on parallel lines to that of Grosseteste himself. In their commentaries both men attenuated the apophaticism of the Greek author to produce what they regarded as a more liveable, affective "humanistic" theology of mystical experience, one more adapted to their native Latin theological culture. See the following article by J. McEvoy: "Thomas Gallus (*Abbas Vercellensis*) and the Commentary on the *De Mystica Theologia* Ascribed to Iohannes Scottus Eriugena. With a Concluding Note on the Second Latin Reception of the Pseudo-Dionysius (1230–1250)," in *Traditions of Platonism. Essays in Honour of John Dillon,* ed. J. J. Cleary, Ashgate, 1999, pp. 389–405.

5. *Hexaëmeron* I.2.1–3 (pp. 49–52).

6. *De cessatione legalium* III.1.1–2.1 (pp. 119–133). For a discussion, see J. McEvoy, "The Absolute Predestination of Chirst . . ." (1980).

7. S. Gieben, "Robert Grosseteste on Preaching. With the Edition of the Sermon *Ex Rerum Initiatarum* On Redemption," in *Collectanea Franciscana* 37 (1967): 100–141; pp. 128–129.

8. "Unity of will" (etc.) translates "idem velle, idem nolle in rebus honestis" (lit. "to will the same things and to abhor the same things in matters of virtue"), a formula that (with variations) became traditional in Latin after Cicero (*Laelius de amicitia*) and Sallust (*Catal.* 20.4); it is found in Seneca, St. Ambrose, St. Jerome, and St. Augustine, as well as in many other Christian writers.

9. See further J. McEvoy, "Robert Grosseteste on the Soul's Care for the Body: A New Text and New Sources for the Idea" (1993).

10. *De cessatione legalium* III.6.8–9 (pp. 150–151).

11. Edited by S. Gieben (1967).

12. See further McEvoy, "Robert Grosseteste and the Soul's Care for the Body" (1993), pp. 38–40; 50–51.

13. *Hexaëmeron* I.8.2–4 (pp. 58–61).

14. *De finitate motus et temporis*, ed. R. C. Dales (1963).

15. *Hex.* I.VIII.5 (p. 61; English trans., p. 59).

16. For further information, see R. C. Dales, *Medieval Discussions of the Eternity of the World* (1990).

17. For a detailed comment on the *Notula*, see J. McEvoy, "Robert Grosseteste and the Reunion of the Church" (1975). Southern discusses it briefly in *Robert Grosseteste*, Oxford, 2nd ed. (1992), pp. 231–232.

18. Southern, "Richard Dales and the Editing of Robert Grosseteste," in *Aspectus and Affectus: Essays and Editions in Grosseteste and Medieval Intellectual Life in Honor of R. C. Dales*, ed. G. Freibergs, New York (1993), pp. 3–14; see p. 7 for the paraphrase.

19. It is expounded best in his commentary on Galatians 5:22 (ed. J. McEvoy, 1995, pp. 154–155).

20. The source of this doctrine is Romans 8:38–39: "Who shall separate us from the love of Christ?"

21. *De decem mandatis* (ed. Dales and King, 1987, p. 6). For a comment, see J. McEvoy, "Robert Grosseteste's Use of the Argument of Saint Anselm," in McEvoy, *Robert Grosseteste: New Perspectives* (1995), pp. 257–275.

22. *Expositio in Galatas*, ed. J. McEvoy (1995), pp. 116–117; see McEvoy, "Robert Grosseteste on Educative Love," in McEvoy, *Robert Grosseteste: New Perspectives* (1995), pp. 289–311.

23. J. McEvoy, "Grosseteste's Reflections on Aristotelian Friendship: A 'New' Commentary on *Nicomachean Ethics* VIII.8–14," in McEvoy, *Robert Grosseteste: New Perspectives* (1995), pp. 149–168.

10. PASTORAL WRITINGS

1. As a sample of Grosseteste's style of popular preaching, a recently edited sermon has been reproduced in English translation in appendix 1.

2. E. B. King, "Durham Cathedral MS A. III.2 and the Corpus of Grosseteste's Homiletical Works," in McEvoy, *Robert Grosseteste: New Perspectives* (1995), pp. 277–288.

3. The work has been edited by J. Goering and F. A. C. Mantello (1984).

4. Edited by S. Wenzel (1970).

5. Edited by J. Goering and F. A. C. Mantello (1987).

6. Edited by J. Goering and F. A. C. Mantello (1986).

7. Edited by J. Goering and F. A. C. Mantello (1985).

11. ANGLO-NORMAN WRITINGS

1. W. Rothwell, "The Role of French in Thirteenth-Century England," in *The Bulletin of the John Rylands Library* 56 (1974): 445–466.

2. *Walter of Henley and Other Treatises on Estate Management and Accounting*, Oxford, 1971.

3. Studied by Goering and Mantello in *Viator* 18 (1987): 253–273.

4. I wish to thank Dr. Eamon Ó Ciosán (NUI Maynooth) for his help with this translation.

5. It was published by P. Meyer in *Romania* 29 (1900), pp. 61–72, from the *Rawlinson MS Poet. 241*. A new edition and critical study are a desideratum.

6. Edited by J. Murray (1918). I am indebted for some of my information about the work to a private letter from Miss Ruth J. Dean, as well as to a conversation with her pupil Professor Maureen Bolton of Notre Dame University.

7. "Ha! tres gloriuse Reine / Marie, Mere e Virgine, / Pur Pité ne puis nomer / Tes doulurs ne rementiver. / Meis lores est tut acomplie / De Simeon la prophetie, Kar plus ke al cors fu naffree / Par mi l' alme de une espee. / Mes cent feiz ta joie dubla / Kant il de mort resuscita. / Riens n'eüst valu la passion / Ne fust la resurrection."

8. See chap. 9 for a discussion of this favorite idea of Grosseteste.

9. K. Sajavaara, *The Middle English Translations of Robert Grosseteste's* Chateau d'Amour, Helsinki, 1967, p. 100. (The foregoing summary owes much to this work.) The reader should consult Southern, *Robert Grosseteste* (1992), pp. 225–230.

10. A new edition is being prepared at the University of Toronto by Evelyn Mackie, with Joseph Goering.

12. THE EARLIEST FRANCISCAN MASTERS AT OXFORD

1. *Fratris Thomae vulgo dicti de Eccleston Tractatus De Adventu Fratrum Minorum in Angliam*, ed. A. G. Little (1951).

2. See chap. 3.

3. For a balanced view, consult S. Gieben, "Robert Grosseteste and the Evolution of the Franciscan Order," in McEvoy, *Robert Grosseteste: New Perspectives* (1995), pp. 230–232.

4. A. G. Little, *Fratris Thomae Tractatus De Adventu* (1951), introduction, p. xxxi. It should not be forgotten that it was St. Francis himself who permitted St. Anthony of Padua, who was already a doctor of theology at the time of his Franciscan conversion, to continue to teach, and to become, in effect, the order's first theologian.

5. They are edited in Grosseteste's *Hexaëmeron*, ed. Dales and King (1982), pp. 341–350. The most comprehensive study of Adam Marsh and his achievement is an unpublished Ph.D. thesis: Roger M. Haas, *Adam Marsh (de Marisco), a Thirteenth-Century English Franciscan*, Rutgers, the State University of New Jersey, New Brunswick, 1989.

6. For further information and the edition of the document, see Gieben, "Robert Grosseteste and Adam Marsh on Light" (1993).

7. On Hugh and his friendship with Marsh and Grosseteste, see chap. 3.

8. Edited at the Pontifical Institute of Mediaeval Studies, Toronto, but not published.

9. D. E. Sharp, *Franciscan Philosophy at Oxford in the Thirteenth Century* (1930), surveyed Thomas's discussion of a number of metaphysical issues (pp. 47–112).

10. This chapter was edited by E. Longpré, in *Archives d'Histoire doctrinale et littéraire du moyen-âge* 1 (1926): 269–308.

11. R. C. Dales, *Medieval Discussions* (1990), p. 81.

13. THE ARRIVAL OF THE *SENTENCES*

1. B. Smalley, *The Study of the Bible* (2nd ed., 1951), p. 277.

2. Ibid., p. 272.

3. The sermon has been edited by R. J. Long in *Mediaeval Studies* 34 (1972): 71–98 (see pp. 96–97 for the text translated here). It has been carefully analyzed by S. Brown, "Richard Fishacre on the Need for 'Philosophy'" (1988). For a general appreciation of Fishacre, see Long, "Richard Fishacre, dominicain." Fishacre's commentary on the *Sentences* is being edited by S. Brown, J. Goering, R. J. Long, and M. O'Carroll.

4. The letter reads: "Mandamus quatenus dilectum filium fratrem R. de ordine Praedicatorum apud Oxoniam docentem in theologica facultate a lectione ordinarie libri Sententiarum non debeas prohibere, sed potius inducas eundem ut secundum gratiam sibi datam continentiam profundam et veritatem necessariam ipsius libri auditoribus aperiat studiosis, cum in eo catholicorum doctorum inveniantur testimonia fide digna quae depulsa erroris calligine tenendam fidelibus asserant veritatem." Edited by G. Abate, "Lettere *secretae* d'Innocenzo IV e altri documenti in una raccolta inedita del saec. XIII," in *Miscellanea Franciscana* (1955): 347, n. 149.

5. S. Brown, "Richard Fishacre" (1988), pp. 32–34.

6. Edited by R. J. Long in *Mediaeval Studies* 40 (1978): 30–55; on the heresies, see Long's edition in *Archives d'Histoire doctrinale et littéraire du moyen-âge* 60 (1993): 207–279.

7. R. J. Long, "Richard Fishacre's Way to God" (1988), edits extracts from Rufus's commentary (pp. 176–182).

8. Extracts from the MS have been edited by R. J. Long in *Archivum Fratrum Praedicatorum* 60 (1990) 15–31.

9. As did Rufus after him. The dependence of their commentaries on Grosseteste was brought to light by R. C. Dales, in an important article printed in *Viator* 2 (1971): 271–300.

10. R. J. Long, "The First Oxford Debate on the Eternity of the World," in *Recherches de Théologie et Philosophie médiévales* 65.1 (1998): 52–96, edits a question by Fishacre on this subject.

11. O. Lottin, in *Revue des Sciences philosophiques et théologiques* 24 (1935): 275.

12. R. J. Long kindly communicated to me his unpublished study of this question, as well as the text of Fishacre's discussion of the eternity of the world.

NOTES TO PAGES 169–191

13. Translated in P. Raedts, *Richard Rufus of Cornwall and the Tradition of Oxford Theology* (1987), pp. 1–2. Raedts's monograph, the first devoted to Rufus, has advanced our knowledge of him considerably.

14. Prof. Rega Wood has undertaken the edition.

15. T. Noone, in *Franciscan Studies* 49 (1989), pp. 55–91.

16. Noone argues the case for it, against Raedts.

17. Raedts, *Richard Rufus of Cornwall*, chap. 4.

18. In II Sent., d.1, qu.1; edited by S. Brown, in *Miscellanea Mediaevalia* 21.1 (1991) 259–280.

CONCLUSION

1. *Statuta Antiqua Universitatis Oxoniensis*, ed. S. Gibson, Oxford, 1931, p. 49.

2. "The incorporation of Aristotle's method and content into theological discussion was much stronger at Paris than at Oxford, even though Oxford was 'ahead' in commenting on the works of Aristotle." S. Brown, "The Eternity of the World Discussion at Early Oxford" (1991), p. 268.

APPENDIX 1

1. "Robert Grosseteste on the Cross and Redemptive Love. With the Text of His Sermon on Galatians 5:24 and Notes on Its Reception," in *Recherches de Théologie et Philosophie médiévales*, 66.2 (1999): 289–315.

APPENDIX 2

1. Grosseteste's ideas on spiritual freedom are studied by J. McEvoy in "Robert Grosseteste on Liberty," and in *Studies in Honor of Edward B. King*, ed. R. G. Benson and E. Naylor, Sewanee (Tennessee), 1991, pp. 187–208.

APPENDIX 3

1. See p. 137 and n. 22.

BIBLIOGRAPHY

This list begins with selected items relative to chapter 1. References for chapters 12 and 13 are also given separately.

The chapters dealing most directly with Robert Grosseteste (chaps. 2–11) have been grouped together, and the references subdivided into the following categories: bibliographies, manuscripts, editions of works, selected studies. The last-named section includes monographs, collective works, and articles published in professional periodicals. Throughout the chapters, those nonessential references that occur only once are normally given in full in endnotes but not repeated in this general bibliography.

Items marked with an * have been reprinted in the following work: James McEvoy, *Robert Grosseteste, Exegete and Philosopher* (Variorum Collected Studies Series: CS 446), Aldershot, 1994.

1. FROM SCHOOLS TO UNIVERSITY

Editions

Alexander Nequam, *Speculatio Speculationum*, ed. R. Thompson, London, 1990.
Edmund of Abingdon, *Speculum Religiosorum* and *Speculum Ecclesiae*, ed. Helen P. Forshaw, London, 1973.
Iohannes Blund, *Tractatus de Anima*, ed. D. A. Callus and R. W. Hunt, London, 1970.

Studies

Catto, J. I., "Theology and Theologians 1220–1320," in *The History of the University of Oxford*, ed. T. H. Aston, vol. 1, *The Early Oxford Schools*, ed. J. I. Catto, Oxford, 1986, pp. 473–497.

Goering, J., *William de Montibus (c. 1140–1213)*, Toronto, 1992.

Hunt, R. W., *The Schools and the Cloister: The Life and Writings of Alexander Nequam (1157–1217)*, ed. and rev. M. Gibson, Oxford, 1984.

Lawrence, C. H., *St. Edmund of Abingdon*, London, 1960.

Southern, R. W., "From Schools to University," in *The History of the University of Oxford*, ed. T. H. Aston, vol. 1., *The Early Oxford Schools*, ed. J. I. Catto, Oxford, 1986, pp. 1–36.

2–11. ROBERT GROSSETESTE

Bibliographies

Gieben, S., "Bibliographia universa Roberti Grosseteste ab an. 1473 ad an. 1969," in *Collectanea Franciscana* 39 (1969): 362–418.

———, "Robertus Grosseteste: Bibliographia 1970–1991," in *Robert Grosseteste: New Perspectives on His Thought and Scholarship*, ed. J. McEvoy (Instrumenta Patristica 24), Steenbrugge, 1995, pp. 415–431.

McEvoy, J., "Robert Grosseteste: Recent and Forthcoming Editions and Studies," in *Bulletin de philosophie médiévale* 35 (1993): 121–129. (Printed also in McEvoy, *Robert Grosseteste: New Perspectives* [1995], pp. 394–405.)

Thomson, S. H., *The Writings of Robert Grosseteste, Bishop of Lincoln 1235–1253*, Cambridge, 1940.

Manuscripts

Cambridge, *MS Gonville and Caius College 380*.
Leiden, *MS Bibliotheek der Rijksuniversiteit, Voss.gr.F.2*.
London, *MS College of Arms, Arundel 9*.
London, *MS Lambeth Palace 499*.

Editions

Baur, L., *Die philosophischen Werke des Robert Grosseteste, Bischofs von Lincoln* (Beiträge zur Geschichte der Philosophie des Mittelalters, 9), Münster i. W., 1912.

Dales, R. C., *Roberti Grosseteste Episcopi Lincolniensis Commentarius in VIII Libros Physicorum Aristotelis*, Boulder, 1963.

————, "Robert Grosseteste's Treatise De Finitate Motus et Temporis," in *Traditio* 19 (1963): 245–266.

Dales, R. C., and S. Gieben, eds., *Robert Grosseteste, Hexaëmeron* (Auctores Britannici Medii Aevi 6), London, 1982. (Complete English translation: *Robert Grosseteste: On the Six Days of Creation. A Translation of the Hexaëmeron*, by C. F. J. Martin [Auctores Brit. Med. Aevi 6(2)], Oxford, 1996.)

Dales, R. C., and E. B. King, eds., *Robert Grosseteste. De Cessatione Legalium* (Auctores Britannici Medii Aevi 7), London, 1986.

————, *Robert Grosseteste. De Decem Mandatis* (Auctores Britannici Medii Aevi 8), London, 1987.

Gieben S., "Robert Grosseteste on Preaching. With the Edition of the Sermon *Ex Rerum Initiatarum* on Redemption," in *Collectanea Franciscana* 37 (1967): 100–141.

————, "Robert Grosseteste at the Papal Curia, Lyons 1250. Edition of the Documents," in *Collectanea Franciscana* 41 (1971): 340–393.

Goering, J., and F. A. C. Mantello, eds., *Robert Grosseteste. Templum Dei. Edited from MS 27 of Emmanuel College, Cambridge* (Toronto Medieval Latin Texts 14), Toronto, 1984.

————, "The *Meditaciones* of Robert Grosseteste," in *Journal of Theological Studies*, N. S. 36 (1985): 118–128.

————, "The Perambulavit Iudas (Speculum Confessionis) Attributed to Robert Grosseteste," in *Revue bénédictine* 46 (1986): 125–168.

————, "*Notus in Iudea Deus*: Robert Grosseteste's Confessional Formulary in *Lambeth Palace MS 499*," in *Viator* 18 (1987): 253–273.

————, "The Early Penitential Writings of Robert Grosseteste," in *Recherches de Théologie ancienne et médiévale* 54 (1987): 52–112.

Goering, J., "Robert Grosseteste at the Papal Curia," in *A Distinct Voice: Medieval Studies in Honor of Leonard E. Boyle, O. P.*, ed. J. Brown and W. P. Stoneman, Notre Dame, Ind., 1997.

Lewis, N., "The First Recension of Robert Grosseteste's *De Libero Arbitrio*," in *Mediaeval Studies* 53 (1991): 1–88.

Mantello, F., "Optima Epistola: A Critical Edition and Translation of Letter 128 of Bishop Robert Grosseteste," in *A Distinct Voice: Medieval Studies in Honor of Leonard E. Boyle, O. P.*, ed. J. Brown and W. P. Stoneman, Notre Dame, Ind., 1997, 277–301.

*McEvoy, J., "The Sun as *Res* and *Signum*: Grosseteste's Commentary on Ecclesiasticus ch. 43, vv. 1–5," in *Recherches de Théologie ancienne et médiévale* 41 (1974): 38–91.

————, ed., *Roberti Grosseteste Expositio in Epistolam Sancti Pauli ad Galatas*, Opera Roberti Grosseteste Lincolniensis, vol. 1 (Corpus Christ. Cont. Med. 130), Turnhout, 1995.

Mercken, H. P. F., *The Greek Commentaries on the* Nicomachean Ethics *of Aristotle in the Latin Translation of Robert Grosseteste*, vol. 1, Leiden, 1973; vol. 2, Leuven, 1991.

Murray, J., *Le Château d'amour de Robert Grosseteste, évêque de Lincoln*, Paris 1918; reprint Geneva, 1973.

Rosemann, P. W., *Tabula*, Opera Roberti Grosseteste Lincolniensis, vol. 1 (Corpus Christ. Cont. Med. 130), Turnhout, 1995.

Rossi, P., ed., *Robertus Grosseteste. Commentarius in Posteriorum Analyticorum Libros*, Introduzione e testo critico (Testi e studi 2), Florence, 1981.

Wenzel, S., "Robert Grosseteste's Treatise on Confession, *Deus Est*," in *Franciscan Studies* 30 (1970): 218–293.

Selected Studies

Callus, D. A., ed., *Robert Grosseteste, Scholar and Bishop*, Oxford, 1955.

———, "Robert Grosseteste as Scholar," in Callus, *Robert Grosseteste*, pp. 1–69.

Crombie, A. C., "Grosseteste's Position in the History of Science," in Callus, *Robert Grosseteste*, pp. 98–120.

———, *Robert Grosseteste and the Origins of Experimental Science, 1100–1700*, Oxford, 1953.

Dales, R. C., *Medieval Discussions of the Eternity of the World* (Brill's Studies in Intellectual History 18), Leiden, 1990.

De Jonge, M., "Robert Grosseteste and the *Testaments of the Twelve Patriarchs*," in *Journal of Theological Studies* 42 (1991): 115–125.

Dionisotti, A. C., "On the Greek Studies of Robert Grosseteste," in *The Uses of Greek and Latin: Historical Essays*, ed. A. C. Dionisotti, A. Grafton, and J. Kraye, London, 1988, pp. 19–39.

———, "Robert Grosseteste and the Greek Encyclopaedia," in *Rencontres de cultures dans la philosophie médiévale. Traductions et traducteurs de l'antiquité tardive au XIVᵉ siècle*, ed. J. Hamesse and M. Fattori, Louvain-la-Neuve–Cassino, 1990, pp. 337–353.

Gieben, S., "Robert Grosseteste and Adam Marsh on Light in a Summary Attributed to St. Bonaventure," in *Aspectus et Affectus: Essays and Editions in Grosseteste and Medieval Intellectual Life in Honor of Richard C. Dales*, ed. G. Freibergs, New York, 1993, pp. 17–35.

———, "Robert Grosseteste and the Evolution of the Franciscan Order," in McEvoy, *Robert Grosseteste: New Perspectives*, pp. 215–232.

Haren, M., *Medieval Thought: The Western Intellectual Tradition from Antiquity to the Thirteenth Century*, Basingstoke, 2nd ed., 1992.

Holland, M., "Robert Grosseteste's Greek Translations and College of Arms

MS Arundel 9," in McEvoy, *Robert Grosseteste: New Perspectives*, pp. 121–147.

Hedwig, K., *Sphaera Lucis. Studien zur Intelligibilität des Seienden im Kontext der mittelalterlichen Lichtspekulation* (Beiträge zur Geschichte der Philosophie und Theologie des Mittelalters, n.s.18), Münster i. W., 1980, chap. 5: "Robert Grosseteste: *Sphaera Lucis*," pp. 119–156.

King, E. B., "Durham Cathedral MS A. III.2 and the Corpus of Grosseteste's Homiletical Works," in McEvoy, *Robert Grosseteste: New Perspectives*, pp. 277–288.

Koyré, A., "The Origins of Medieval Science: A New Interpretation," in *Diogène* (1956): 1–22.

Loewe, R., "The Medieval Christian Hebraists of England: The *Superscriptio Lincolniensis*," in *Hebrew Union College Annual* (Cincinnati) 28 (1957): 205–252.

*McEvoy, J., "Robert Grosseteste and the Reunion of the Church," in *Collectanea Franciscana* 45 (1975): 39–84.

*———, "Robert Grosseteste's Theory of Human Nature. With the Text of His Conference *Ecclesia Sancta Celebrat*," in *Recherches de Théologie ancienne et médiévale* 47 (1980): 131–187.

*———, "The Absolute Predestination of Christ in the Theology of Robert Grosseteste," in *"Sapientiae Doctrina." Mélanges de théologie et de littérature médiévales offerts à Dom Hildebrand Bascour, O.S.B.*, Leuven, 1980, pp. 212–230.

*———, "Language, Tongue, and Thought in the Writings of Robert Grosseteste," in *Sprache und Erkenntnis im Mittelalter*, ed. A. Zimmermann, *Miscellanea Mediaevalia* 13.2 (1981): 585–592.

———, *The Philosophy of Robert Grosseteste*, Oxford, 2nd ed., 1982.

*———, "Robert Grosseteste on the Ten Commandments," in *Recherches de Théologie ancienne et médiévale* 58 (1991): 167–212.

———, "Robert Grosseteste on the Soul's Care for the Body: A New Text and New Sources for the Idea," in *Aspectus et Affectus: Essays and Editions in Grosseteste and Medieval Intellectual Life in Honor of R. C. Dales*, ed. G. Freibergs, New York, 1993, pp. 37–56.

———, ed., *Robert Grosseteste: New Perspectives on His Thought and Scholarship* (Instrumenta Patristica 24), Steenbrugge, 1995.

———, "Grosseteste's Reflections on Aristotelian Friendship: A 'New' Commentary on *Nicomachean Ethics* VIII.8–14," in McEvoy, *Robert Grosseteste: New Perspectives*, pp. 149–168.

———, "Robert Grosseteste's Use of the Argument of Saint Anselm," in McEvoy, *Robert Grosseteste: New Perspectives*, pp. 257–275.

———, *Gli Inizi di Oxford (1150–1250). Grossatesta e I Primi Maestri* (Eredità

Medievale. Storia della teologia medievale da Agostino a Erasmo da Rotter-dam), Milan, 1996.

——, *Robert Grosseteste et la théologie à l'université d'Oxford (1150–1250)*. Traduit de l'anglais par Éliane Saint-André Utudjian (Initiations au Moyen Âge), Paris, 1998.

——, "Robert Grosseteste on the Cross and Redemptive Love. With the Text of His Sermon on Galatians 5:24 and Notes on Its Reception," in *Recherches de Théologie et Philosophie médiévales* 65.2 (1999): 79–102.

Moreton, J., "Robert Grosseteste and the Calendar," in McEvoy, *Robert Grosseteste: New Perspectives*, pp. 77–88.

Rosemann, P. W., "Robert Grosseteste's *Tabula*," in McEvoy, *Robert Grosseteste: New Perspectives*, pp. 321–355.

Rossi, P., "Robert Grosseteste and the Object of Scientific Knowledge," in McEvoy, *Robert Grosseteste*, pp. 53–75.

Smalley, B., *The Study of the Bible in the Middle Ages*, Notre Dame, 2nd ed., 1951.

Southern, R. W., *Robert Grosseteste: The Growth of an English Mind in Medieval Europe*, Oxford, 2nd ed., 1992.

Speer, A., "Licht und Raum. Robert Grossetestes spekulative Grundlegung einer scientia naturalis," in *Raum and Raumvorstellungen in Mittelalter*, ed. J. A. Aertsen and A. Speer, *Miscellanea Mediaevalia* 25 (1998): 77–100.

Wasserstein, D., "Grosseteste, the Jews, and Medieval Christian Hebraism," in McEvoy, *Robert Grosseteste: New Perspectives*, pp. 357–376.

12. THE EARLIEST FRANCISCAN MASTERS AT OXFORD

Lawrence, C. H., "The Letters of Adam Marsh and the Franciscan School at Oxford," in *Journal of Ecclesiastical History* 42 (1991): 218–238.

Little, A. G., ed., *Fratris Thomae vulgo dicti de Eccleston Tractatus De Adventu Fratrum Minorum in Angliam*, Manchester, 1951.

——, Introduction, *Fratris Thomae Tractatus De Adventu*, pp. xi–xxxi.

Longpré, E., "Thomas d'York et Matthieu d'Aquasparta," in *Archives d'Histoire doctrinale et littéraire du moyen-âge* 1 (1926): 269–308.

Sharp, D. E., *Franciscan Philosophy at Oxford in the Thirteenth Century*, Oxford, 1930.

13. THE ARRIVAL OF THE *SENTENCES*

Brown, S. F., "Richard Fishacre on the Need for 'Philosophy,'" in *A Straight Path: Studies in Medieval Philosophy and Culture. Essays in Honor of Arthur Hyman*, ed. R. Link-Salinger and others, Washington D.C., 1988, pp. 23–36.

——, "The Eternity of the World Discussion at Early Oxford," in *Mensch und Natur im Mittelalter*, ed. A. Zimmermann, *Miscellanea Mediaevalia* 21.1 (1991): 259–280.

Long, R. J., "The Science of Theology According to Richard Fishacre: Edition of the Prologue to His *Commentary on the Sentences*," in *Mediaeval Studies* 34 (1972): 71–98.

———, "Richard Fishacre's Way to God," in *A Straight Path: Studies in Medieval Philosophy and Culture. Essays in Honor of Arthur Hyman*, ed. R. Link-Salinger and others, Washington D.C., 1988, pp. 174–182.

———, "The Moral and Spiritual Theology of Richard Fishacre: Edition of *Trinity College MS O.1.30*," in *Archivum Fratrum Praedicatorum* 60 (1990): 5–31.

———, "Richard Fishacre, dominicain, †1248," in *Dictionnaire de spiritualité*, 13: 509–512.

Noone, T. B., "Richard Rufus of Cornwall and the Authorship of the *Scriptum Super Metaphysicam*," in *Franciscan Studies* 49 (1989): 55–91.

Raedts, P., *Richard Rufus of Cornwall and the Tradition of Oxford Theology*, Oxford, 1987.

INDEX